FINANCIAL SECTOR OF THE AMERICAN ECONOMY

T0303976

edited by

STUART BRUCHEY
ALLAN NEVINS PROFESSOR EMERITUS
COLUMBIA UNIVERSITY

THE MYTH OF BLACK CORPORATE MOBILITY

DR. ULWYN L.J. PIERRE

Routledge
Taylor & Francis Group
New York London

First published 1998 by Garland Publishing Inc.

This edition Published 2013 by Routledge
711 Third Avenue, New York, NY 10017
2 Park Square, Milton Park, Abingdon, Oxfordshire OX14 4RN

First issued in paperback 2014

Routledge is an imprint of the Taylor and Francis Group,
an informa business

Library of Congress Cataloging-in-Publication Data

Pierre, Ulwyn L.J.
 The myth of black corporate mobility / Ulwyn L.J. Pierre.
  p. cm. — (Financial sector of the American economy)
 Revision of the author's thesis (Ph.D.—Columbia University, 1992)
 Includes bibliographical references and index.
 ISBN 0-8153-3138-X (alk. paper)
 1. Afro-American executives. 2. Afro-Americans—Promotions. 3. Discrimination in employment—United States. I. Title.
II. Series.
HD38.25.U6P54 1998
331.6'396073—dc21

98-42967

ISBN 13: 978-1-138-86386-6 (pbk)
ISBN 13: 978-0-8153-3138-4 (hbk)

This book is dedicated to my collegiate peers, now deceased, who in striving to rise above the stereotypes associated with being black have made the ultimate sacrifice in their pursuit of truth and knowledge—the tools of empowerment. May their experience serve future generations as an enduring testament that in the pursuit of excellence one has to be strategic and balance the cost of success with the quality of life to be enjoyed.

Contents

Foreword

When inconsistencies and injustices occur, people respond in different ways. Some stay on the sidelines and criticize. Some pretend not to see the wrongdoings. And some find reasons to convince themselves that the particular atrocity was somehow well-deserved or another person's fault. However, there are a few who tend to do something, no matter how small, to rectify the situation.

When I contemplate whether I should engage myself in an effort to right a wrong that can have an impact on the lives of others, or even just one person, and move him or her to take positive action, Bishop Martin Niemoller's poem comes to mind (Bartlett 1992):

> In Germany they came first for the Communists, and I didn't speak up because I wasn't a Communist. Then they came for the Jews, and I didn't speak up because I wasn't a Jew. Then they came for the trade unionists, and I didn't speak up because I wasn't a trade unionist. Then they came for the Catholics, and I didn't speak up because I was a Protestant. Then they came for me, and by that time no one was left to speak up (684).

As human beings we can no longer wait for someone else to address crises or injustices taking place in our families, schools, workplaces, and the larger community. We must be emboldened to do the best we can to facilitate positive change, however minor the intervention. We must hope that others who are slower to act will eventually be motivated to follow or lead other efforts to facilitate the needed improvement.

This book addresses one such needed change in the corporate arena—the continuing inequality of opportunities for success that blacks experience relative to their similarly qualified white peers.

When I came to the United States via Canada, I had already been exposed to the literature that chronicled the history of blacks and their minorities. However, I soon realized that I had not fully understood or internalized the information. These events were outside the realm of my experience and imagining. As a black person originally from Trinidad, West Indies, my indoctrination into the *real* United States began upon my arrival into this country. I began experiencing and witnessing incidents that previously existed only within the pages of a book. Now they were becoming a reality.

The injustice that had the greatest impact on me was the underutilization of human resources, especially among blacks and other minorities. I witnessed the movement of individuals from hope to hopelessness. I saw little black boys and black girls internalizing the negativism of being labeled "minority" and learning to have blurred visions of themselves and their futures. I observed my peers being systematically destroyed by the ongoing mistreatment inflicted on them, because they dared to possess lofty dreams. I saw very few of us survive the traumas and injustices administered to America's so-called "minorities." I saw very few of us have the opportunity to maximize our true potential.

I also read and constantly heard the educational and corporate argument about blacks not being qualified, and as a result, their success—academically and professionally—was impacted negatively. I also read and heard the argument from the other side, by many blacks and other researchers, that race tends to be a significant factor that stymies black and minority success. I found myself wanting to stay a spectator of this horrific "game." However, because of the fact that I was now living in America and I was black, I became an unwilling participant.

As stereotypes of blacks and other minorities were kept alive through various media, certain kinds of questions appear to still require explanation. I interviewed many people of all races, searching for answers to this question: Why do America's minorities continue to receive unequal treatment, despite legislative and judicial redress, and despite the reality that diverse immigrant groups have helped to make this country a global superpower? I was amazed to discover that many blacks also had internalized stereotypes about themselves that most whites held about blacks and acted upon.

Going back to the literature, I continued reading the criticisms leveled at the research in this area. These criticisms included claims that many researchers failed to document whether comparison groups were similarly qualified; or that some studies were qualitative and therefore perceived not to be objective; or that the samples were too small; or statistical analyses were not adequately conducted.

I thought, if it is true that people are America's most precious resource (Federal Glass Ceiling Commission 1995), then why are America's minorities in such a predicament? Why is the potential of this group not embraced and unleashed? Why is so much time and effort expended to muffle their contributions? In light of the tragic waste in the utilization of human capital and the devastation this causes to people's dreams and potential, I felt moved to contribute to this area of research and undertook my dissertation.

Years later, when Garland Publishing, Inc. asked me to invest more time, thought and energy into transforming my dissertation into this book, I had to think long and hard. The process of completing my dissertation was extremely arduous—filled with obstacles, challenges, injustices, and subjectivity. When the process was finished, I buried the ordeal and did not want to unearth it. However, because of what is currently taking place in America—the attempts to repeal affirmative action, California's Proposition 209, my own experiences and exposure within corporate America, the discriminatory rhetoric that continues to be given voice, and the lack of moral fiber and apathy that have their jaws on America's conscience—I felt it was important to continue to add my voice to this area of research. Especially compelling was that the findings of my study provide a clear understanding of some of the key elements needed to facilitate equal opportunities for employees' mobility in corporate America.

Many years have passed since I completed my dissertation. During that time I have put to use, as much as possible, the findings of this study. I have also been motivated and encouraged to expand my research and work in the area of organizational change. Opportunities continue to abound for me to assist in the optimization of America's human capital through my company, Pierre & Associates, Inc., founded in 1987. My associates and I provide a wide range of human resource management and organizational development services to our clients. Through our expertise, experience, and our systemic and holistic approach to change, we are able to have a significant and positive impact on how corporations develop and utilize their diverse human resources, maximize their effectiveness and productivity, and successfully leverage their competitive advantage. While corporate leaders and managers realize that in this global economy, optimization of human resources is not an altruistic endeavor but just good business, many are challenged to find effective ways to achieve desired results.

This need on the part of corporations spawned a whole new area of diversity, as they continue to experience challenges in developing and implementing interventions that produce measurable bottom line results. Many diversity practitioners continue to place most of the emphasis on changing individual behavior. Based on the results of this and other research, and my work with corporate clients, focus should also be placed heavily on changing current corporate and organizational policies, processes and systems that continue to reinforce old and discriminatory behavior. If diversity training and associated initiatives continue to be implemented myopically, bottom line results will not be realized. Therefore, these initiatives will wane because corporate leaders will see no benefit or return on their investment in their human resources. Another subsequent effect is that corporate leaders, managers, and employees in general will continue to blame the victims. From their perspectives, they did all they could to address a biased situation and yet these programs had minimal, if any, impact on the victims' career success. Another side effect is the further strengthening and internalization of existing stereotypes, as well as the reduction of opportunities for career advancement for blacks and other minorities.

While reading this book, some may feel challenged by the nature of the issues presented. As human beings, we have a tendency to be defensive in areas and situations that make us uncomfortable. As you read this book, I hope you do not slip into a defensive posture but rather that you become reflective and thoughtful. We all can make a positive contribution. America need not be a nation whose workers' potential is underutilized because they are restrained by criteria that are non-work related, such as race, gender, and religion. We can transform America into a place where we are judged not by the color of our skin, but by the content of our character, and where we are not stymied by unequal opportunities. At the moment, this nation's operating posture is win-lose. If we move to a win-win posture there are benefits to be derived by all.

Preface

Although initially completed in 1992, this study is still timely. The tenor in this country continues to be conservative where matters of race are concerned. The repercussions of long-term institutionalized racism continue to be negative and visible for blacks and other minorities. Attempts during the 1990s to repeal affirmative action and other civil rights programs seek to drive back efforts to override the majority population's use of non-work related factors as criteria to shut out historically disenfranchised groups from equal opportunities in areas such as jobs and hiring contracts.

This study sought to discern the degree to which this tendency is still alive and well in America's corporations. The research conducted between 1989 and 1992 for my doctoral dissertation has been updated with more recent studies, evidence, and citations to determine more about corporate mobility after 1992. This update also seeks to corroborate or refute prior arguments made about the practices occurring in America's corporate environments. I have also used findings and conclusions of current studies to determine whether the findings and conclusions of my original research are still valid in the corporate environment of the late 1990s. A review of current literature revealed no major inconsistencies with the literature from the late 1980s and early 1990s referenced during the time the study was undertaken. This means that study findings are still valid and reliable and that conclusions and recommendations are still relevant with respect to black upward mobility in today's corporate arenas.

Study findings revealed that race-related factors still influence the career success of blacks, irrespective of their academic and professional qualifications. This being the case, one has to question the attempts to repeal laws and dismantle programs that were originally designed to prevent or end discrimination in environments where this type of discriminatory behavior and activities precipitated these laws and programs. It also stands to reason, since this type of behavior is still "alive and well," that efforts should be directed at implementing laws that have more "teeth" and programs that effectively eradicate this type of discriminatory behavior.

It is generally acknowledged that blacks are significantly underrepresented in upper-level positions within the corporate hierarchy and they experience slower rates of upward mobility. To date, the arguments on both sides (by corporate leaders and whites versus many blacks and researchers) continue to be the same relative to the reasons for this underrepresentation. The corporate argument—that blacks experience slower rates of upward mobility because they lack the requisite skills, qualifications, and experience—has been gaining momentum. This anti-affirmative action momentum is attributable to what has been occurring in the United States at large, and in particular, in states such as California and Texas, and in the U.S. Senate and House of Representatives. For example, congress from 1993 to 1998 stalled or opposed President Clinton's nominations for posts such as federal judges and those who would head the civil rights division of the Justice Department. In 1996-1997, the federal government was forced to shut down because Congress and the President could not agree on certain budgetary matters, some of which were related to civil rights. In 1997, voters in California and Texas passed ballot initiatives that effectively ended affirmative action laws in those states. This action had an immediate impact on hiring and state university enrollment.

Coupled with this momentum against affirmative action is a consequent spillage into the corporate arena, fueled by the news media. Data, research, and the increase in discrimination lawsuits against corporations that outwardly give credence to valuing diversity but act as though they have the freedom to discriminate, all speak to the fact that race is still a significant barrier that negatively impacts the career advancement of blacks and other minorities. Conversely, the argument held by other researchers as well as many blacks and other minorities purports that factors other than education, professional qualifications, and performance (i.e., race-related factors) limit the rates of upward mobility of blacks and other minorities.

This particular study departs from most empirical research in that it focuses on "qualified" black managers and their similarly "qualified" white peers rather than on black workers in general. This comparative approach is intended to provide further clarity on the "requisite skills and qualifications" argument and to deepen the understanding of why "qualified" blacks perceive that their mobility is inhibited.

In this study, corporate upward mobility is quantified using two measures: average Compound Annual Growth Rate in salaries (CAGR) and average rate of vertical promotion as experienced among employees. To determine whether any differences existed in the rates of upward mobility between blacks and their similarly "qualified" white managers, data on the employment experiences of three matched sample groups (white managers, black managers who participated in specialized training, and black managers who did not participate in such training) were collected and analyzed. Information was also obtained from the supervisors of the trained black managers in order to document these managers' on-the-job performance levels. Additionally, a group of black senior corporate executives, identified as corporate success stories, was interviewed to identify factors other than "requisite skills and qualifications" that can specifically influence black upward mobility.

The study found that of the three matched study groups, the two groups of black managers experienced significantly slower rates of upward mobility than the group of their similarly qualified white managers. Additionally, analysis of interviews with black senior corporate executives revealed that differences in the socioeconomic and cultural backgrounds between blacks and whites, as well as negative stereotypes and their subsequent discriminatory effects, can limit the career advancement of black employees in the corporate arena.

Since this book is about the *myth* of black corporate mobility, the definition of "myth" found in *Webster's Encyclopedic Unabridged Dictionary* (1994) is particularly relevant to this discussion. A myth is an unproved collective belief that is accepted uncritically and is used to justify a social institution" (946). Myths have a profound influence over a society collectively and individually, as witnessed by the long held view of blacks' inferiority that was used to justify slavery in the U.S. and elsewhere. Nearly a century of struggle by abolitionists as well as a civil war were required before substantive change—the end of slavery—occurred, and still, the myth of blacks' inferiority persisted. Individuals still believed in whites' superiority and institutions of all kinds–governmental, religious, and corporate, to name a few—continued to practice racism.

Taken from another angle, the myth of the availability of or access to corporate upward mobility for qualified blacks and other minorities fuels their belief in their advancement. The scarcity of blacks at the top levels of corporations demands that blacks and other minorities accept–uncritically, perhaps naively—America's word that in this country, individuals can reach their greatest potential if they are qualified, work hard, and pull themselves up by their bootstraps. Even if blacks perceive race-relators such as slow rates of upward mobility and lack of access to mentors and networks, the myth requires gullibility from them. To participate in the corporate arena, many blacks feel like a boxer who is told, after strenuous training, years of bouts won and titles earned—"You are not ready for the world championship, but maybe someday you will be." In other words, the fight feels skewed in favor of one person over another, yet the perceived rewards are enticing so the myth continues to be kept alive.

But the reality—the paucity of upper level executives who are black or who belong to another minority group, and the slow rate of upward mobility experienced by these groups' members—makes the experience of career advancement to upper levels of management into an illusion. What appears to be the reality is that when it comes to promotions to higher corporate levels, irrespective of academic credentials, and meeting professional and performance corporate standards, those levels are still a bastion of entitlement held for white males in particular. Data from the Federal Glass Ceiling Commission sponsored by Republican members of Congress (March 1995) reinforces this assertion. Report findings show that white men hold 44.8% of administrative and managerial positions in banking, 51.6% in business services, 47.6% in communications, 74.6% in construction, 71.9% in the utilities, 58.5% in transportation, 62.9% in manufacturing, and 47.5% in public administration, while blacks hold only 2.3% in all private sector industries and 3.9% in public and private sectors combined. Report findings also revealed that despite the fact that white men comprise 43% of the workforce, they hold 95% of senior management positions, while African Americans hold 0.6%, Hispanic Americans hold 0.4%, Asian Americans hold 0.3% and women hold between 3 to 5%.

Proponents of affirmative action assert that those who oppose affirmative action have failed to produce the quantitative data of harm or economic damage that were the catalyst for the creation and substantiation of affirmative action programs. The author agrees with Jackson-Leslie (1995) who indicated that it is unfortunate that the media's coverage of this issue has been reduced to sound bites, "race baiting, and allegations of quotas, reverse discrimination, of racial preferences, and those less qualified" (24). In any case if recent lawsuits for discrimination are any indication, such as Bari-Ellen Roberts' suit against Texaco for discrimination, affirmative action has major obstacles to overcome (Johnson 1997). Other lawsuits against Denny's Restaurants and R.R. Donnelley and Sons, Inc. also serve to reinforce this point. Since the media shape public opinion and America, they have a responsibility and should be held accountable to eliminate stereotypes and barriers by accurate and balanced reporting. There must be honest discussion. The media must stop putting their own spin on events and distorting data which only serves to reinforce existing stereotypes.

Let's stop the rhetoric about rights, unfair quotas, and reverse discrimination that dramatize our headlines. Let's stop the hypocrisy about blacks and minorities not being qualified if, in fact, when these qualifications exist among these groups, they do not have a significant positive impact on their advancement to top corporate ranks. Let our discussion be about root causes and let our actions be about eradicating root causes and barriers.

SUMMARY AND ORGANIZATION OF BOOK

By examining career advancement of qualified blacks and comparing their rates of upward mobility to those of similarly qualified white peers, key factors emerged from this study which seemed to influence blacks' upward mobility and should concern particular audiences (e.g., those groups similarly underutilized, corporate leaders and managers, change agents, consultants, employees in general; indeed all of America's everyday citizens). Contrary to the "requisite skills and qualifications" argument, these key factors pointed away from work-related criteria for advancement and towards race-related inhibitors of mobility. The idea that upward mobility for blacks is available as long as they are qualified has always been a myth that deserves airing.

The contention that blacks in corporate America are experiencing significantly slower rates of upward mobility than their white counterparts opens up the field for additional research, study, and *action* and poses some serious questions as to why qualified blacks continue to perceive limited access to upper-middle through top level positions.

The data and research that formed the backdrop and foundation of this study completed in 1992 have been updated and expanded to include today's societal, economic, and corporate realities. The author believed that it was prudent to do this update, especially for Chapters I and II, to determine whether the situation and realities that existed prior to the early 1990s still exist. If this is the case, then this study's findings, conclusions, and recommendations would still be valid, relevant and pertinent to addressing issues and challenges regarding the upward mobility of qualified black employees in American corporations.

Chapter VI, "Conclusions, Recommendations and Implications of the Study," has also been refined so that these areas are in the context of new developments or improvements that have occurred in programs, initiatives, research, or policies in areas such as human resources, organizational behavior and development, government regulations, organizational change, training and development, corporate career advancement, and the economy. Contextual and editorial changes with few updates occurred in the other chapters.

This book is organized as follows: *Chapter I* puts the issue in historical and socioeconomic context and speaks to the purpose of the study. *Chapter II* analyzes literature on the subject of corporate upward mobility and provides information on factors that are believed to influence the career advancement of employees in general, and of blacks in particular. *Chapter III* presents a model, based on information obtained from the review of the literature, that outlines the determinants of black upward mobility within the corporate arena. The chapter also presents the study design and methodology. *Chapter IV* provides a statistical analysis of quantitative data obtained from black and white corporate managers who occupied positions in the same companies and in the same job classification or organizational level. *Chapter V* analyzes descriptive/qualitative data obtained from a sample of black senior corporate executives in order to begin to identify factors that can inhibit or enhance the upward mobility of blacks within the corporate arena. Finally, *Chapter VI* summarizes the results of the study and discusses the implications. In this final chapter, recommendations and conclusions are given for addressing those factors that influence the upward mobility of black employees within corporate America.

GENERALIZABILITY OF STUDY

The issues raised and discussed, conclusions drawn, and recommendations made are relevant to groups and individuals (e.g., other minorities, women, the differently abled, and others) who encounter similar challenges as those experienced by black employees in corporate America and other sectors of the economy. If your talents and potential are underutilized in your work environment because of factors that are non-work related, this book will provide you with useful and practical information.

For corporate executives and managers, this book moves beyond the media sound bites and race-baiting, and hopefully provides an honest discussion of issues that impede the ability to maximize the use of all available human resources. Since people are purported to be a company's most valued asset and competitive advantage, it is hoped that the information shared would lead to a clearer understanding of the issues.

I hope that both the quantitative and qualitative analyses provided to support findings will assist you in reducing the defensiveness caused by preconceived notions and faulty data that are normally touted to protect the status quo. It is hoped that this balanced discussion of the issues will enhance your growth and development and will facilitate you in being a more effective leader and manager of a diverse work force.

With diversity initiatives echoing throughout work environments and continuing to be drowned out by the torrent of racism, consultants who focus on the areas of affirmative action, equal employment opportunity, and diversity will find this study of particular importance. Since diversity is a process and not an event and should be linked to a corporation's strategic business objectives, this study would be of great importance to consultants who facilitate organizational change within the private and public sectors.

Because students are the future employees and leaders of tomorrow, they must understand the issues and be equipped with the skills and experience to function effectively in diverse work environments. Important conduits of this information and experience are their teachers and professors. Thus, the information communicated in this book will assist these purveyors of information to more fully understand the issues and be equipped with the quantitative and qualitative data and numerous support data to logically and objectively explain the issues and provide an environment where understanding and experiential learning occur.

Since the corporate arena is a microcosm of society, the values, beliefs, norms, and stereotypes within work environments is a reflection of what exists in the larger society. Thus, this book should be of interest to all citizens who live in an America that keeps stereotypes alive and perpetuates the underutilization of segments of society.

Acknowledgments

This book emanated from my dissertation which was completed at Columbia University, New York, in 1992. The dissertation represented a personal commitment to empowerment and to the pursuit of excellence. The list of those whose labor and commitment contributed to the dissertation's completion is extensive. They represent the corporate sector, the educational arena, friends, relatives and many ordinary people who became sources of insight and inspiration. I owe a debt of gratitude to each of them that I cannot adequately express in words.

The time and patience given by my dissertation committee, chaired by Professor Francis Ianni and composed of Dr. Samuel Johnson and Professors John Delaney and John Hughes, were pivotal. Professor Delaney's critical review of earlier drafts and Professor Ianni's assistance in bringing the dissertation process to closure are especially appreciated.

Further acknowledgment and appreciation is extended to Dr. Roger Fox for his invaluable support and assistance throughout the process. This experience reinforced the true power of a mentor. Many thanks to Floyd Brady without whose commitment to empowering minority youth this project would not have been kept alive. I am deeply grateful to Jerry Tarrer, Paul Brady, and Ernesto Constantino for their constructive criticism and intellectual stimulation, as well as Ruthie Wilson and Marcia Hospedales for their continual encouragement, unfailing support, and caring. I also appreciate the generous assistance and support of Dr. Sanders and Su He. Thanks to Dr. Bailey and others who reviewed parts of the final dissertation manuscript and provided helpful feedback.

In the movement of this scholarly piece to a book, there are others to whom I want to express my gratitude.

I thank Mary Lewis, my friend and editorial consultant, who encouraged me to embrace and enjoy this process. She also helped me to stay on track with respect to time commitments and offered her journalistic capabilities in ensuring that the arguments were logical and clearly expressed. The book became quite a marathon for me and she was a much valued and patient coach. A significant participant in the final laps of this marathon was Dennis Aldycki, who consistently demonstrated that a task worth doing is worth doing right the first time. I thank him for his assistance, unfailing support, commitment, and the long hours–right up to the final delivery. I also wish to extend my thanks to Ramiro Atristain for his input in the situational context portion of this book.

It is said that people are as rich as the people in their lives. I am lucky to be surrounded by people who care. In particular, I am deeply grateful to Philip Hendel for his unconditional support, caring, and encouragement extended throughout this process. He also helped to remove obstacles that might have impeded the completion of this book. I would be remiss not to extend my deepest appreciation to Aaron Busch, a masterful thinker, innovator, and practitioner. His consistent support and input have helped refine my thinking and contributed to the success of my consulting business. The results of this and other research we conducted have also helped to solidify my holistic approach to organizational change as well as diversity, and produce positive bottom line results for our clients.

Special appreciation is also extended to my mother, brother, sister, aunt, and other family members who provided invaluable moral and financial support throughout the dissertation process. I owe them a debt of gratitude for their sound advice, love and unfailing faith in me. They are my Rock of Gibraltar, and they continue to encourage me to be the best I can be throughout all my endeavors.

Last but not least, I acknowledge my unfailing faith in God, who continues to protect me and allow me to be free, because with Him all things are possible.

Tables

Charts

The Myth of Black
Corporate Mobility

CHAPTER I

General Introduction

The United States has always been a haven for immigrants. Culturally diverse people from Europe, Africa, Latin America, Asia, the Caribbean, and other places have come to the U.S. in search of a new way of life, economic prosperity, and an escape from religious and political persecution. These diverse groups have helped to shape the character of American life as it exists today. Descendants of European immigrants continue to form the dominant white American culture. However, blacks, Americans of African descent, remain America's most visible minority group, separate in many ways from the dominant society (Nixon 1983).

Until the mid-1950s, in many states blacks were not allowed, by law, equal access and opportunities to such things as adequate housing, medical care, job opportunities, and career advancement within the corporate arena. During the late 1950s, several states began passing fair employment acts which forbade private employers, labor unions, and employment agencies from hiring, promoting, or dismissing workers on the basis of race, color, creed, or national origin.

Between 1960 and 1964, activist groups such as the NAACP began filing lawsuits alleging discriminatory actions perpetuated against blacks in several areas, including employment. Additionally, these activist groups, including blacks led by civil rights spokesmen such as Dr. Martin Luther King Jr., engaged in civil disobedience to protest the unfair treatment black Americans historically had received (Salmon 1979). As a result, in 1964 Congress passed a Civil Rights Act that included the establishment of the Equal Employment Opportunity Commission (EEOC) to administer and enforce federal equal employment laws (Fernandez 1975). This Act provided the strong legislative foundation needed for the elimination of discrimination based on race, color, religion, sex, or national origin (Hall and Albrecht 1979; Fernandez 1993). Thus, the Civil Rights Act of 1964 and the lawsuits that followed were designed to address "inequitable practices that keep the earnings of blacks and women below those of similarly qualified white men" (Farley 1984, 124).

To ensure compliance with the 1964 Civil Rights Act by corporations and other business enterprises, several additional legislative initiatives were undertaken. Perhaps the most significant came in the form of affirmative action programs. Affirmative action began officially when President Lyndon B. Johnson signed Executive Order 11246 on September 24, 1965. That order required employers holding federal contracts to make an affirmative effort to ensure that applicants were hired and employees were promoted and treated without regard to their color, race, religion, or national origin. Affirmative action was designed to overcome continuing discrimination and ultimately to provide equal job opportunities for both minorities and whites. In 1968, Executive Order 11246 was amended by Executive Order 11375 to include women (Sobel 1980; Villere and Hartman 1989; Gleckman et al. 1991). The goals of affirmative action were to be accomplished through employers' implementation of specific programs or plans which included "measurable indications of improvement by minorities and females in various employment areas including hiring, promotion, and training" (Villere and Hartman 1989, 23).

In the past, affirmative action had been "generally perceived by the public as any program whose purpose is to overcome the effects of past discrimination against minorities or women by increasing their numbers in employment and public programs" (Rasnic 1988, 176). In this vein, Jackson-Leslie (1995) sees affirmative action as "an organized effort to provide increased employment opportunities for women and ethnic minorities for past as well as present patterns of discrimination" (24). Patterson (1995) contends that this anti-discrimination strategy was designed to compensate for opportunities denied *talented* minorities and women, thus intending to curb the systematic exclusion of these groups from opportunities. While affirmative action laws and its subsequent programs played an important role in the employment of African Americans, it did not go the full extent in eradicating the injustices it was designed to correct—discrimination and its effects still reign supreme in America (Barclay 1996; Charme Zane 1994).

Affirmative action, however, continues to come under increased scrutiny and criticism (Crosby and Clayton 1990; Heilman 1994). Many view affirmative action as providing preferential treatment for America's "protected groups" (i.e., minorities and women). Some argue that this preferential treatment is morally wrong and unfair to other members of American society. For instance, some opponents of affirmative action claim that providing preferential treatment for certain groups appears to be contrary to the original intent of equal opportunity, in that it violates Title VII of the Civil Rights Act of 1964. Additionally, affirmative action opponents argue that allowing special treatment to make up for wrongs committed against ancestors provides "remedies to individuals who are not themselves victims" of discrimination (Villere and Hartman 1989, 26-27). However, regardless of these alleged weaknesses, some gains have been made. Substantial pressure was put on corporate America to hire minorities and females in the years following both the Civil Rights Movement and the enactment of affirmative action legislation (Hall and Albrecht 1979). Since the 1960s, the number of minorities, blacks in particular, employed within the corporate arena has increased substantially. Between 1975 and 1979, for example, the representation of women and minorities in banking management and the electronics industry increased by 52 percent (Hall 1979, Villere and Hartman 1989).

Between 1967 and 1992 the relative percentage increase of blacks in the work force was 50%. During roughly the same twenty-year period, there has also been a substantial relative increase in the percentage of blacks employed in managerial positions. Federal statistics show that between 1972 and 1982 the number of blacks classified as managers and officials increased by 83%. Equal Employment Opportunity Commission statistics show that while blacks accounted for 1.9% of the managerial positions in 1970, they accounted for 4.8% of managerial positions in 1985. In 1989 approximately 5% of all managers in the nation were black.

This represents a 500% increase since 1966 and a 30% increase since 1978 (Hymowitz 1989; McBride 1987; Braham 1987; DiTomaso and Thompson 1988; Gleckman et al. 1991). Yet the news is not all good. In 1990 blacks still accounted for 5% of all officials and managers and in 1993 they accounted for 5.1%. As recently as 1996, blacks represented approximately 12.6% of the population yet accounted for only 5.3% of all officials and managers (U.S. Department of Commerce, Statistical Abstract 1997).

Despite the overall increased presence of blacks within the corporate arena, many believe there still exists a cause for concern (Fernandez 1981; Work 1984; U.S. Department of Labor 1991). In terms of absolute numbers, blacks were and still are severely underrepresented in the managerial ranks (Dovidio and Gaertner 1996; Hartmann 1997; U.S. Department of Labor 1997). Those blacks who held managerial positions appear to be concentrated in lower and middle level management with very little representation at the upper rungs of the corporate ladder. A 1979 survey conducted by Korn/Ferry International found that blacks represented only 0.2% of the senior executives of American corporations. A later survey also conducted by Korn/Ferry International showed that in 1985 the representation of blacks in the senior executive ranks was only 0.3%. Indeed, from 1980 to 1990 there was only a very slight increase in the representation of minorities in the top executive positions in America's 1,000 largest corporations (Korn/Ferry International 1990).

More recent statistics (Federal Glass Ceiling Commission 1995) revealed that black men hold only 2.3% of executive administrative and management jobs in all private sector industries (black women hold 2.2%) and 3.9% of these jobs in the private and public sectors combined (black women holding 4.6%). Broken down by industry, data from the Federal Glass Ceiling Commission sponsored by Republican members of Congress (March 1995) show that white men hold 44.8% of administrative and managerial positions in banking, 51.6% in business services, 47.6% in communications, 74.6% in construction, 71.9% in the utilities, 58.5% in transportation, 62.9% in manufacturing, 47.5% in public administration, while blacks hold only 2.3% in all private sector industries and 3.9% in public and private sectors combined.

More damaging statistics on minority representation revealed by this commission show that while white males comprise 43% of the work force, they hold 95% of senior management positions. That compares with African Americans, who hold 0.6% of those positions; Hispanic Americans, who hold 0.4%; Asian Americans, 0.3% and women with between 3% and 5%. These data suggest that very little progress has been made in increasing black representation at the upper levels of management. The data also reveal that while affirmative action laws and programs had some impact on the employment of blacks and other minorities at lower corporate levels, they had minimal impact in moving these groups up the corporate ladder to senior executive ranks.

Some corporate leaders argue, with what they perceive to be some amount of justification, that the main reason blacks are underrepresentation at upper levels of management is the small number of blacks in the labor pool with the requisite academic and professional backgrounds to function in the corporate arena (Zweigenhaft 1984). In a corroborative study conducted by DiTomaso, 218 of America's top, publicly owned companies (as indicated by *Forbes* in its list of top 500 U.S. companies) were surveyed for their opinion of minority advancement (DiTomaso et al. 1988). According to DiTomaso, "responses were well distributed across industry type, with the primary concentration in durable and nondurable goods manufacturing; transportation, communications, and other public utilities; and finance, insurance, and real estate" (120). The most frequent response by these corporate leaders for factors that hinder the success of blacks in the corporate arena was the "insufficient number of qualified candidates" in the labor pool (DiTomaso 1988, 135). The U.S. Statistical Abstract (1997) revealed additional educational data, for blacks and whites with four or more years of college for the years 1990 and 1996, that can support the above assertions. The data reveal that only 11.3% of blacks in 1990 and only 13.6% of blacks in 1996 over the age of 25 had completed four or more years of college, while 22% of whites in 1990 and 24.3% of whites in 1996 over the age of 25 had completed four or more years of college (U.S. Department of Commerce 1997).

These data, examined in isolation, reinforce a popularly expressed belief that too few blacks entering the work force have the educational requirements that corporations need to fill positions at higher levels of the corporate hierarchy. Corporate leaders argue that most blacks major in education and the social sciences and that too few blacks have degrees in business administration, engineering, and the hard sciences (DiTomaso and Thompson 1988). For example, Spilerman (1988) explains that:

> . . . in recruiting for management and professional positions and in promotion decisions to middle level management, many firms seek not simply individuals with college credentials but candidates with particular majors. Mathematics, engineering, computer science, economics, and business school backgrounds are generally the most valuable, not only for positions that require the formal skills associated within these majors but more widely because they signify a familiarity with analyzing complex information. In contrast, majors in education, humanities and the social sciences are usually less attractive to industrial and financial organizations (30).

Again, statistics show that there may be some truth to these assertions. In a study conducted by Spilerman (1988), only 16.6% of the master's degrees awarded to blacks in 1979 were in quantitative areas such as the physical sciences, engineering, and business; the rest were in areas such as education, social sciences, and the humanities. These statistics are considerably lower than those of whites and Asians, who respectively had 24.3% and 45.6% of their master's degrees in quantitative areas (Spilerman 1988). While the education argument is offered as justification for the lack of blacks' upward mobility, others such as the U.S. Department of Labor 1992 Report, "Pipelines of Progress," purported that attitudinal and organizational barriers have a far more deleterious effect on minority career advancement than qualifications or career choice.

Additionally, many researchers, corporate leaders and average citizens believe that blacks do not have the relevant experiences needed to succeed at higher levels in U.S. companies. There is some evidence to support this belief. Statistics reported by the U.S. Equal Employment Opportunity Commission for 1989 show that only 4.5% of the black labor force population in private industry held executive, administrative, or managerial positions as compared with 13.3% for the white labor force population and 11.4% for the labor force as a whole. Corporate leaders and others continue to argue that this discrepancy occurs because blacks lack relevant professional experience and thus find it more difficult to climb the corporate ladder successfully. Adams (1993) and the Federal Glass Ceiling Report (1995) indicated that minorities continue to be steered into traditional academic and occupational tracks that are not aligned with the courses and skills considered vital for movement into the executive ranks. This perceived lack of experiences of qualified minorities is due in part to their limited access to relevant developmental opportunities and experiences needed for advancement (Wernick 1994). The end result is that blacks and other minorities are underrepresented at higher levels of the corporate structure.

However, there is much evidence that blacks who are "qualified" or who arguably have all the requisite skills and academic and professional backgrounds needed for career advancement are still not moving up the corporate ladder at the same rates as their white peers. A survey conducted in 1986 by Edward W. Jones, Jr., found that out of 107 black managers who had received MBAs from the nation's top five graduate business schools, 98% believed that there was no equal opportunity for black managers in the corporate arena. Indeed, 84% of the respondents maintained that their mobility was inhibited because of their race, despite the fact that they were well qualified (Jones 1986). A 1987 survey of black managers conducted by Richard Clarke Associates, Inc., reported that 97% of the respondents held college degrees and more than 50% held graduate degrees. In comparison, a 1986 *Fortune* Magazine survey of CEOs who were all white, representing America's Fortune 500 companies, found that 97% of respondents held college degrees while 63% held graduate degrees (McComas 1986). These surveys suggest that black managers hold academic credentials broadly similar to the CEOs of America's leading corporations. Indeed, black managers in the 1987 Clarke survey considered themselves qualified to hold upper level positions within their respective corporations. Yet, 56% felt that they could not reach the top levels of their corporations because of their race. In fact, 62% of the respondents believed that their mobility in general was inhibited because of their race.

While it is important to recognize that these responses are perceptions which may be biased, it is also important to give attention to the concerns that these black employees express. Their concerns are significant because of the large percentage of respondents who expressed this opinion, the consistency of research findings, and recent evidence that these perceptions may be based on truth. In providing some support to the latter, another U.S. Department of Labor Study (1991), "The Impact of the Glass Ceiling on African American Men and Women," found that "the level of education has only a very limited impact on the likelihood of blacks' employment in top positions" (2). Another study conducted by the U.S. Department of Labor in 1991 indicated that of the nine Fortune 500 companies examined, minorities had made significant progress at the entry level and first levels of management. But, they had not experienced similar progress at mid-level and senior executive levels of management, despite "their increased experience, credentials, overall qualifications, and a greater attachment to the work force" (6).

Even more recent studies by Fernandez (1993), Wernick (1994), America and Anderson (1996), and the U.S. Department of Labor (1997) support this reality. Fernandez (1993) also contends that black managers tend to be older, have longer tenure with their companies and on average tend to be more educated than their peers. The Glass Ceiling Commission Report of 1992 by U.S. Secretary of Labor Robert Reich indicated that hiring blacks does not ensure equality of opportunity to move up in the corporate hierarchy. A U.S. Department of Labor Report (1997), "Are There Cracks in the Glass Ceiling?", shared findings from the fiscal year 1993-1994 corporate management reviews. These reviews indicated that severe problems existed in terms of discriminatory hiring and compensation practices which negatively impact salaries and promotions for minorities. These findings imply that equality of educational attainment alone is not sufficient for blacks to shatter the glass ceiling.

If salary is any indication of mobility, then blacks may be justified in their concern. A 1990 study conducted by the U.S. Census Bureau reported that black men 25 years and older who have four or more years of college education earned a third less than their white male counterparts who had equal amounts of education (U.S. Census Bureau 1991). A U.S. Department of Labor Study (1991), "The Impact of the Glass Ceiling on

African American Men and Women," indicated that inequality in income for blacks at corporate levels is worse within some industries. For example, in finance, real estate and insurance industries, blacks in top positions earned slightly more than half the salaries of whites in similar positions. In the wholesale trade and professional services industries, blacks earned less than half the salaries of whites in similar positions.

The March 1995 Current Population Survey conducted by the U.S. Census Bureau indicated that at the higher end of the income level distribution whites also enjoyed higher level earnings for 1994. Fifteen percent of whites, versus three percent of blacks, had incomes of more than $60,000. This survey also indicated that income differences in 1994 existed, even with the same levels of educational attainment. Earnings for whites were $41,475 versus $33,899 for blacks. The earnings differential was even wider when comparisons were made between white males ($48,591) and black males ($36,072). In fact, Jeffries and Schaffer (1996) contend that "increases in education do little to close the earnings gap between blacks and whites" (58). A U.S. Department of Labor Report (1997) noted that while the highest paid women in companies studied in 1994 had only the 20th highest salary, the highest paid minority ranked 127th. Another study, the Federal Glass Ceiling Commission (1995) found that black men who hold executive positions earn 79% less than their white male counterparts with similar degrees in similar positions. Based on this reality, the labor market must find a way to eliminate the old "tradition" which has always assured that blacks will earn significantly less than whites for doing the same job and having the same credentials and experience (Price 1996).

Despite the implementation of legislative and company initiatives, qualified blacks who manage to enter the corporate arena do not experience rates of upward mobility or earnings comparable to their white peers (Fernandez 1981; Work 1984; Jones 1986; Collins 1997). Many black employees believe that, after the years of supposed commitment made by corporations to equal opportunity in the aftermath of the civil rights era, blacks are still underrepresented in key positions and upper management levels of the corporate hierarchy (Braham 1987). Many argue that there is a "glass ceiling" which blacks hit as they move up the corporate ladder. That is, black upward mobility is limited and no amount of motivation, work performance, credentials, and experience can break through this barrier (Reibstein 1986; U.S. Department of Labor 1991 and 1992).

The 1991 study of nine Fortune 500 companies conducted by the U.S. Department of Labor (initiated by the Secretary of Labor) provided support for the existence of a "glass ceiling" or position level within these corporations, beyond which few blacks had either advanced or been recruited. Other researchers and studies that reinforce the existence of this "glass ceiling" include Igbaria and Wormley (1995), Federal Glass Ceiling Commission (1995), and the U.S. Department of Labor (1997). Loden (1996) contends that racism remains one of the most toxic, lethal, and emotionally charged problems in our society and overwhelms diversity initiatives in the workplace which are designed to address some of these issues. The U. S. Department of Labor's Glass Ceiling Initiative (1997) further supports this viewpoint and states that attitudinal and organizational barriers are impenetrable between minorities and the executive suite and inhibit their advancement of upper levels of management irrespective of their performance, qualifications, and merit.

Arthur, Hall, and Lawrence (1989) and Freedman (1995) contend that within the corporate arena the upward mobility process is generally viewed as a fair contest among individuals in which the most deserving employees—the best performers—receive rewards in the form of promotion and salary increases. The Ugorji 1997 study revealed that on the issue of promotion, African Americans had significantly higher means in experiencing such behaviors as "steered me away from management track titles," "discouraged me from seeking promotional opportunities" and "kept moving the goal post with respect to promotion" (253).

Black employees who viewed their upward mobility as being "stymied are increasingly disillusioned about their chances for ultimate success" (Jones 1986, 84). In spite of the legal advances achieved during the civil rights era, these "qualified" blacks have a growing sense of disappointment, frustration, betrayal, and anger. They believe that, despite having the required educational credentials and professional experience, they are not experiencing comparable rates of upward mobility as their white peers (McBride 1987; Kanter 1988; Fernandez 1993). While these perceptions do not enable one to conclude conclusively that the mobility process is unfair, the preponderance of data and research point to an unfair contest for qualified black employees.

Blacks' lack of corporate mobility should be of great concern because of the range of reactions by these employees to their reported unfair treatment. Many researchers report that some black managers simply opt out of the corporate arena as a consequence of their dismay and frustration over limited opportunities for career advancement in America's white-run corporations (Enkelis 1984; James 1988; Loden 1996). In many instances, black employees who leave the "white" corporate arena are among the more competent employees (Braham 1987). On June 7, 1988, *The Wall Street Journal* reported that, in interviews with blacks who had left predominantly white corporations, their most frequently expressed concern was that of limited opportunity and an inability to accomplish similar levels of career advancement as their comparably qualified white peers. Many researchers of this issue believe that an exodus of talented blacks from the corporate arena is due primarily to what blacks perceive to be slow rates of upward mobility brought about by unfair treatment and inequality of opportunity because of their race.

These blacks are seeking alternative arenas, such as entrepreneurship or other corporations, where they perceive that they have better opportunities to apply their skills and maximize their potential. Others are seeking employment with black-owned firms (McBride 1987; James 1988; Adams 1993; Bates 1994). America and Anderson (1996) advise blacks to stop wasting time, believing the myths and confronting racial discriminators. Instead, they must sharpen their skills, build professional credibility, access networks, and either move up or move out.

This exodus of competent black employees out of corporate careers, their lack of representation at upper management levels, the underutilization of these human resources, and the perceived slow rates of upward mobility because of the glass ceiling and other related factors should be an important cause of concern for business leaders.

Shattering the "glass ceiling" is an economic imperative and if it does not occur, it will have a deleterious impact on businesses' bottom line and the future economic stability of America's families (Federal Glass Ceiling Commission Report 1995). As Price (1996) indicated, "all Americans must be equipped and encouraged to contribute to America's well being" (7). As America approaches the year 2000, changing demographics, a more diverse customer base, and increasing competition in the national and international arenas will have important implications for American businesses. The glass ceiling can only be broken by corporate leaders and top management who have the power to change the organizational climate and instill new values (Dimpka 1992).

The next section of this chapter provides a brief outline and analysis of the situation that researchers predict American businesses will face during the late 1990s and beyond if they fail to maximize the use of all available human resources. It will outline how the underutilization and exodus of talented and competent blacks from the corporate arena could have severe consequences for the future of America's corporations. Additionally, this information will provide a context for interpreting the data presented in this study and for developing implications and recommendations.

SITUATIONAL CONTEXT

The underutilization of any talent, regardless of race, gender, creed and the like, adversely impacts long-term organizational success (Bell 1996). Corporate America is slowly realizing the need to maximize the use of its human resources. This realization comes as a result of changing demographics, increasing competition, and technological changes taking place on both the national and international fronts (Farrell, Weber, and Schroeder 1990; Federal Glass Ceiling Commission 1995). Countries should prepare themselves for the future as a result of burgeoning robust economies in countries that were previously economically stagnant and the subsequent shift to global markets (Neely and Carter, Fall 1990/1991).

Robert D. Kennedy, Chairman and CEO of Union Carbide Corporation, contended that business survival depends on how well managers read trends and anticipate the problems that can arise in the future. Further, he stated that companies were ignoring very important signs of concern in their most critical resource—the supply of skilled employees in the work force (*The Wall Street Journal,* 1990). If women and minorities are not utilized more efficiently, the U.S. may experience problems in filling the high skilled, high paying positions, that in the future, are expected to grow faster (Silvestri and Lukasiewics 1992). As the labor pool contracts, companies that have not developed the competency in successfully managing diversity will find it difficult to compete with other companies in recruiting and hiring new, younger workers with the needed skills (Cox, Lobel, and McLeod 1991; Baker 1995). The U.S. Department of Labor's Glass Ceiling Initiative (1997) reported that "diversity is good and necessary for a profitable business" (3). Klagge (1997) agrees with this assertion. However, in spite of the economic benefits derived from valuing diversity, the business case for diversity is seldom acknowledged or emphasized in corporate initiatives (Loden 1996).

Although the "U.S. remains the premier economic power," the rest of the world is quickly catching up (Pennar 1990, 62). As of the late 1990s, the American economy was the healthiest it had been in three decades and the U.S. has been enjoying one of the highest standards of living in the world (President Clinton's Economic Report 1997; Price 1998). Some indicators of this prosperity are reflected in the following statistical data:

- unemployment rates have decreased by nearly 33% in the last four years (1994-1997) and inflation averaged 2.8%—both factors are at their lowest in three decades;
- business investment increased more than 11% per year–the fastest since the 1960s;
- between 1993 and 1995 the poverty rate experienced the largest two-year drop in more than 20 years, as presented from economic indicators;
- during 1997 the productivity growth rate of 4.2% was slightly faster than production growth.

However, with major economic challenges still facing the U.S., America must learn from its past. Since the 1980s, America's corporate leaders have been increasingly faced with downsizing and rapid technological change. Concern has mounted about the growing shortage of skilled labor (Bernstein, Anderson, and Zellner 1987), due in part to employees lacking the necessary skills and qualifications required to be productive within the corporate arena and the work force in general (Bernstein, Anderson, and Zellner 1987; Farrell, Weber, and Schroeder 1990; Hudson Institute, Workforce 2020 1997). Silvestri and Lukasiewcz (1992) contend that opportunities to move into occupations that are higher paying will generally demand post-secondary education. Since the fastest growing jobs demand the highest levels of education, for blacks to compete in the labor market over the next 15 years, they must meet these higher level requirements (Kutscher 1992).

Badi G. Foster, President of Aetna Life & Casualty Co.'s Institute for Corporate Education, argued that companies were already finding shortages in skills that are critical for employees' productive performance (Bernstein, Anderson, and Zellner 1987; Judy 1997). Further, American corporations have been expressing concern that in the near future, there may not be an available supply of qualified managers needed to run their companies effectively (Bernstein, Anderson, and Zellner 1987). One of the consequences of this shortage of qualified workers is that America may experience difficulty in competing effectively in world markets. To enjoy the fruits of a growing economy, the U.S. must continue to be a major player in the world economy (Neely and Carter, Fall 1990/1991). Thus, America's corporations cannot afford the loss of any qualified and competent managers.

During the 1970s through the late1980s, the United States' position as a key competitor was challenged throughout the global market as countries such as Japan and Germany gained on the U.S. at a rapid rate. Pennar (1990) found that "from 1973 to 1989, annual gains in output per hour averaged 5.5% in Japan compared to 2.6% in the U.S." (62). Within the United States, companies were facing increased competition from outside sources (Mandel 1990). The number of jobs within the U.S. generated by foreign companies was growing fast. In 1988, 3.7 million Americans worked for foreign companies within the U.S., whereas in 1991 that number had increased to more than 4.5 million (Hoerr, Spiro, Armstrong, and Treece 1990).

Productivity within industries is a major factor that determines the robustness of the U.S. economy (Neely and Carter, Fall 1990/1991). Because of a troubled infrastructure and a poor education system, U.S. companies no longer saw themselves optimally competitive in the global market (Farrell, Weber, and Schroeder 1990). Citing the fact that the American productivity growth rate fell from an average annual gain of 2.8% between 1958 and 1969, to a gain of 1.4% between 1970 and 1986, Farrell, Weber, and Schroeder (1990) contend that production standards must be improved if the United States is to compete successfully in the global market. Mandel and Bernstein (1990) cite Robert Z. Lawrence, an economist at the Brookings Institution, as stating that if America does not become more competitive in the global marketplace, during the 1990s its standard of living could be reduced by 3%—erasing the gains made in the 1980s.

In spite of an excellent current economic outlook, rapid changes are still taking place in the American economy, technology, and society. In President Clinton's Economic Report (1997), he recommends that "instead of ignoring or lamenting these changes, the Nation must embrace them, transforming problems into opportunities" (28). A case in point comes to mind—changing demographics in the American work force. Cox, Jr., and Smolinski (1994) and Federal Glass Ceiling Commission Report (1995) noted a strong positive correlation between companies that had a high representation of all racial and gender groups and the impact on the bottom line. America not only has to invest in its labor force and develop and implement technological advances, it also has to begin to fully utilize all of its available human resources (Pennar 1990; Neely and Carter, Fall 1990/1991; U.S. Department of Labor 1997). This need for American corporations to fully exploit their human resources becomes clear when examining the nation's changing demographics. In 1987 demographers predicted that several major changes in the U.S. work force would take place by the year 2000 (Hudson Institute 1987):

- The labor force will grow at a slower rate than at any time in the last 60 years;
- The dwindling numbers of new entrants will require a search for workers among groups of individuals previously ignored (also U.S. Department of Labor 1997);
- In 30 years minorities will comprise 39% of the U.S. population (also Mercer 1990);

- Nearly a third of all new entrants in the work force will be non-white;
- More than 15% of the labor force will be people of color by the end of the next decade. From now until the end of the century 85% of work force growth, *including immigrants*, will come from women, blacks, and people of Hispanic or Asian origin;
- One-third of all new jobs will require a college degree.

Chusmir and Ruf (1992) contend that minorities are becoming an "increasingly important source of badly needed skilled individuals to fill jobs between today and the year 2000" (56).

Demographers also predict that due to a decrease in annual growth rates, white males will account for only 15% of the new workers entering the work force by the year 2000 (Hudson Institute 1987). By the year 2000, white males will account for 45% of the work force, a significant decrease from the 51% representation of 1980 (Dreyfuss 1990). At the same time, women, blacks, and other minorities will account for 55% of the work force (Dreyfuss 1990). The nature of the corporate work force is shifting from one in which white males are the majority, into one in which women and minorities are the majority. Because of demographic changes in the U.S. work force—an increase in black representation from 10% to 12% is expected by the year 2000—and the growing need to employ qualified and competent workers, corporations cannot afford the loss of any qualified black employees (U.S. Department of Labor, Bureau of Labor Statistics 1990). But who will be the group still controlling the top jobs in corporate America?   Data show that white males make up 43% of the population but still hold 95% of senior management positions (Federal Glass Ceiling Commission 1995).

To add more understanding to the need for better utilization of all groups, it is important to understand the market arena and the need for efficiency. In his 1975 book on equality and efficiency, Arthur Okun (1975) argued that certain trade-offs exist between equality and efficiency. Okun explained that equality should be promoted only to the point "where added benefits of more equality are fairly matched by the added costs of greater efficiency" (90). For instance, he argued that attempting to create equality by equalizing such things as capital and income would create inefficiencies that would be too costly for society to sustain (e.g., Okun stated that equalizing income would eliminate incentives and thus create inefficiency). Yet, Okun argued for the promotion of equal opportunity because it promotes increases in efficiency. According to Okun, one way in which promotion of equality of opportunity increases efficiency is by allowing for the use of those qualified individuals who otherwise would go underutilized. The point here is that corporations can increase their efficiency, and thus their productivity, by promoting equal opportunity within their work environments.

Given the changing demographics of this country and other realities, American corporations will need to seek out labor and resources in areas that have been underutilized in the past—especially as it relates to meeting the needs of their increasingly diverse customer base, domestically and internationally (Doka 1996; Loden 1996). In particular, in order to increase their efficiency, if they are not already doing so, corporations need to provide equal opportunity for career advancement to qualified black employees and other groups similarly underutilized. Any exodus of qualified blacks and other minorities from the corporate arena can have severe consequences for businesses as they search for competent workers to manage their corporations as America approaches the year 2000. America needs all of its qualified workers so that the nation's corporations can remain competitive (Neely and Carter 1990/1991; Fernandez 1993). It will be particularly important for businesses to retain qualified minority employees because of their predicted increase in the proportion of the work force by the year 2000. While corporations are aware of the benefits of diversity, the changes in U.S. demographics argument alone does not motivate their leaders to pursue real and sustainable organizational change (Loden 1996).

However, some corporations are making attempts to address the issue of the slow rates of upward mobility experienced by black employees. These corporations appear to be aware of and concerned about the issue of black upward mobility, and some have taken actions to address this issue (U.S. Department of Labor 1991, 24). For example, in 1988 Wilbert S. Crump, Director of Equal Employment Opportunity for Allied-Signal, Inc., explained that during the 1980s an objective of Allied-Signal was to accelerate the entry of minorities and women into middle and more senior level positions. To accomplish this objective, Crump stated that:

> . . . in 1980 the chairman [of Allied-Signal, Inc.] and his executive committee adopted a proposal wherein the hiring and promoting of minorities and women into significant-level executive positions would be incorporated into the annual action plans of senior managers eligible for incentive compensation. In effect, this program ties incentive compensation to the accomplishment of equal opportunity goals. One of the unique features of this program is that it goes beyond the achievement of government-mandated EEOC requirements (Crump 1988, 257).

Another example of a corporation attempting to address black upward mobility was demonstrated during the 1980s by the efforts of Exxon Corporation. Robert A. Hofstader, Manager of the Education and Development Unit of Exxon Research and Engineering Company (an affiliate of Exxon Corporation) described the creation of an Affirmative Action and Advisory Committee in 1981. This committee was comprised of senior management at the company and "assumed the responsibility to pay attention to the full utilization, retention, and upward mobility of the company's women and minorities" (Hofstader 1988, 249). Exxon developed this committee based on "long standing business objectives of effecting a work environment conducive to the fullest productivity of the company's human resources" (249).

Other efforts by a U.S. corporation to address the issue of slow rates of black upward mobility were demonstrated by McNeil Pharmaceutical (an affiliate company of Johnson & Johnson). Gail Judge, Vice President of Personnel for McNeil Pharmaceutical explained that in 1986 Johnson & Johnson developed a corporate committee of senior black managers to help the company probe the underrepresentation of blacks in upper management. In addition, in 1984 Johnson & Johnson engaged a consulting firm to conduct an "interpretive analysis of retention of black managers" (Judge 1988, 246). According to Judge, each effort was conducted in an attempt to thoroughly diagnose and address the issue of black upward mobility.

A 1991 study by the U.S. Department of Labor reported that chief executive officers became personally involved in the efforts to address the slow rates of upward mobility that minority and female employees have been experiencing in the corporate arena. According to the study,

> . . . one large defense contractor briefed the Department's executive staff of their efforts. With the strong support of the CEO and other corporate officers this company has determined to aggressively recruit minorities and women through external recruitment efforts, including executive searches; make "deputy" assignments, when possible, using these positions as training grounds for developing minorities and women as "high potential" managers; executive mentoring and sponsoring high potential or high performing minority or female managers and professionals; and increase executive accountability and responsibility for cultural changes at every level through a creative incentive compensation plan (24).

The study also reinforced that top executives were giving a lot of their time and attention to the issue of black upward mobility. These executives were communicating their commitment by identifying special studies and task forces to develop and implement programs to address issues related to the slow rates of upward mobility experienced by qualified minorities and women.

Another study conducted by the U.S. Department of Labor (1992), "Pipelines of Progress," spoke about a Fortune 500 company that reorganized and placed all of its responsibilities for equal employment opportunity in an integrated human resource structure. Some of the initiatives they undertook were incorporated into their strategic plan for the achievement of work force diversity. Among the initiatives were: a) the scheduling of a diversity conference involving senior management, b) the management of the development of a strategic plan by the Senior Vice President of Human Resources, and c) a diversity planning session which convened and involved directors from each business unit. This report named still another company, Southern Bell of Georgia, which since its inception has included high potential women and minorities in its High Potential Development Program to make certain that they are not overlooked when advancement opportunities occur. In 1991, this company received the U.S. Department of Labor's Exemplary Voluntary Effort (EVE) Award. Other companies that have actively tried to eliminate the glass ceiling are Columbia Broadcasting System, Cummins Engine and Procter and Gamble. They tried to eliminate barriers to advancement for all qualified employees through the use of internships, job postings, mentoring, career development, succession planning, and the formation of a Female Retention Task Force (U.S. Department of Labor 1997). Clearly, some corporations have been making serious efforts to address issues concerning black upward mobility in corporations.

However, irrespective of the efforts of some highly visible corporations, blacks continue to perceive their upward mobility within the corporate arena as being inhibited. They argue that, despite having acquired the requisite education and experience for corporate upward mobility, success eludes them. These black employees argue that they are not experiencing levels of career advancement comparable to their similarly qualified white peers because of inequality of opportunity. Lending some support to these claims are government data from the U.S. Equal Employment Opportunity Commission (1989), the U.S. Census Bureau (1990), the U.S. Department of Labor (1991), Fernandez (1993), the Federal Glass Ceiling Commission (1995), Igbaria and Wormley (1995), and the U.S. Department of Labor (1997), which show that minorities and women are still significantly underrepresented in upper-middle through top levels of management. Thus, additional examinations must be made into the claims of these blacks in an attempt to understand better their situation and the reasons why they continue to perceive their opportunities to be limited. Additional examination also needs to be made as to the results of the initiatives of the corporations previously featured. Have they achieved their stated goals? If not, then why not? and if yes, then what factors facilitated that achievement?

To increase their own economic success, American corporations need to continue to examine the mobility process of their minority group employees in comparison to that of their similarly qualified white employees and their own intentions and efforts. The intent of this examination should be to ensure a fair work environment, in which all employees have an equal opportunity for career development and advancement, based on their qualifications, experience, and performance and in which their corporations can fully maximize the use of all of their human resources. The Federal Glass Ceiling Commission (1995) contended that "America's vast human resources are not being fully utilized because of glass ceiling barriers" (6). These issues are particularly noteworthy since, in most corporate arenas, their employees are their most valuable asset and competitive advantage.

Past and current analyses of research and statistical data revealed no substantial difference in the issues and conditions that qualified blacks face with regard to corporate upward mobility between the time this study was originally completed and the publication of this book. In fact, with changing demographics, increasing competition, technological changes, a more diverse customer base, and shortages in the supply of skilled labor, it behooves America in general and corporations in particular to maximize the talents and potential of all of its human resources.

PURPOSE OF STUDY

A number of surveys have shown that many blacks working in the corporate arena believe that blacks experience slower rates of upward mobility than their white peers, despite having met the requisite academic and professional qualifications and performance standards needed for corporate upward mobility. Research and statistical data have also given credence and support to the assertion made by these black employees. Thus, the primary purpose of this study is to gain some understanding as to why "qualified" black employees within the corporate arena may experience limited opportunities for career advancement to mid- and upper level management positions, despite their qualifications.

To begin, this study reviewed relevant literature addressing the issue of black mobility in the corporate arena, in an attempt to identify those factors that can influence the mobility of employees in general and of blacks in particular. Then, the study examined the rates of upward mobility of similarly qualified black and white managers, while controlling for those factors that the literature suggests influence the upward mobility of all employees. The managers participating in this study were deemed "qualified" in the sense that they possessed the skills and qualifications reported as requirements for advancement to middle and upper level management positions in most industries. This analysis is an attempt to investigate whether any differences actually exist in the rates of upward mobility between qualified blacks and their similarly qualified white peers.

A comparison between similarly qualified black and white managers should provide some means of exploring the credibility of the assertion by black managers that they are experiencing slow rates of upward mobility despite their qualifications. For example, if in this comparison it were found that whites experienced faster rates of upward mobility than the equally qualified black peers, then this finding would support blacks' perceptions that their opportunities for career advancement are limited despite their qualifications. It is hoped that this analysis will provide some insight into whether other factors, beyond those that are central to the upward mobility of all employees, do indeed contribute to any differing rates of upward mobility between qualified blacks and their similarly qualified white peers.

Next, a qualitative analysis was conducted that examines the perceptions of a national sample of qualified and experienced black senior corporate executives. This analysis attempted to identify any key factors that can influence the upward mobility of qualified black employees in the corporate arena. It is hoped that the perceptions of these executives could provide some understanding of the types of factors influencing the mobility of qualified blacks in the corporate arena and as a result add some insight into why blacks may experience limited opportunities and their mobility may be inhibited, despite their qualifications.

The model developed for the purposes of this study attempts to depict how qualified blacks can experience rates of upward mobility that are slower than those of their similarly qualified white peers within the corporate arena. The model is based on those factors that the review of the literature revealed to have a substantial influence on blacks' corporate upward mobility. The framework will point out important issues relevant to blacks' upward mobility that deserve thoughtful study.

This study is unique in that it looks specifically at black employees who are known to possess the requisite skills and qualifications which corporations traditionally have identified as prerequisites for employment and upward mobility. Many studies on this topic have not been as specific or as focused as this one on this particular factor. In addition, unlike many other studies, this study analyzes experiences of individuals employed at several corporations, examines perceptions and opinions of black employees as well as factual data, controls for some key variables that have the potential to influence upward mobility, and attempts to establish the credibility of the study's participants by documenting their academic and professional backgrounds. Additionally, this study provides a model that corporations can use to identify and isolate those factors within their respective companies that can account for differences in the rates of career advancement of black employees relative to their similarly qualified white peers.

Because of the predicted increase in the representation of blacks in the work force, the definite need for corporations to maximize the use of their available human resources, and other realities, it will be increasingly important to provide corporations with information that will help them identify those factors that can inhibit and enhance the upward mobility of black employees. This type of information will assist corporations in developing self-assessment instruments for identifying and analyzing the enhancers and inhibitors to black upward mobility and to other groups similarly situated within their particular corporate work environments. This data will also be useful as corporations seek to put some teeth into their diversity initiatives and address root causes of some of the challenges they are facing in their particular environments.

The attempts to identify enhancers and inhibitors of upward mobility for blacks will also provide corporations and industries with information that can be used to develop and implement appropriate and relevant policies, programs, and strategies for: a) addressing the impact of identified inhibitors on black upward mobility; b) creating a situation in which equally qualified black and white employees can experience equal opportunity for career advancement; c) creating a work force that better represents the country's diverse cultural make-up; and d) creating an environment where corporations can take full advantage of the available human capital—both white and non-white. Thus, the resulting information can aid corporations in managing ethnically diverse employee populations and in making the necessary changes to create more effective work environments and, hopefully, a more productive work force.

CHAPTER II
The Review of the Literature

In the previous chapter, an examination of certain statistical data demonstrated that blacks are clearly underrepresented in upper management positions within U.S. corporations. In an attempt to understand the reasons for this insufficiency, current literature on the issue of black mobility in the corporate arena was examined. Two main viewpoints surfaced. First, corporate leadership argued that blacks are underrepresented at the upper echelon because not enough qualified blacks are available to be promoted into these higher level management positions. Second, blacks employed in the corporate arena argued that there are blacks who have acquired the necessary qualifications, but they are still not being promoted into higher level positions. A number of surveys have shown that many blacks perceive that, despite having attained the requisite skills and qualifications needed for upward mobility, they were not receiving the same opportunities for corporate advancement as their similarly qualified white counterparts (Fernandez 1993; Wernick 1994; Federal Glass Ceiling Commission 1995; America and Anderson 1996;).

From the two apparently contradictory viewpoints of the corporations and the black employees, an important question arises: Why do blacks in the corporate arena, who view themselves as "qualified," perceive an inequality between the opportunities afforded to them and those afforded to their white similarly qualified counterparts?

Because most corporations are hierarchically structured, members of a particular group of employees must experience some degree of upward mobility within the hierarchy in order for that particular group to be represented at various positional levels. As a result, in addressing the issue of black underrepresentation in the corporate arena, it is important to examine issues relating to upward mobility as it pertains particularly to blacks and other minorities as well as employees in general. Thus, the question of the perceived inequality of opportunity for blacks will be addressed with the hope of adding some level of understanding about the problems that black employees experience in their attempts at upward mobility in America's white-run corporations. This chapter, therefore, examines the current major research literature, such as social theories, economic theories, and published works of several researchers which address issues related to upward mobility in general and the specific upward mobility of blacks and other minorities employed within the corporate arena.

This chapter is divided into two sections. The first section examines those key factors that the literature reports to have an influence on the employability (i.e., skills and academic background) and upward mobility of all employees of corporations. The second section of this chapter attempts to uncover those key factors that are reported to have an influence on the upward mobility of blacks in particular within the corporate arena. In fact, the factors identified here are purported to account for differences in the rates of upward mobility between black and white employees who have met the requisite skills and qualifications needed for corporate employability and upward mobility.

REQUISITE CORPORATE QUALIFICATIONS FOR ALL EMPLOYEES

In many areas of business, American companies have been at the forefront in the world market and have led the world in productivity. This dominance of the United States in the world market arena could be attributed in part to the emphasis by corporate leaders on productivity and efficiency. However, much concern has been also expressed about the diminishing productivity of the U.S. worker (Muckler 1982). One of the pillars of economic growth is improvements in human capital. The Council of Economic Advisers to the President (1997) note that "as the economy has changed, the demands imposed on the brainpower of the American work force have increased enormously" (32). As a result, American corporations have been aggressive in their efforts to increase their productivity and remain competitive in the world market. In part, corporate leaders see these efforts as the only way to survive and maintain a strong leadership role in today's extremely competitive marketplace (Francis and Woodcock 1990).

Corporations assert that one of the major components in maintaining high productivity and efficiency standards is a skilled and well-qualified work force (Francis and Woodcock 1990). They believe that their quest to remain competitive must involve maximizing efficiency and productivity by employing, compensating, and promoting those individuals who have the best qualifications (experience, education, and on-the-job performance) to handle particular positions and job directives (Francis and Woodcock 1990).

Individuals seeking career advancement are advised to become more competitive, more productive, more efficient, and more valuable to corporations by increasing the levels of investment in their own human capital (Irons and Moore 1985; Judy 1997). Human capital is defined, in part, as the essential accumulation of knowledge, skills, and on-the-job experience (Sowell 1971). Level of education and relative professional experience are considered to be the two most important factors determining an individual's ability to perform at higher levels in the corporate hierarchy and to further his or her level of career advancement within a business environment.

As was previously indicated, the upward mobility process is viewed as a fair contest among individuals in which the most deserving employees—i.e., the most qualified and the best performers—receive rewards in the form of promotions and salary increases (Arthur, Hall, and Lawrence 1989). Thus, the perception that an employee lacks strong academic qualifications and professional experience negatively influences his or her upward mobility as the individual competes for promotions, salary increases, and bonuses.

Within the hierarchically oriented corporate setting, those individuals at the top rungs of the corporate ladder provide leadership for corporations. Those employees who succeed in the mobility contest and make it to the top rungs of the corporate ladder are the individuals whom corporations have deemed best qualified to run America's companies effectively and are more likely to have a positive impact on the bottom line. Francis and Woodcock, in their 1990 book on organization values, explain that:

> ...an inadequate manager can wreak havoc—both by sins of commission and by sins of omission. The successful organization understands the vital importance of getting the best possible candidates into management jobs and of continuously developing their competence (510).

Thus, the quality of individuals who fill management roles is very important, since they are the ones to ultimately fill higher level leadership positions. The best qualified workers are generally considered to be the most educated, trained, experienced, dedicated, and hard working (Arthur, Hall, and Lawrence 1989).

In one particular study, Blau and Duncan (1974) found that when examining factors that exert some form of force upon an individual's career advancement or status, educational attainment was found to have the greatest amount of direct influence on career achievement or success. Richard Judy, in his 1997 book "Workforce 2020: Work and workers in the 21st Century," also cites this finding. In fact, when individuals first enter the job market, corporations evaluate the knowledge, skills, and expertise which they have acquired from their formal education and use this evaluation in making employment and promotion decisions.

Within a work setting certain skills, information, abilities, etc., are important in facilitating movement to higher level positions and status (Becker and Strauss 1956). Indeed, because certain occupational positions are characterized by particular norms that must be understood and certain standards and qualifications that must be met, if an individual is to be successful in a particular role, educational attainment acts as one of the major means by which an individual is oriented to meeting such qualifications and standards. In general, the higher the status of a position within a corporate setting, the higher the educational requirements (Salmon 1979; President Clinton's Economic Report 1997).

Both the level of professional experience and the nature of experiences one accumulates while working within the corporate arena have a direct influence on one's career advancement. In his study on experience and its effects on an individual's earning ability, Mincer (1974) argues that an individual's earnings increases with his or her level of accumulated post-schooling experiences (i.e., those relative experiences an individual accumulates outside of formal education). In addition to the amount of professional experience an individual acquires, the quality and type of experience an individual garners also directly influence his or her career growth. For example, some researchers argue that, in most companies, there is a difference in the value of experiences acquired in line positions as opposed to staff positions.

Line positions are important because they involve employees in the actual manufacturing, selling, or distribution of products or services for which the company is organized and thus have a direct impact on the company's profitability (Schuman and Olufs III 1988; Wernick 1994). Staff positions in corporations are normally functional areas which provide support to line positions and have fewer ties to the top levels of a corporation (Collins 1997). As a result, staff positions tend to offer little opportunity for contact with the powerful individuals at a corporation who can mentor or play a significant role in an employee's career advancement. These positions usually require the supervision of fewer people and fewer resources, providing the employee in this position with little opportunity to gain the skills necessary to operate effectively in a line position (DiTomaso and Thompson 1988).

In general, many researchers contend that line positions tend to provide more opportunities to obtain positions at the top rungs of the corporate ladder, while staff positions offer fewer opportunities (Holsendolph 1972; Argyle 1972; Kanter 1977; Fernandez 1988; Schuman and Olufs III 1988; DiTomaso and Thompson 1988; Wernick 1994). Thus, it would appear that an employee who desires to achieve higher level positions would tend to have greater opportunity for career advancement by working in line positions that provide better and more relevant experiences.

The successful organization understands that in its constant drive to stay competitive and in pushing the organization toward higher performance levels, it must promote and reward the top quality performers with the needed education and relevant experience levels (Francis and Woodcock 1990). Wernick (1994) and Freedman (1995) offer a similar viewpoint. Clearly, the argument is that the practice of promoting efficiency by promoting the most qualified employees is useful and necessary for corporations to maintain their national and international competitiveness.

An examination of the literature has revealed that certain educational requirements must be met and certain professional experience must be obtained by all employees seeking to move up the corporate ladder. Corporations seek to promote individuals who are perceived to be the most qualified and the most efficient. Since educational attainment and professional experience are the two major criteria used in judging one's qualifications and ability to perform a particular function, it is apparent that blacks, like all other workers, must first meet certain educational and professional experience requirements before they can be considered for promotion.

While this section focused on educational and on-the-job experience as factors that influence the mobility of all employees, the next sections will have a different focus. They will examine literature that addresses those factors, other than education and professional background, that influence the upward mobility of black employees in particular.

FACTORS SPECIFIC TO BLACK EMPLOYEES

The Stereotyping of Blacks

Society embraces a value system that defines and establishes the expected paths through life for the individuals comprising its population (Schein 1978). Social forces are the unwritten beliefs, values, assumptions, attitudes, conventions, behaviors, customs, and institutions that together provide individuals with meaningful lives. These forces coalesce to form the societal culture (Garcia 1982; Francis and Woodcock 1990).

The influence of these social forces is pervasive and touches every aspect of the lives of the individuals who make up a society. They affect the conscious and unconscious behavior of individuals and influence the subjective and objective characteristics of their behavior. Often, these cultural influences are intangible and hard to pinpoint. However, their power is very strong and is so inextricably tied to everyday life that social forces sometimes become difficult to distinguish from human nature (Ferguson 1980).

One arena in which social forces, integral to societal culture, play a major role is within the organizational realm of corporate America. In fact, corporate America can be described as a microcosm of the larger American society (Nixon 1983; South 1994; Butler 1995; Federal Glass Ceiling Commission 1995). Because corporations and the individuals who run them exist within the larger setting of American society, many of the beliefs, attitudes, and customs prevalent in American culture have a substantial impact upon the cultures that exist within American corporations (Work 1984). Organizational culture can be defined as "established ways of thinking and doing things" (Butler 1995, 245). Thus, the culture of an organization influences how employees behave, think, and solve problems relative to race and gender and unfortunately, these traits lead to discriminatory behavior (Butler 1995). These practices are always costly for the corporation and ultimately impact the corporate bottom line (Loden 1996).

Webster's Dictionary (1981) defines a stereotype as "a standardized mental picture that is held in common by members of a group and that represents an oversimplified opinion, attitude, or judgement" (1132). Because individuals within a corporation are products of the larger society, they bring into corporate cultures their own attitudes, beliefs, assumptions and stereotypes (Work 1984; Charme Zane 1994). Jones asserts that all people maintain some form of stereotypes. He further argues that people often use stereotypes to remember certain individual characteristics and to help classify particular persons or groups of people. Jones (1986) states that most of the time stereotypes are "mere shadow images rooted in one's history and deep in the subconscious" (88).

Controlled experiments have revealed that the insertion of the word "black" into a sentence has resulted in individuals changing their responses to certain statements (Scullock and Brooks 1970). Fernandez (1993) contends that while stereotypes exist about all minorities, the most pronounced and resilient pertain to blacks and as a result blacks tend to bear the greatest brunt of racism. In fact, Fernandez (1993) states that "overwhelmingly positive concepts of blacks have not prevailed in any period of white American history" (224). Thus, there is a certain power inherent in the use of stereotypes. For example, Fernandez (1981) argues that myths and stereotypes act as one of the means by which whites maintain their social, economic, and political position in this society. Indeed, many blacks would probably agree that when whites use stereotypes about blacks, one result is a wielding of domination or perceived power (Howard 1996).

In fact, in a Clarke (1987) study on the perceptions of qualified black managers within major U.S. corporations, 57% of 497 study participants stated that they felt their white peers did not regard them as equals. In fact, 49% of these black managers believed that they have been treated differently due to their race. Clarke's study goes on to reveal that 44% of the black managers felt that their color had been a factor in their not receiving an expected promotion or raise (Clarke 1987). The study argues that these results appear to point to an existence of racial stereotyping.

In his study on the perception of minorities and women within the corporate arena, Fernandez (1981) found that 46% of the surveyed black managers felt that race was a harmful factor of their future promotions. In another study on upward mobility, Fernandez (1988) surveyed 13 companies and found that many of the white upper level managers recalled that almost every discussion concerning the upward mobility of members of minority groups contained statements referring to some type of presumptive characteristics, along with generalized statements indicating the lack of skills or qualifications of minorities. Many blacks employed at corporations claim that negative stereotyping of them by whites is one of the reasons why they are unable to move to the upper rungs of the corporate ladder (Salmon 1979; Nixon 1983; Jones 1973; Work 1984, Dimpka 1992; Cross et al. 1994; Wernick 1994).

While the statistics cited are not overwhelmingly large, it is a considerable percentage and substantial enough to generate concern. Additionally, the consistency of research findings gives further voice to these concerns. While in no way conclusive, this information appears to lend some support to the following observation made by Jones (1973) and Nixon (1983) in their studies on black managers in the corporate arena.

> Overwhelmingly, writers assert that because the corporation is a microcosm of the larger society, whites have difficulty perceiving blacks as competent management personnel. Such perceptions present a major barrier because it is difficult for black managers to differentiate problems that are attributed to them as persons, managers, or as blacks (108-116; 8).

Further evidence that blacks view their upward mobility as being inhibited by racial stereotypes is presented in a 1986 Jones survey of 107 black alumni of the five top business schools. He found that 98% agreed with the statement that stereotypes and subtle prejudice pervade their own companies. Eighty-four percent of the respondents felt that their race had hurt their appraisals, pay, recognition, and ultimately their promotions (Jones 1986). In another study of about 70 black executives and 1,000 less-senior blacks, most possessing MBAs, Jones found that 95% believed their advancement had been hindered because of their race (Jones 1986). One black executive of a major U.S. white-run corporation was quoted by *Newsweek* as saying, "What I have found in my career . . . is being constantly required to prove my worth, over and over again. In almost every instance, a new boss or a supervisor starts with some preconceived ideas" all seemingly grounded in race (*Newsweek*, May 23, 1983, 61).

Butler (1995) argues that stereotypes derail the career advancement of people of color when they influence judgments and decisions that lead to differential treatment. The 1995 Federal Glass Ceiling Report "Good for Business," sheds light on the negative impact of differential treatment. For example, this report indicated that African Americans with professional degrees earn 21% less than their white peers who are in the same job categories and hold the same degrees. Thus, unlike their white peers, blacks must find mechanisms and ways to demonstrate to employers that racial stereotypes about blacks are not applicable to them (Holzer 1996; Kirschenman, Moss, and Tilly 1995).

Furthermore, many black employees have argued that because whites adhere to negative stereotypes about black people, such as their being less qualified, poor performers, and hired and promoted because of affirmative action solely to fill quotas and not based on merit, whites would not associate with them and denied them access to informal networks (Fernandez 1981; Nixon 1983; Jones 1986; Clarke 1987; McBride 1987; Leinster 1988; Baker 1995). Heilman, Lucas, and Block (1992) argue that compounding these fervently held stereotypes is the stigma of incompetence associated with the "Affirmative Action" label. As a result, people who hold this view tend to view minority selection (employment and promotion) as preferential treatment and not attributable to qualifications of minorities.

It should be noted that in examining the perceptions of black employees, Fernandez (1981) comments that it is important to take into consideration that, "because of their socialization and experiences," some blacks will interpret specific acts as racially stereotypical when they really are not (64). However, he also warns that because racial stereotyping can be subtle and difficult to detect, the perceptions of these black respondents cannot be written off as merely the complaints of incompetent employees. Too many qualified blacks are claiming the existence of negative racial stereotypes to merely discount the validity of their claims. While perceptions in no way prove or disprove the existence of racial stereotypes, or that they contribute to the underrepresentation of blacks at the higher levels of the corporate hierarchy, they do raise a cause for concern.

Indeed, because of: a) research literature showing the large numbers of blacks who argue that stereotypes based on race impedes their upward mobility, and b) research that attests to the fact that stereotyping is indeed a reality that negatively impacts the advancement of blacks, this study includes racial stereotyping as one possible negative factor that can influence the mobility of blacks within the corporate arena.

Corporate Recruitment and Performance Appraisal Processes

Beliefs, assumptions, values, and stereotypes have been found to influence corporate culture and, in turn, influence the corporate recruitment and performance appraisal processes. Performance evaluations are considered essential to effective management (Fernandez 1981; Cross 1996). Appraisals of current job performance often play a significant role in an organization's assessment of an employee's promotability (Greenhause, Parasuraman, and Wormley 1990). Thus, they should be implemented accurately, consistently and fairly (Somerick 1993).

Both the recruitment and the performance appraisal processes should also be objective. Ideally, to minimize confusion, bias, or discrimination, both the recruitment and appraisal processes should be based on some objective operational standards set by the corporation (Henderson 1984). These objective standards should serve as reference points for measuring the relative value of an employee or potential employee (Henderson 1984). The recruitment process should objectively measure an individual's ability to successfully adapt to a company's culture and effectively contribute to that company's operation. The appraisal process should be performance based and should objectively measure the output and performance of the employee in question (Devries, Morrison, Shullman, and Gerlach 1981; Forbes and Piercy 1991).

However, almost any recruitment or performance appraisal program has some degree of subjectivity. To a large extent, subjectivity and informal practices result from the fact that the recruiters or evaluators are humans who bring to the recruitment and appraisal processes their own socially acquired attitudes, behavioral patterns, and beliefs (Henderson 1984; Cameron 1989; Kochman 1994). Henderson (1984) explains:

> Possibly the most critical barriers to accurate and valid measurement of employee performance lie deep within the genetic and learned makeup of all people. A wide variety of emotional, psychological, intellectual, and physical problems that, at first glance, may appear to be separate and irrelevant factors may combine in any number of different ways during the performance appraisal process to completely neutralize or lay waste to any program designed to measure employee performance (2).

However, Henderson explains that much of the difficulty presented by the subjective nature of human beings can be removed through the use of a clear and objective performance appraisal process. Unfortunately, many black employees perceive the recruitment and appraisal processes in use at their companies as impeding their upward mobility (Ugorji 1997). Jones (1986) and Butler (1995) argue that stereotyping adds additional subjectivity to the performance appraisal process. In fact, biases, stereotyping, and informal practices in the performance appraisal process cam impede minority career advancement (Forbes and Piercy 1991; Landau 1995; Collins 1997).

Some blacks argue that because their white supervisors bring their stereotypes and prejudices into the performance appraisal process, their performance rating is compromised by their supervisors' beliefs about blacks (Jones 1986; Sackett, DuBois, Wiggins Noe 1991; Dimpka 1992; Igbaria and Wormley 1995; Landau 1995; Ugorji 1997). Raters are more likely to fall back on racial stereotypes in evaluations, especially when there is little information about the candidate (Hoy 1994). Lack of career advancement for people of color as well as differences in cultural backgrounds may lead to miscommunication, misinterpretations, and misevaluations (Baker 1995).

Blacks have continued to express discontent with their companies' performance appraisal processes. A 1987 survey of the perceptions of blacks in the corporate arena found that 22% of 497 participating black managers stated they felt that assessments of their job performances had been unfair (Clarke 1987). While initially 22% may not appear to be a large percentage, when considering the fact that the appraisal process is supposed to be fair and objective and it plays a significant role in an organization's assessment of an employee's promotability, it indeed is a cause for concern. In another survey of black managers, Jones (1986) found that 90% of 107 black alumni of the top five business schools indicated they believed that blacks are treated worse in performance appraisals than whites at the same level.

Work (1984), in his study of upward mobility, and Tomaskovic-Devey (1994) in his study on race, gender, and ethnic inequality contend that the beliefs, prejudices and stereotypes held by some recruiters and raters may cause some hiring and promotion decisions to lead to what is referred to as statistical discrimination. Statistical discrimination occurs when employers and managers use readily available traits of a group (race, dress, speech, etc.), rather than an individual's qualifications, as an inexpensive screening device—means of excluding presumably less productive employees from either the corporate arena itself or from certain positions therein (Thurow 1975; Work 1984; Tomaskovic-Devey 1993; Katz 1994; Moss and Tilly 1995). In this situation, the decision to discriminate against an individual is based on the perceived average characteristics of the group to which he or she belongs. These characteristics can include tardiness, absenteeism, high turnover rates, lack of education, lack of communication skills, and lack of relevant experience (Thurow 1975).

Statistical discrimination can be damaging to the upward mobility of blacks and other minorities because it has the potential to lead to well qualified and deserving individuals being overlooked for hiring or promotion (Work 1984). For example, when statistical discrimination occurs, even if a black individual possesses none of the above undesirable characteristics and meets all of the formal requirements for the job in question, because of group affiliation, he or she often is not hired or promoted (Thurow 1975). In some cases where this form of discrimination is practiced to "maximize efficiency," employers' judgments are essentially correct and well founded, in the sense that many members of the group actually exhibit the stereotypical characteristics attributable to them. However, the generalized judgments are incorrect with respect to any particular qualified individual within the group (Thurow 1975). When this type of discriminatory behavior occurs during the recruitment and performance appraisal processes, it can have a negative impact on the career advancement of the individual involved.

One negative impact is the pattern of steering minorities into staff positions that have little access and visibility to senior executives and that are removed from strategic business decisions (Federal Glass Ceiling Commission 1995). Another study by Greenhause, Parasuraman, and Wormley (1990) which compared similarly qualified black and white managers found that "race had direct negative effects on job performance evaluations" (79). While the intent is to select the "best" person, informal selection practices make it easier to reinforce racial, ethnic, and gender stereotypes and biases which serve only to inhibit the advancement of interested and educationally qualified employees (Wernick 1994). Indeed, other studies have shown that white raters evaluate the job performances of blacks less favorably than those of whites (Kraiger and Ford 1985; Dimpka 1992; Igbaria and Wormley 1995). Hanner, Kim, Baird, and Bigoness (1994) affirm that evaluators still may rate blacks as average, irrespective of the actual level of performance. Jackson-Leslie (1995) stated that in 1993, employment testers proved the "black job applicants with equivalent and even slightly higher skills are routinely rejected in favor of white applicants" (28). A U.S. Department of Labor Report (1997) noted that artificial barriers exist in both the recruitment and performance appraisal processes and as a result they negatively impact career advancement and developmental opportunities for minorities.

The above literature does not prove conclusively that blacks are discriminated against in the recruitment and performance appraisal processes. However, it does suggest that the underrepresentation of blacks at top levels of U.S. corporations might be due in part to the assumptions, beliefs, and stereotypes that exist about blacks within the society at large and thus within corporate culture. The results of these studies suggest that white employees, who conduct most of the hiring and performance ratings, may approach the recruitment and appraisal processes with some stereotypical beliefs concerning blacks' alleged inferior qualifications and performance levels. For this reason, biased recruitment and performance appraisals are considered as factors that can possibly influence the upward mobility of blacks in the corporate hierarchy.

The Corporate Socialization Process

The socialization process in organizations is important, since it is one through which an individual learns the duties and dynamics associated with an organization's position; and as a result, structures his or her relationships with other individuals with whom he or she will work (Chao 1988; Francis and Woodcock 1990). Studies of corporate upward mobility have shown that the ability to socialize and form supportive relationships in the workplace are positively associated with career mobility (Thomas and Kram 1988; Chao et al. 1994). Chao (1988) and Chao et al. (1994)

reinforce this viewpoint and claim that socialization is important to upward mobility, because it not only allows individuals to develop and build supportive alliances on the job but also it facilitates relationship-building efforts that aid in two main areas: (1) acquiring the necessary knowledge, skills, and abilities needed to perform a job, and (2) learning the way the organization functions in terms of its culture. Individuals who are not able to socialize effectively within their work environments are not able to fully learn the functions of their roles or of the corporations at which they work. These individuals tend to experience low levels of productivity and eventually peak at lower level positions or eventually leave the company (Chao 1988). Lee (1980) and Nixon (1983) explain that:

> . . . successful integration or "fit" into corporate culture depends on how well the individual learns the customs, folkways, and appropriate behaviors. The higher one climbs the corporate ladder, the more the individual must be attuned to the subtleties of the job, company and policies. It is expected that participation and acceptance into corporate life accompanies the climb. Thus, successful integration is a prerequisite to upward career advancement (109; 3).

Loden (1996) contends that an environment that is welcoming and rewarding engenders superior human performance. Thus, a sense of belonging is important to effective job performance. Individuals in the corporate arena need to function comfortably and effectively as important members of the company and exhibit a high level of commitment to their work. As a general rule, employees whose attitudes and beliefs coincide with those of the company and its culture are more likely to experience career advancement than those whose attitudes and beliefs differ (Caplow 1954). Ideally, within a corporate setting, those individuals who hold roles of power tend to share the same basic values. Thus, almost all successful individuals in the corporate arena are more likely to be individuals who are perceived to have conformed to the corporate culture, to have successfully socialized into the corporate culture of their particular companies, and to have been accepted as integral to that culture (Francis and Woodcock 1990). In American corporations, the dominant culture is white-Anglo (Carnevale and Stone 1994).

Corporate culture is defined as the pattern of beliefs, values, assumptions, and expectations shared by the members of a particular organization (Huse and Cummings 1985). Butler (1995) defines it as "the established ways of thinking and doing things" (245). Through the presentation of a group of shared assumptions, corporate culture provides employees with information about aspects of their employment and work such as: a) how work is to be performed, completed, and evaluated; b) what is acceptable and unacceptable behavior; c) what is and is not of value within the corporation; d) how certain groups are perceived; and e) how employees relate to each other. These shared assumptions also determine such things as company policy and practices, norms, behaviors, dress, etc. (Huse and Cummings 1985; Leibowitz, Farren, and Kaye 1986). These assumptions influence the values which underlie employee relations and manager/subordinate activities and interactions (Schein 1978).

In general, most corporate cultures are formally and informally established by those who founded the corporations or by the individuals who run the corporations, particularly the Chief Executive Officer (CEO) and his or her senior staff. Together, they communicate the beliefs, norms, and values of the corporation to the other members of the company. The founder and/or the CEO as well as his or her senior staff members determine such things as whether a company is team oriented, whether it is culturally diverse, whether key assignments are equitably distributed, whether the company provides employees with training, the quality and type of training the company provides, and the criteria for promotion to key positions (Huse and Cummings 1985).

Before any employee can move into higher levels of the corporate hierarchy, he or she must be viewed as having a high level of commitment to his or her respective company and an ability to conform to the corporate culture. This commitment and conformity can be divided into three components: (1) identification with the organization by adopting its values and goals, (2) involvement with the job and a display of willingness to devote a large portion of one's life to work related activities, and (3) demonstration of a high degree of loyalty to the organization (Chao 1988). Francis and Woodcock (1990) explain that:

> ... a well organized and well motivated group can achieve more than the sum of individuals who comprise the group. One person's talent can balance the weaknesses of another. It is vitally important that people feel they belong. The successful organization insures that it derives the benefits of effective teamwork (131).

Successful corporations view themselves as a close family working toward common goals. Individuals who are not able to socialize properly are perceived as ineffective, low in company commitment, and thus are excluded from the central functions of the corporation (Francis and Woodcock 1990; Chao et al. 1994).

The individual working within a culture in which he or she "fits" and understands the norms and rules, feels comfortable and secure in knowing that he or she can compete with others at the company and be judged on the same standards (Kiechell III 1982). Effective socialization also allows the individual to learn appropriate and inappropriate behaviors in specific interactions, circumstances, and environments (Chao et al. 1994). The mobility of qualified blacks in the corporate arena is also influenced by the socialization process that occurs for all employees of corporations. However, corporate leaders and researchers (Work 1984; Fernandez 1987; Braham 1987; Ford 1988; DiTomaso et al. 1988; Alexander 1990) point out that many black employees experience difficulty in "fitting" into a corporate setting, and that this difficulty impedes their mobility up the corporate ladder. The literature reveals that because of whites' stereotypes about blacks and differences in socioeconomic and cultural backgrounds of black and white workers, blacks experience considerably greater difficulty than their white peers in socializing within or "fitting" into a particular corporate culture. According to researchers and corporate leaders, the difficulties experienced by blacks in attempting to "fit" into or socialize within a particular corporate culture, can influence their mobility at their respective work environments (DiTomaso et al. 1988; Butler 1995).

Not only do blacks themselves feel that they have difficulty in "fitting in," but also some whites have expressed the same concern about blacks. In a study of white corporate leaders' perceptions about the mobility of their black workers, DiTomaso et al. (1988) argue that survey participants placed the ability of blacks to "fit in" high on the list of factors that can hinder the career advancement of black employees. In a 1975 study of black managers in four California corporations, a large percentage of white employees revealed that they felt that blacks had difficulty in interacting effectively or socializing with whites in higher business circles (Fernandez 1975).

In particular, blacks express that they often experience difficulty in completely socializing or integrating with the majority of their co-workers (i.e., white peers). Clarke's 1987 survey of 497 black managers in top American white-run corporations revealed that 42% of the participants indicated that they often feel isolated from others in their work group and sometimes feel like an outsider within their companies. In a 1983 study on black managers, Nixon surveyed 303 black managers from American white-run corporations and concluded that the study empirically supports the thesis that many blacks in the corporate arena suffer from extreme isolation and exclusion (Nixon 1983). In this situation there are only losers—people, group productivity, and the organization suffer (Carnevale and Stone 1994).

Two main viewpoints have been offered to explain the difficulties blacks apparently encounter in socializing and integrating into corporate cultures. One of these views pertains to the stereotypical beliefs which many blacks claim whites have about them. Fernandez (1987) contends that many blacks feel that some whites perceive blacks as poor performers, unqualified, lazy, and disloyal. According to Fernandez (1987), this perception leads blacks to experience difficulties in being accepted by white employees as part of the team and thus part of corporate culture.

The second viewpoint pertaining to the inability of blacks to "fit in" corporate culture has more to do with life-styles and cultural differences (DiTomaso et al. 1988). Ford (1988), after studying the upward mobility of minority managers, suggests that blacks experience difficulty in "fitting" into a corporate setting because they lack an understanding of corporate culture, politics, and social surroundings. He argues that blacks lack this understanding because they come from different social backgrounds, and they lack the information about corporate culture and politics which their white peers may have received from family and friends (Ford 1988; DiTomaso et al. 1988). Some argue that many whites have been exposed to the norms and nature of corporate culture through friends and parents, and that blacks entering the corporate arena have had no such exposure and as a result many face difficulties in adjusting. In his 1975 study on black managers, Fernandez conducted interviews with whites in four California corporations. These whites stated that blacks' mannerisms, social mores, dress, and speech produce a "cultural gap" between them and blacks. Salmon (1979) points out:

> . . . a source of dissatisfaction unique to black executives is the fact that the "informal organization" is centered around "white norms" which reinforce black-white differences, thereby creating barriers to interaction. The inference is that because of the absence of interaction the black executive finds socialization into the job an unusually difficult process (23).

As a result of being unable to effectively socialize within the corporate setting, many blacks argue that they find themselves outside of the main functions of corporations or as members of social margins existing on the periphery. In their 1983 study, Buono and Kamm described social margins as areas in which individuals experience uncertainty and are refused full participation in the dominant group's culture or institutions. The Federal Glass Ceiling Commission (1995) purported that business leaders also identified cultural differences as significant barriers to minority advancement.

There is enough evidence to indicate that blacks feel or are actually isolated from their company's central functioning. Because some blacks feel isolated and unable to effectively integrate into or socialize within their company's corporate culture, and because of the importance placed on the corporate socialization process, it is necessary to consider this process as a factor that can influence the upward mobility of blacks in the corporate arena.

Access to Corporate Network Systems

It is generally accepted within the corporate arena that networks are critical to the career advancement of employees (DiTomaso, Thompson, and Blake 1988). Yet, many blacks find themselves excluded from these networks (Fernandez 1993; Baker 1995; Barclay 1996). The importance of this issue forces an examination of the role of networks in the corporate arena. Work (1984) states that:

> Membership in networks determines the distribution of quality assignments, the organizational perception of employees, and, ultimately, career advancement and upward mobility. Moreover, networks translate corporate needs into information and career actions for their members and, further, communicate employee performance appraisals in ways that determine membership (96).

Society has evolved into what Naisbitt calls an "information society" in his 1982 book *Ten Megatrends*. In an information society people interact with each other in a continuous flow of information. Without communication systems, this flow of information halts. Therefore, since networking systems are part and parcel of communication systems, it is important to maintain these systems that are developed by individuals and institutions (Naisbitt 1982).

The networks operating within most corporations are both formal and informal in nature. The formal networks are developed and governed by corporate regulations. These networks communicate pertinent corporate information such as:

> . . . an organization's broad plans and objectives, its policies and practices, specific kinds of work force data, personnel vacancies, financial results, the competitive picture, relevant notices and directives, (and) planned training sessions (Work 1984, 85).

The formal networks are hierarchically ordered and information is communicated from the top of the corporate ladder downward. Due to the hierarchically ordered nature of the formal network system, the flow of information is slow as it must go through each level of the corporate hierarchy (Work 1984).

Although accessing and maintaining formal corporate networks are important for moving up the corporate ladder, informal networks seem to play an even more critical role in one's success in the corporate arena (Lee 1980; Federal Glass Ceiling Commission 1995). Informal networks allow individuals to go outside of defined formal corporate relationships or skip tiers of the corporate hierarchy in order to participate in the communication of pertinent information (Irons and Moore 1985). For example, if an employee is asked to produce a stock market report and determines that important information is needed to complete it, the employee can utilize formal networks and the formal communication process of the corporate hierarchical system to obtain the information he or she needs. However, the employee can expedite the search for information and thus the development of the report by accessing informal relationships, thereby avoiding the often lengthy and tedious formal communication processes.

In his 1982 work on megatrends, Naisbitt argues that networks exist to "foster self-help, to exchange information, to change society, to improve productivity and work life, and to share resources" (Naisbitt 1982, 193). Networking systems allow individuals to interact one-on-one in a peer relationship, thereby improving the efficiency of transmitting or receiving information. In most cases, information provided by these networks may be more difficult and time consuming to obtain outside of the network systems, therefore they are a vital component of a corporation's culture. Thus, when individual employees are excluded from these systems their upward mobility is inhibited and causes invisible barriers for qualified, interested employees (Wernick 1994).

For example, a 1991 study by the U.S. Department of Labor found that in some Fortune 500 companies, vacancies for positions beyond a certain level were not posted and could only be learned about through word of mouth or through networking. Individuals with limited access to upper level networks did not find out about these vacancies and thus were disadvantaged in having the access needed to identify available positions and apply for them. Tomaskovic-Devey (1994) contends that promotions at higher levels of the corporate hierarchy are more dependent on trust, social similarity, and access to powerful informal corporate networks.

The barriers to an individual's involvement in networks occur, in part, because networks are based upon communication between people. Sometimes, the personal interactions that are necessary in maintaining participation within a network may be more difficult to accomplish when there are racial differences between the parties (Baker 1995). Stereotypes concerning blacks and other minorities that exist among majority group members can prevent the inclusion of minority group members into these networks. Thus, when racial differences are features of a relationship, the individuals involved may find it difficult to form positive identifications and to develop a significant level of trust and openness (Thomas and Kram 1988). As a result, the majority members of a network who are of the same race tend to exclude members of different races from their networks.

Many minority workers argue that one of the major reasons for their lack of upward mobility is their exclusion from the social and political networks within corporations that can provide them with resources and information vital to accomplishing their jobs (DiTomaso et al. 1988). For example, in a 1988 article, George Davis indicated that of the 108 black MBAs surveyed, 102 indicated or alluded to exclusion from a company's informal networking structure as the greatest problem faced by black managers. Jeffries and Schaffer (1996) contend that:

> . . . a legacy of systematic exclusion, discrimination, and residential isolation has severely limited black Americans' access to the information networks—the social capital—that are so crucial to labor market success (65).

This lack of access to a company's internal networking systems deprives many qualified blacks of valuable information that can lead to an increase in their performance, productivity, and ultimately their upward mobility. For these reasons, the inability of many blacks to successfully access white corporate networks is considered a factor with the potential to influence the mobility of blacks in the corporate arena.

Access to Mentors

Perhaps one of the easiest ways for an individual to learn his or her organizational role, enhance socializing skills, learn to identify with company goals, and gain access to networks within a corporation is through the help of a mentor. Baker (1995) contends that having a mentor or a sponsor is key to an employee's career advancement. Mentors are a vital resource within the structure of corporate culture. A strong mentoring relationship can provide personalized instruction for the protege, as he or she learns the demands of the job and how to function within an organization's culture (Kram 1985; Bell 1996). Thus, mentoring, whether it is formal or informal, is a powerful socialization technique that helps to develop productive employees (Chao 1988; Shea 1994; Chao et al. 1994; Butler 1995). Any individual, regardless of race or position within the corporate hierarchy, benefits from the tutelage and guidance of a mentor who is experienced and has a high level of concern for the protege's career.

A study by Russell Reynolds Associates, Inc. (1990) shows that the overwhelming majority of corporate executives believed that mentoring helped to advance their careers. Shea (1994) and Bell (1996) reinforce these findings and contend that employees reap benefits from being mentored. Benefits include improved personal productivity, better decision making, and enhanced job performance. A 1991 study by the U.S. Department of Labor found that programs which identify qualified individuals and include them in developmental mentoring serve as a means to provide experiences that enhance the credentials and promotability of the participants. The study cites two cases where mentoring programs were in effect:

a. One company left individual managers to groom their own successor. Such a process allowed the manager to provide developmental opportunities to an identified successor.
b. In another company, mentoring took place in the form of upper level managers choosing individuals from a list of those identified as high potentials to "sponsor"[1]. When an inquiry was made into what

sponsoring denoted, the response was to "make it happen" for the high potential employee (21-22).

These approaches are some of the means by which corporations identify qualified and high potential employees and groom them for leadership positions (Federal Glass Ceiling Commission 1995).

Thus, to be an effective mentor one has to be knowledgeable of corporate dynamics, must have power within the corporation, and must be acutely attuned to what is needed to achieve higher level positions within the corporation (Bell 1996). In grooming leadership, those at the top of the pyramid look for replacements they can trust, who know the business, have contributed to bottom line profits, are visible and credible, are accessible to upper management and executives, demonstrate organizational savvy, and have varied experiences in the core areas of the business (Wernick 1994). The mentor's experience and understanding of the corporate structure and functioning assist the protege in understanding the informal and political processes of the corporation and many of its subjective standards (Kram 1985; Nixon 1983; Carnevale and Stone 1994; South 1994; Baker 1995; U. S. Department of Labor 1997). Researchers contend that when influential members of an organization seek employees to sponsor, mentor, or promote, they are more inclined to select employees who are:

> like themselves in general appearance (e.g., dress, manner, speech) and who, in addition have demonstrated specific ability to conform to hierarchic expectations ... and to maintain the interest of the group. (Caplow 1954, 72)

A great deal of research has shown that obtaining mentors within the corporate arena is particularly important but especially difficult for blacks and other minorities (Cambell 1982; Davis and Watson 1982; Dickens and Dickens 1982; Graves 1982; Ford 1988; Fernandez 1993; Shea 1994; Baker 1995; Butler 1995). In fact, a 1988 survey of minority workers pointed out that a large percentage of respondents indicated that it was much harder for minorities to find mentors than it was for whites (Fernandez 1988). This same study surveyed more than 200 of America's top corporations and found that the majority of the corporate respondents believed that one of the main inhibitors to the success of minorities is their lack of access to corporate mentors.

DiTomaso et al. (1988) also found that a great many black managers felt their mobility was inhibited because of their lack of access to mentors. Indeed, in this survey of the perceptions of white corporate leaders about the mobility of blacks in the corporate arena, he found that corporate leaders place the difficulty blacks have in obtaining mentors high on the list of factors inhibiting black mobility. Furthermore, it should be noted that a 1986 study suggested that even in cases where blacks had mentoring relationships, black employees often were not able to benefit fully from a relationship with whites serving in this role (Thomas 1986). This study and a subsequent one suggest that, while white mentors were able to help blacks with the technical aspects of their jobs, a lack of trust or understanding between the mentor and the protege prevented the white mentors from fully aiding the black proteges in the socialization process (Thomas 1986 and 1990).

Mentor-protege relationships work only when there is trust which comes from experience and involves some risk (Bell 1996). In fact the risk of mentoring outside one's race is further intensified and managers must be fully aware that they have to work much harder to combat these risks (Butler 1995; Bell 1996). Indeed, understanding that the risk of sponsoring individuals for important jobs is great, any feeling of mistrust or misunderstanding in a mentor-protege relationship could cause the mentor to hesitate in promoting the protege (Thomas 1986; Kram 1988; Arthur, Hall, and Lawrence 1989). Similar findings were revealed in a 1991 study by the U.S. Department of Labor which also found that blacks within the corporate arena still lack access to mentors and sponsors.

Much emphasis is placed on the ability of employees to find mentors. Many researchers and corporate personnel argue that mentors are valuable and important in facilitating an individual's climb up the corporate ladder. Pfleeger and Mertz (1995) contend that for members of underrepresented groups who show promise, being mentored results in positive measurable improvements in their status and condition. Thus, since mentors, vital resources within corporate culture, tend to fill a variety of roles which can influence an employee's career advancement, the difficulty blacks have in accessing mentors is considered an important factor that can influence the upward mobility of blacks in the corporate arena.

Participation in Special Corporate Training Programs

Sheridan et al. (1990) contend that gaining entrance to a company through a prestigious training program and a powerful department can provide early momentum to one's career. Many researchers explain that special training for blacks and other minorities is the best approach for addressing the difficulties they experience in upward mobility as well as for correcting their lack of representation at the higher levels of American corporations. These training programs are usually designed to provide business experience, oral and written communication skills, individual and group leadership skills, time management, interpersonal and socialization skills, etc. (Irons and Moore 1985). In addition, these programs provide individuals with the tools that allow them to assess their weaknesses and strengths, minimize their weaknesses, highlight their strengths, and direct and develop their career plans to achieve both personal and professional goals (Chao 1988).

Corporate leaders also argue that special corporate training is important because it allows minority individuals to compensate for the difficulties they may experience in the corporate world. A study conducted by the Upward Mobility Committee of the Program to Increase Minorities in Business (PIMIB) reported these difficulties as[2]:

- the perception that one's own values do not fit into the corporate culture;
- the employee's expectations versus the reality of qualifications and timing;
- ethnic culture and language differences;
- lack of access to informal networking;
- lack of responsibility or opportunity to identify and develop mentor relationships;
- hesitancy to participate in multi-cultural social interactions;
- insufficient understanding that the individual is responsible for his or her development;

- lack of education and training ranging from general knowledge to specific skills;
- hesitancy to break away from the peer group;
- negative image of business;
- lack of sufficient understanding of the components and demands of management careers;
- family pressures.

That same study found that training aimed at helping blacks and other minorities address these and other difficulties could enable these group members to become more efficient, and thus experience greater rates of upward mobility in their particular corporate settings. Because of the substantial positive impact that these special training programs are purported to have on the employability and career advancement of talented blacks and other minorities, this factor is considered important in influencing the upward mobility of blacks in the corporate arena.

CONCLUSION

The above review of the literature specified certain factors that many theorists, researchers, and corporate leaders identified as influencing the upward mobility of all employees. The literature indicated that in order to achieve upward mobility within corporate work environments, all employees must meet specific requisite skills and qualification standards set by corporations. These standards include acquiring certain levels of academic qualifications and professional on-the-job experience and participation in special training.

The literature reviewed also provided an analysis of certain identified key factors, beyond requisite skills and qualifications, that are reported to influence the upward mobility of blacks in the corporate arena. In the discussion of various points of view, the literature indicated that such factors as stereotyping, biased recruitment and appraisal processes, the nature of the corporate socialization process, the lack of access to networks, and the lack of access to mentors can each prevent qualified blacks and other minorities from achieving levels of career advancement comparable to those of their similarly qualified white peers. Special corporate training was offered as an effective mechanism to address deficiencies and barriers minorities are thought to experience.

In order to assess the influence of these factors on the upward mobility of blacks who have met the requisite skills and qualification standards established by most corporations, a mobility model was developed and tested. In the next chapter, this model is depicted and described. The next chapter also provides the specific details as about the manner in which this assessment was conducted.

NOTES

1. Here, sponsor and mentor are used interchangeably.
2. Though white employees can experience many of these difficulties, the PIMIB study focused specifically on difficulties experienced by minority group members.

CHAPTER III

The Methodology

Some of the literature reviewed in Chapters I and II indicated that blacks are experiencing slower rates of upward mobility than their white peers and are subsequently underrepresented at higher levels of the corporate ladder. The review of the literature in Chapter II suggested several critical factors in the mobility process that can influence the upward promotion of all employees in the corporate arena. In addition to those factors, the literature suggested a number of factors that can influence corporate mobility of blacks in particular.

This chapter outlines a model that will address both groups of factors and will depict how these factors can affect the outcome of black corporate mobility. This model serves two purposes:

1. It shows two main paths that explain the slower rates of mobility of black employees.
2. It investigates whether qualified blacks find their upward mobility stymied by factors revealed in the literature as influencing their promotability.

Chart 3-1 provides a representation of the model, developed for the purpose of this study.

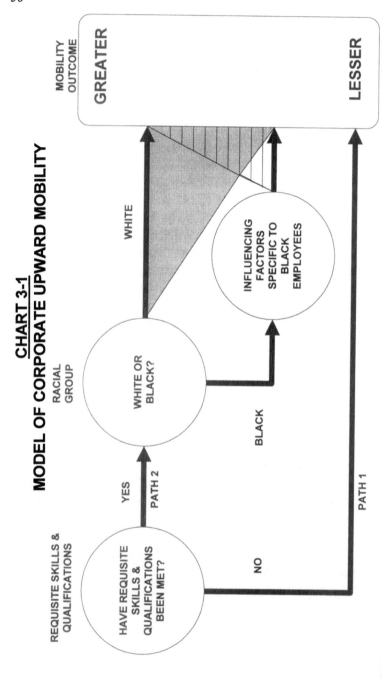

CHART 3-1
MODEL OF CORPORATE UPWARD MOBILITY

The first determinant of upward mobility reflects the requisite skills and qualifications set by corporations and identified by researchers and corporate leaders as important for all employees in securing employment and in increasing their chances at upward mobility in the corporate arena. These criteria include the level of skills, abilities, expertise, and practical knowledge acquired from formal education and professional experience. They also include the performance levels achieved to meet corporate standards. These criteria must be met by all employees. If these criteria are not met by an employee, then the model predicts that the mobility rate and outcome of that employee will be greatly reduced (Path 1).

However, if the requisite skills and qualifications criteria are met by either black or white employees, then these employees experience the second determinant of mobility, which depends on racial group membership. In particular, qualified black employees tend to experience certain additional factors, not normally experienced by qualified white employees, that inhibit their rates of upward mobility. The primary factors include: a) the beliefs, values, and assumptions based on societal stereotypes about blacks which are a part of corporate cultures; b) the application of unfair and subjective corporate recruitment and appraisal processes; c) blacks' inability to adapt to corporate culture, due to differences between blacks' socioeconomic and cultural backgrounds and the majority population; d) blacks' lack of access to corporate network systems; and e) blacks' lack of access to corporate mentors.

Within this second determinant of upward mobility, the independent effect of each of these factors is examined. Attempts are made to determine how each factor influences the upward mobility of qualified blacks in the corporate arena. According to the literature reviewed in Chapter II, each of these factors negatively influences the mobility of blacks and thus reduces their rates of upward promotion. Since majority group members, on average, do not experience these influencing factors, their relative mobility rates tend to be greater than those of black employees.

It should be pointed out that the paths leading to mobility outcomes are not static. In other words, each outcome is distributed over a range which represents a general level of mobility that each group tends to experience relative to the other group, as indicated by the literature reviewed in Chapter II. Indeed, it is not impossible that under unusual circumstances, an individual who has traveled one particular path can experience mobility outcomes commonly associated with another path. For instance, a black employee who travels along Path 2 can, under special circumstances, experience higher mobility outcomes than the literature predicts would generally be associated with the range of mobility outcomes for a typical, qualified white employee. However, this employee's mobility would be quite unusual. Thus, the purpose of the model is to depict what generally happens to blacks in the corporate arena.

In summary, the model outlines two distinct paths that could possibly lead to the slow rates of upward mobility that blacks are said to experience. Path 1 depicts qualifications and skills required by all employees, but not met. Like any employee who lacks specific qualifications and skills, if blacks do not meet these expectations and standards, the model predicts that they will experience significantly slower rates of upward mobility than individuals who possess these qualifications and skills. Path 2 depicts the individual's racial group. If one is black, one can experience certain inhibiting factors that negatively influence his or her rate of upward mobility, irrespective of meeting the requisite skills and qualification standards. Qualified white employees, because they are less likely to experience these inhibiting factors or experience them to a lesser degree, tend to experience greater mobility than their qualified black peers.

The first path of the model (see Chart 3-2) raises questions pertaining to blacks' opportunities for employment and advancement in the corporate arena. For example, to what extent do blacks possess or not possess the requisite skills and qualifications to enter the corporate arena and achieve career advancement? If they do not possess these skills and qualifications, how can they improve in these areas? Taken alone, Path 1 inadequately reflects the contextual factors that impact the lesser mobility outcomes of qualified blacks in the corporate world. However, because this study is investigating the claims of qualified blacks (i.e., those blacks who have overcome the obstacle of the first path) that they are not moving

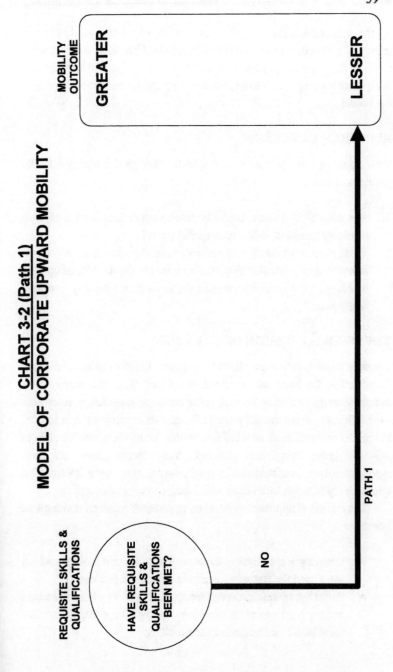

CHART 3-2 (Path 1)
MODEL OF CORPORATE UPWARD MOBILITY

REQUISITE SKILLS & QUALIFICATIONS

HAVE REQUISITE SKILLS & QUALIFICATIONS BEEN MET?

NO

PATH 1

MOBILITY OUTCOME

GREATER

LESSER

up the corporate ladder despite their qualifications, this study focuses most of its attention on Path 2 (see Chart 3-3). Therefore, the following sections discuss: the research questions, overall design of the study, and the quantitative approach used to investigate the second mobility path of the model.

RESEARCH QUESTIONS

Two research questions were posed to test the model outlined in the previous section:

1. Are blacks' corporate mobility rates slower than those of their similarly qualified[1] white managerial peers?
2. What inhibiting factors do qualified blacks experience, based on their minority group membership, that account for slower rates of upward mobility in the corporate arena relative to their similarly qualified white peers?

THE OVERALL DESIGN OF THE STUDY

The model outlines factors related to corporate mobility of all employees identified in the literature reviewed in Chapter II. In this study, these factors were quantified and tested, using statistical methods, to determine their influence on the mobility rates of corporate employees. In addition, the model presents another set of factors that, on average, apply solely to minority group employees. Because these factors have not been systematically operationalized in the literature, they were investigated qualitatively through interviews with black corporate executives.

The statistical approach to addressing research question number one involves:

- Defining and analyzing the measures of upward mobility which were used for statistical analyses of quantitative data;
- Selecting sample groups (Groups 1, 2, and 3) whose members occupy positions at the same job classification or organizational level in the same companies and cities;

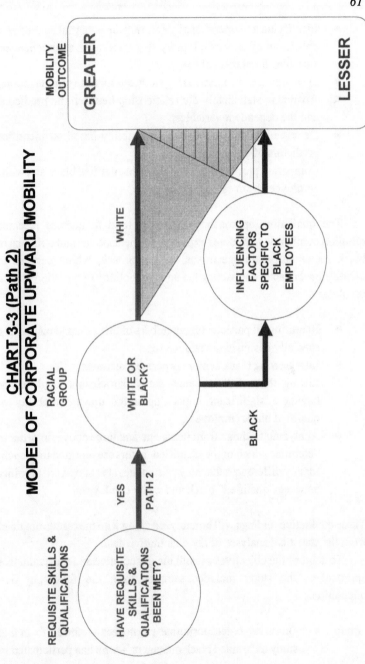

CHART 3-3 (Path 2)
MODEL OF CORPORATE UPWARD MOBILITY

- Identifying and operationally defining the potential quantifiable predictors of upward mobility that were used as independent variables for statistical analyses;
- Developing and administering study questions to sample groups;
- Analyzing statistically the relationship between the predictors and the dependent variables;
- Determining study groups' comparability based on identified predictors of upward mobility;
- Comparing the mobility rates between qualified black and white employees from sample groups.

The qualitative approach, which was used to address research question number two, involves exploring the perceptions and opinions of black senior corporate executives. This approach, which pertains to identifying the factors impacting the upward mobility of qualified blacks, involves:

- Requiring all participating members of this group to complete a specially designed questionnaire;
- Interviewing black senior corporate executives;
- Listing those factors which study participants identified as having a significant impact upon the upward mobility of qualified black employees;
- Analyzing findings from items one and three above, in order to determine which of the identified factors are reported to account for any differences that may exist in the rates of upward mobility between "qualified" black and white employees.

These qualitative findings will be analyzed along with the results obtained from the statistical analyses of the quantitative data.

To achieve the objectives of both the quantitative and the qualitative approaches, the study includes samples from the following five populations:

Group 1   Qualified black corporate employees—referred to in this study as "trained black managers"—who had participated in

Group 2
a "special training program"[2] prior to their initial employment;

Qualified black corporate employees—referred to in this study as "black managers"—who occupied comparable positions (same job classification or organizational level) in the same companies and cities as the trained black managers' sample group, but who did not receive that type of special training prior to their initial employment;

Group 3
Qualified white corporate employees—referred to in this sample as "white managers"—in comparable positions (same job classification or organizational level) in the same companies and cities as the trained black managers' sample group;

Group 4
Supervisory personnel of the "trained black managers";

Group 5
Black senior corporate executives.

Further details of the study's overall design are delineated in the next section.

PREDICTING UPWARD MOBILITY STATISTICALLY: A QUANTITATIVE APPROACH

This empirical model utilizes a quasi-experimental design (Campbell and Stanley 1967). The design does not require randomly assigned treatment and comparison groups (Kidder 1981). Under the preferred conditions of a fully controlled experiment, random assignment of subjects to experimental and control groups assures initial group similarity for virtually all independent variables. Instead, the quasi-experimental design provides an alternative when the ability to randomly assign individuals to treatment conditions is not possible. Quasi-experimental designs permit data to be gathered and analyzed in social settings, while impeding many threats to internal validity (Kidder 1981).

In studying the impact of upward mobility factors on the experiences of employees in corporate America, neither random assignment of subjects nor controls for all extraneous variables is possible. One cannot readily control for who is or is not black, who receives a particular type of career preparation, or who obtains employment in specific corporate settings. This makes the reliance on a quasi-experimental design necessary so that a variety of extraneous independent variables, other than the treatment variables being tested, may not be found to account for the differences between the experimental and control groups. Construction of a research design that controls for the influence of extraneous variables was a major methodological objective of this study.

DEFINING UPWARD MOBILITY MEASURES

For the purposes of this study, corporate upward mobility is defined by two measures: the compound annual growth rate (CAGR) in salaries and the Rate of Vertical Promotion. It is defined in this way, since salary and promotion are considered by most Americans to be the main measures of career advancement (Fernandez 1975; Irons and Moore 1985; Thomas 1990; Pfleeger and Mertz 1995; U.S. Department of Labor 1997). Several studies on the mobility of minorities and women within the corporate arena have used one or both of these variables (Fernandez 1975; Salmon 1979; Rosenbaum 1984; Work 1984; U.S. Department of Labor 1991; U.S. Census Bureau 1991; Freedman 1995). It should be noted that decisions regarding the economic value of a position or the size and importance of a promotion may differ from one industry to another or from one company to another. These distinctions will be taken into account in the statistical analyses of data by controlling for type of industry and size of company.

Since the purpose of this study is to measure employees' rates of upward mobility over their entire working career, instead of from one year to the next, there is a need to show the average compound effect of certain factors operating throughout their employment history. Thus, calculations of the average compound annual growth rate (CAGR) in salaries (in real dollars) and the average rate of vertical promotion are appropriate measures of upward mobility. Further, because the rate of vertical promotion is indicative of salary growth, rate of vertical promotion was used as a supplemental measure of upward mobility. This measure of upward mobility is important, since employees may also judge their success by a qualitative improvement in status or position.

In the next two sections, a more detailed discussion will be presented about these two dependent variables (salary growth and rate of vertical promotion).

Salary Growth[3]

Since the employees sampled were hired at varying points in time and worked for different lengths of time (i.e., two years as opposed to five years, etc.), salary growth was analyzed so that an adjustment was made for these differences. To control for these factors, the yearly average salary growth was used. Hence, salary growth was defined as the CAGR in salaries (in real dollars) and was derived from an adaptation of the compound annual growth rate's formula, which has been widely used to analyze rate of growth (Del Grande, Duffe, and Egsgard 1970; Dottori, Knill, and Stewart 1979). This equation is as follows:

$$\text{Amount} = \text{Principal} \times (1 + \text{Rate})^{\text{Time}}$$

In this study, this formula is modified by substituting ending salary for amount, beginning salary for principal, and years employed for time, to solve the equation for CAGR (the rate). This modified formula is as follows:

$$\text{CAGR in Salaries} = \sqrt[\text{years employed}]{\frac{\text{Ending Salary}}{\text{Beginning Salary}}} - 1$$

This measure reflects three situations: a) salary increases due to cost of living increases even if there were no promotions obtained; b) salary increases gained as a result of lateral promotions; and c) salary increases gained as a result of vertical promotions.

In order to calculate CAGR in salaries accurately, participants had to have had their work career histories within the same time period so that salary comparisons across groups were primarily influenced by the same historical events and macroeconomic effects, such as inflation, recessions, corporate salary growth trends, changes in the broader job market, etc. As an added control for this measure, inflation was accounted for by converting nominal wages into real dollars, with 1988 being the base year (U.S. Bureau of the Census 1990).

Rate of Vertical Promotion

Movement up the career ladder can be measured in two ways: the average number of years necessary to make each vertical move, or the average number of vertical promotions made within a year or more. Since most people tend to view their rates of vertical promotion in terms of how long it takes them to move from one job classification, grade, or organizational level to another, the average number of years taken to make a vertical promotion was used in this study and was calculated as follows:

$$\text{Rate of Vertical Promotion} = \frac{\text{Number of Years Worked}}{\text{Number of Vertical Moves}}$$

Employees who made no vertical moves[4] or only lateral moves were not included in the analysis of the rate of vertical promotion, because the absence of a vertical promotion prevents the calculation of an unbiased estimate for the prediction of vertical promotion. Additionally, this formula would assign a zero for vertical movement to individuals who have worked for differing periods of time and have not experienced a vertical move. For example, individuals with two years, five years, or 15 years of work experience who have not made a vertical move would be similarly classified. However, each scenario reflects a different mobility situation and a different potential rate for vertical promotion. Data on whether a move was lateral or vertical were gathered from the questionnaires shown in Appendix A.

Since the rate of vertical promotion may differ, based on the extent or size and importance of a promotion in a large or small organization, type of industry and company size were controlled for in the study. In addition, the three comparison groups were chosen from the same companies and cities in the same position levels. Since most employees in the sample began their careers at entry level and had obtained middle level management at the time of the study, more similarity was anticipated in terms of size and importance of promotions across the range of positional levels.

In order to determine whether any trends existed in size and importance of a promotion among Groups 1, 2, and 3 in the study, preliminary analyses were conducted on the type of industry and the size of company. Additionally, position level at the time of initial employment and at the time of the study were analyzed across these three study groups, since the rate and importance of a promotion between entry and middle level management may be different than between middle and upper level management. The preliminary analyses found no trends in size and importance of a promotion across Groups 1, 2, and 3. The three sample groups used in the quantitative analysis of this study reflected the following similarities:

- Approximately 60% of all participants from each of the three study groups worked for multiple companies, in multiple industries, and in various cities. No significant differences were present between the three study groups in terms of the variable "industry type" either at the time of their initial employment or at the time of the study[5].
- Approximately 85% of all participants from each sample group worked for companies of similar size. In fact, no significant differences were present for these groups in terms of the variable "company size"—measured by the natural log of the number of employees employed at the company nationwide[6].
- The majority of the sample selected for the three study groups began their careers at entry level or upper entry level positions and progressed as far as middle management positions. No significant differences were present across study groups in terms of their beginning position level at the time of their initial employment and their ending position level at time of the study[7].

SAMPLE SELECTION FOR THE THREE MATCHED STUDY GROUPS

Some researchers contend that because of the traditionally poor educational backgrounds of blacks, to meet the requisite skills and qualifications standards set by corporations for employability and upward mobility, blacks must receive special corporate training to complement their educational and professional backgrounds (Irons and Moore 1985; Chao 1988). Thus, a group of qualified black managers who graduated from a special corporate training program was selected to participate in the study[8].

In selecting the three study groups (Group 1, Group 2, and Group 3), identified earlier in the overall design of the study, the intent was to have each of the trained black managers identify a black peer and a white peer at the same job classification or organizational level and from the same company and city. It was necessary to control for position level between the three groups because of the different rates of promotion and salary increases that occur between entry and middle management levels and between middle to top management levels. The trained black to black peer comparison was used to identify the effects of special training on upward mobility. The black peer to the white peer comparison was used to identify race related effects on upward mobility.

Group 1, the trained black managers, consisted of 117 individuals[9] who completed a four-year special corporate training program specifically designed to increase the employability and upward mobility of minority graduates in corporate America. These individuals attended this program between 1970 and 1983, prior to obtaining their first full-time jobs. It should be noted that initially 613 minority graduates were identified as possible participants in the study. Of these potential participants, 443 (72%) were black and the remaining 170 (28%) were either Hispanic or Native American. Some of these potential participants could not be contacted by the staff of the training program, others did not complete the 29-page questionnaire, and others were participants in another study which targeted the same sample group and thus were unavailable for participation in this study.

The selection criteria for these trained black managers ensured that the group possessed the characteristics identified in Chapter II as vital to enhancing an employee's upward mobility. These criteria included:

- Completion of the special corporate training targeted at blacks and other minorities which provided participants with the requisite skills, expertise, and experience for employment and upward mobility in the corporate arena;
- Professional corporate experience acquired prior to full-time employment, which included meeting the minimum level associated with that experience based on set standards developed by the particular corporations and the special corporate training program. In order to document the on-the-job performance of the trained black managers in relation to their corporate peers, data from the supervisors of the trained black managers (Group 4) were obtained and analyzed. These data documented the performance levels of the trained black managers as judged by their supervisors;[10]
- Attainment of at least a bachelor's degree at an accredited institution of higher education; and
- Full-time employment at a corporation for a minimum of four years. Researchers such as Salmon (1979) contend that corporate employees receive a promotion on average every four years. Since the computation of an individual's rate of vertical promotion requires that the individual has had at least one vertical move between job classification, grade, or organizational levels, a four-year minimum was used for purposes of this study.

The 117 blacks selected for Group 1 were a representative sample because no significant differences were found in the academic and professional backgrounds, training experiences, and job status between those who chose to participate in the study and those who did not. Moreover, members of this sample group, like all the graduates of the training program, met specific academic, professional, and training requirements before completing this program (see Appendix B).

Group 2, "black managers," consisted of a sample identified by "the trained black managers." This sample was selected based on a request made to the trained black managers to identify black individuals who occupied positions comparable to their own (within the same job classification, grade, or organizational level). These individuals had to meet the following criteria:

- They had to be black and to have completed college. The latter criterion was important for making comparisons across the three groups on such factors as academic qualifications, prestige of school attended and academic major;
- They had to be employed within the same company and city, and;
- They must not have participated in any special corporate training program for minorities designed to complement their educational and professional backgrounds.

To reduce any systematic selection biases, all selection criteria were checked twice to ensure that the trained black managers had strictly adhered to the stated selection criteria.

The availability of this comparative sample of individuals was contingent upon the ability of the group of trained black managers to identify black peers in positions comparable to their own within their respective work environments[11]. In many cases the trained black managers were either unwilling to identify black peers in comparable positions or unable to identify any black peers in a position comparable to their own within their particular companies, since no black peer existed at that level at their companies. Seventy-three trained black managers were the only black employees at their respective levels in their companies. For approximately 3% of the 73 trained black managers, they were the only person in that particular job at that level in the company (e.g., only one assistant comptroller existed at the company). The 117 individuals in Group 1 were able to identify 44 black managers who met the three criteria. Sixteen of these 44 black managers did not participate in the study, either because they did not wish to invest the time or did not want to participate due to the nature of the study. This process eventually yielded a group of 28 black managers who were used in this study.

Group 3 consisted of white managers who also were identified by the trained black managers. These white managers occupied positions similar to the trained black managers (i.e., within the same job classification, grade, or organizational level) and met similar criteria established for the group of black managers. The only difference in the selection criteria for Group 3 was race. Again, to reduce any systematic biases in the selection of this group by the trained black managers, the same double-checking procedure was conducted as the one employed for the black managers (Group 2).

The availability of the comparative data was again contingent upon the ability of the group of trained black managers to identify white peers in positions comparable to their own within their respective work environments.[12] Twenty-seven of the 117 trained black managers (23%) did not have white counterparts at their levels in their respective companies (e.g., assistant comptroller, manager of affirmative action relations). Thus, 90 white managers who met the selection criteria were identified. Of these white managers, 27 chose, however, not to participate in the study, offering similar explanations as the non-participants in Group 2.

The remaining 63 white managers who participated in the study had a tenure of work experience ranging from one to 29 years in contrast to the work experiences of both Group 1 and Group 2 which did not exceed 14 years. This resulted in the absence of a black comparison group for 12 members of the white managers' sample with work experience between 15 and 29 years. Because of several factors resulting from changes in macro-economic and socioeconomic conditions between differing time periods, many of which would be difficult if not impossible to quantify and thus control, no individual with more than 15 years of work experience from the white managers' group was used when comparisons of salary growth rates or rate of vertical promotion were conducted. The 1960s were a boom period with extremely high inflation, while the 1970s saw the U.S. moving into a recessionary period with its dominance in the world economy slipping. These qualitative differences in the economy during 1954-1967 may have affected the white managers' mobility rates in a way not comparable to the rates experienced by the other managers of the sample during 1968-1983 of their employment history. The final sample of 51 white peers in comparable positions was used in this study.

QUANTIFIABLE FACTORS CONTRIBUTING TO UPWARD MOBILITY: IDENTIFICATION OF INDEPENDENT VARIABLES

Data from the above three sample groups were analyzed based upon quantifiable factors that were thought to influence the upward mobility of all employees in corporate work environments. The study was designed so that the influence of each of the three study groups' academic, professional, and demographic background characteristics on corporate upward mobility could be examined and measured. Thus, a comprehensive description of relevant background characteristics is provided in this section. This description serves to delineate those specific background variables of an employee that can possibly affect upward mobility rates between the study groups selected for comparison.

Researchers such as Gross (1964) and Salmon (1979) and reports (U.S. Department of Labor 1991) indicate that race and gender as well as the amount and quality of academic training and relevant professional experience obtained tend to be the primary determinants of the extent to which employees achieve career advancement. Thus, the ten variables used for purposes of statistical analyses were in three categories: demographic variables, academic background variables, and professional experience variables.

Demographic Background Variables

Demographic variables, which include gender and racial group membership, were chosen since they have been identified in the literature and research as playing key roles in the corporate upward mobility process (Work 1984; U.S. Department of Labor 1991). The gender variable is cited in the literature as affecting an individual's rate of upward mobility (U.S. Department of Labor 1991; Wernick 1994). For example, women are often stereotyped as being less capable than their male counterparts (Fernandez 1981), with "capability" being measured by an individual's academic and professional background. This variable is used to control for possible differences between the sexes.

On the other hand, belonging to a minority group has been cited by many researchers (Work 1984; Fernandez 1988; U.S. Department of Labor 1991; Wernick 1994) as playing a major role in limiting the upward mobility of blacks in corporate environments. Thus, it is important to isolate the effect of minority group membership on upward mobility.

Academic Background Variables

Since some researchers contend that blacks experience slower rates of corporate upward mobility than their white peers because of deficiencies in their academic background (DiTomaso and Thompson 1988; Leinster 1988; Spilerman 1988), in this study, academic background factors will figure prominently in assessing the individual's potential for attaining corporate upward mobility. These variables will be identified in this study as academic credentials, school prestige rating, and academic major. The 1997 U.S. Department of Labor Report on the American Workforce noted that these variables were thought to be strongly associated with earnings, employment, and entry into higher paying occupations.

The level of academic achievement is considered a major factor influencing an individual's rate of upward mobility (Gross 1964, Forbes and Piercy 1991). It is widely believed that the more advanced an individual's academic credentials, the greater his or her chances of achieving career advancement (Jencks 1979; Salmon 1979; Wernick 1994) and the greater the impact on earnings (Jeffries and Schaffer 1996; Judy 1997; U.S. Department of Labor 1997). To gain an understanding of the value corporations place on an individual's academic qualifications, a five-point index was developed to illustrate the hierarchy of preferred academic qualifications:

1. Associate Degree and Undergraduate Degree—B.A., B.S., B.Ed., B.B.A.
2. Master's Degree—M.A., M.S., Ed.M., M.A.S.
3. Professional Master's Degree—M.P.H., M.B.A., M.F.A., J.D., M.P.H.

4. Base Degree & C.P.A.—(1) and/or (2) and/or (3) plus C.P.A.
5. Doctoral Degree—Ph.D., Ed.D.

This index was developed from various sectors of the corporate structure, and was based upon input from company representatives with personnel expertise or from individuals who are responsible for determining a company's selection and promotion criteria. See Appendix C for a discussion as to how the academic index was determined.

In addition, because the reputation of the school attended is an important factor influencing an individual's career advancement (Fernandez 1975; U. S. Department of Labor 1997), a review of the various ratings of school prestige contained in such annual college guides as *Lovejoy's College Guide* (1987) by Charles Straughn and *Peterson Guide* (1988) by Kim Kay were considered in selecting the prestige index to be used for the universities attended by study participants. The Lovejoy prestige index was the one used in the study since it is viewed as the most comprehensive of all college guides. Lovejoy's rating criteria are based upon several college admission requirements, such as high school GPA, SAT, and ACT scores, and the percentage of applicants accepted.

An employee's academic major, another academic background variable, is also seen as influencing his or her career advancement and earnings (Forbes and Piercy 1991; U.S. Department of Labor 1997). Within the corporate arena certain jobs or positions require particular skills and knowledge. Generally, one's major reflects the nature or subject matter of the skills and knowledge the individual has acquired through his or her schooling. Therefore, academic major as an indication of the type of skills one has acquired can be seen as influencing an individual's mobility. For example, Salmon (1979) contends that while possessing a business management major may not be critical to gaining initial employment, it becomes important at higher levels where management skills become more important. Therefore, having majored in business is believed to play a crucial role in vertical promotions in the corporate arena (Salmon 1979).

Professional Experience Variables

Mincer (1974) contends that professional experience variables, more so than academic background variables, reflect the achievements employees have made after their entry into the work world. The most common measure of professional experience is an individual's job titles throughout his or her career, because they convey a general sense of a person's duties associated with a particular position. In addition to job titles, other factors that influence the nature of a person's professional experience are the types of industry and the size of the companies for which an individual has been employed.

Job titles typically describe two separate dimensions of a person's job: a) the types of position an individual occupies (i.e., line or staff); and b) the position level an individual occupies in an organization's hierarchy. Leinster (1988) and Wernick (1994) maintain that personnel in line positions, because of their experience with a company's essential workings which can directly impact the bottom line, are considered better qualified for top management positions than those in staff positions who serve more supportive functions. Therefore, the position type variable was included in the statistical analysis as a predictor of career advancement to upper levels of the corporate hierarchy.

While an employee's initial position is indicative of his or her starting point at a company, an individual's position level at the time of the study is indicative of his or her level of career attainment in the corporate hierarchy. Since position level is reflective of an employee's job status within a company, it was included in the statistical analysis as an important predictor of corporate mobility. A three-level hierarchical position scheme (see Table 3-1) that represents corporate position orderings was developed for the purposes of this study:

Table 3-1: Hierarchical Position Scheme

---

1. TOP LEVEL MANAGEMENT

    Chief Executive Officer, President of Company/Partner, Senior Vice President, President of a Division, Executive Vice President, Vice President of Company, Comptroller, Chief Financial Officer

2. MIDDLE LEVEL MANAGEMENT

    Vice President of a Division/Region, Assistant Vice President, Engineer, Manager, Accountant, Analyst, Senior Auditor, Officer, Supervisor, Programmer, Director, Attorney

3. PROFESSIONAL ENTRY LEVEL MANAGEMENT

    Account Executive, Administrative Specialist, Assistant Officer, Assistant Manager, Executive Assistant, Junior Engineer, Junior Supervisor, Senior Sales Representative, Staff Engineer, Account Representative, Assistant Buyer Trainee, Associate Engineer, Junior Staff Accountant, Programmer Trainee, Clerical Support Staff.

It should be noted that title inflation is a possible source of bias. However, this bias is reduced by the use of a broad hierarchical position scheme.

Given that salaries vary according to type of industry (Rosenbaum 1984), an industry variable was included in the statistical analysis. Table 4-11 presents a breakdown of the industries in which the study respondents worked during the periods of their initial employment and their jobs at the time of the study. Finally, since the size of a company can have an influence on the level of compensation employees receive and the rate at which they are promoted within their respective companies (e.g., smaller companies have fewer positions at upper levels—providing fewer opportunities), the variable "company size" was included in this study.

MEASUREMENT OF PREDICTORS

Once the three sets of independent variables of corporate upward mobility were identified, they were operationalized for statistical analysis purposes.

Appendix D provides the details on how each of the ten major variables were measured for purposes of regression analysis. With the exception of "company size," the variables were measured at the time of an individual's initial employment, since an employee's entry point in the corporate hierarchy has a critical impact on where his or her career ends.

QUESTIONNAIRE DESIGN AND ADMINISTRATION

Three separate questionnaires were designed for each of the three matched study groups. The questionnaire (see Appendix A) designed for the trained black managers (Group 1) was intended to reveal the nature and quality of their academic and professional backgrounds, their beliefs and experiences on issues related to black upward mobility, and the nature of their training experiences. The questionnaire (see Appendix A) designed for the black managers (Group 2) was intended to reveal the nature of their academic and professional backgrounds and their beliefs and experiences on issues related to black upward mobility. A third questionnaire (see Appendix A), designed for the white managers (Group 3), was designed to provide information on their academic and professional backgrounds. Because of the comprehensiveness of the questionnaires and the need to ensure data integrity and maximum response rates from all groups, the data collection process took approximately one year (September 1987 to September 1988).

The questionnaire prepared for the trained black managers (Group 1) was the first to be administered, since the subjects of this experimental group had to be matched with subjects of the two comparison groups (black managers and white managers). It was designed based on information from prior literature in such areas as corporate employability, upward mobility, sociology, business, and corporate training.

This questionnaire consisted of four sections. Section 1 secured information on the academic and professional backgrounds of each respondent in order to identify demographic as well as academic, and professional backgrounds of these employees. Section 2 of the questionnaire asked respondents to provide general information on the perceived strengths and weaknesses of the training program in which they participated. Section 3 of the questionnaire posed questions to participants to determine which aspects of the training program were perceived to be effective in their career advancement. Finally, Section 4 asked participants to identify areas where they believed the training program could have provided them with additional assistance and thereby better meet their needs at the time of the study.

The questionnaire was pretested before being disseminated as a means of correcting ambiguous language and questions. Also, the pretest was used to ensure that all pertinent aspects of the training program were appropriately represented in the questionnaire. Appendix E includes the details of the pretesting process. To ensure a maximum response rate, a comprehensive data collection process was implemented. Additionally, to reduce any sources of questionnaire bias, questions regarding the same issue were cross-referenced and responses checked to determine consistency of responses. Appendix E provides a more detailed description of the nine-phase data collection process for Group 1.

The questionnaire for the black managers (Group 2) was also pretested to remove any ambiguous language or questions. The questionnaire used for the black managers was similar, in part, to that prepared for the trained black managers (Group 1). However, Group 2's questionnaire contained questions designed to obtain information on the respondents' academic and professional backgrounds, mobility rates of each respondent, and factors which he/she believed either enhanced or inhibited his or her upward mobility within the corporate arena. A detailed data collection process was implemented to maximize the response rate to the questionnaires. To address issues relating to missing data or inconsistencies in the answers to study questions, the same procedure was employed as in Group 1. Appendix E includes a detailed description of the four-phase data collection process for Group 2.

The questionnaire for the white managers (Group 3) contained a section with various questions limited to obtaining information on demographic characteristics and on academic and professional backgrounds, because pretest results indicated that higher response rates could be achieved from white managers if all questions related to race were removed. The same pretest process that was employed for Group 2 was used for Group 3. Appendix E provides a more detailed discussion of the pretest process. A thorough data collection process was implemented to ensure that maximum effort had been made to collect data from Group 3. Appendix E includes the details of the three-phase data collection process.

STATISTICAL ANALYSES USED

One-way analysis of variance (ANOVA) and chi-square tests were used to conduct comparative analyses between key background variables of the study groups. This information allowed for the formulation of demographic, academic, and professional profiles of all study groups (see Chapter IV).

One of the criticisms made by researchers such as Fernandez (1975) of prior studies is that the findings were generally limited to surveys of perceptions and opinions of minorities or corporate leaders. In an attempt to respond to this criticism, quantitative analyses were conducted of key objective factors influencing upward mobility. The final set of independent variables, which were used for statistical analyses of quantitative data from the three study groups, include:

- demographic background variables (gender and racial group membership);
- academic background variables (degree, major, prestige of school attended); and
- professional experience factors (hierarchical position level, type of position, type of industry, change in industry, and size of company).

Multiple regression analysis was used to determine the impact of factors influencing the upward mobility of blacks within corporate environments, by testing the impact of the three sets of independent variables on the two dependent variables, salary increase and rate of promotion. Chi-square automatic interaction detector (CHAID) analysis was also performed because of its particular suitability to the analysis of categorical data which represents the bulk of the variables used in this quantitative analysis. Frequently used in the business industry, this statistical procedure has been shown to be a valid instrument when categorical data are collected and analyzed (Kass 1980; Perreault and Barksdale 1980; Magidson 1982). Thus, as a complement to the regression analysis, the Chi-Square Automatic Interaction Detector (CHAID) analysis was performed to see if similar findings were obtained when employing the same independent variables used in the regression analysis.

GATHERING INSIGHTS FROM CORPORATE PERSONNEL: A QUALITATIVE APPROACH

Qualitative analysis was performed on the data gathered through the interviews of black senior corporate executives and from their responses to the questionnaire administered. These executives were asked to identify factors that they believe account for the slow rates of upward mobility experienced by blacks in the corporate arena. This study group consisted of a national sample of 50 black senior corporate executives and entrepreneurs (Group 5) between the ages of 30 and 66. Of these 50 executives, 15% held upper-middle positions and 68% held top level management positions in corporate America's prestigious companies. Group 5 also consisted of some black senior executives who had left corporate America and were successfully managing their own companies (17%). Based on their current positions, they successfully met the corporate requisite skills and qualification standards for upward mobility and knew about many of the challenges blacks experience in corporate environments. Thus, this group was perceived to be a valuable source of information regarding the factors that influence blacks' upward corporate mobility. A detailed discussion follows of the rationale for selection of this group, the group's characteristics, and the design and administration of their study questionnaire.

SAMPLE SELECTION

The data availability of this sample was contingent upon the ability to gain access to these corporate executives and entrepreneurs. Upper-level management contacts (white and black) across the U.S. identified these black senior corporate executives as successful executives and entrepreneurs. These executives and entrepreneurs, in turn, made contact with their black peers and requested their participation in the study. Many of the most well-known and highly regarded blacks in the business world were among the 75 black executives and entrepreneurs who were identified as potential participants for this study. However, 25 of the black corporate executives identified did not participate in the study, stating that they either did not have the time to invest or that they were routinely deluged with requests of this nature and as a result were not willing to participate.

QUESTIONNAIRE DESIGN AND ADMINISTRATION FOR GROUP 5

Two assessment instruments were used to obtain information from Group 5: a questionnaire and a structured interview. The questionnaire was used to document the nature and quality of their academic and professional backgrounds. These black corporate executives were asked to identify obstacles, if any, which they and their peers experienced in their climb up the corporate ladder.

Interviews, ranging from 45 minutes to 2 hours, were conducted to obtain detailed information regarding the strategies these black executives employed in addressing any barriers they faced in their climb up the corporate ladder. These individuals were also asked to identify what they believed to be factors that impacted their upward mobility and the upward mobility of blacks in general at various rungs of the corporate ladder (entry, middle, and upper management levels). Finally, opinions were sought regarding the actions corporations could take to eliminate or minimize barriers, if any, to the career advancement of blacks in the corporate arena.

As with previous study groups, the questionnaire and set of interview questions for the black senior corporate executives (Group 5) were pretested to address any ambiguous language and questions. Pretesting was conducted on a small sample of managers holding middle and upper-middle positions at various corporations. Appendix E provides a more detailed explanation of the pretest process for Group 5. Again, because of the comprehensiveness of the questionnaire and interview and the need to ensure data integrity and maximum response rates for Group 5, a comprehensive data collection process, which took approximately one year, was employed. The same procedure used for Groups 1, 2, and 3 in addressing problems of missing data or inconsistences in answers to study questions was implemented for this group. Appendix E provides more details of the six-phase data collection process for Group 5.

QUALITATIVE ANALYSIS USED

Tape recordings and handwritten notes from the interviews of the black senior corporate executives were transcribed. The researcher read each transcript and coded any occurrence of a factor mentioned relating to the upward mobility of blacks in the corporate arena. Generally, since analysis of qualitative data tends to be perceived as being subjective in nature (lacking objectivity), only those particular factors that were mentioned by a majority of the black senior executives were used in the analysis of interview data.

CONCLUSION

In order to investigate thoroughly the upward mobility of qualified blacks in the corporate arena, two approaches (quantitative and qualitative) were used to analyze data obtained from interviews conducted and questionnaires completed by the five study groups.

First, statistical analyses, using a quasi-experimental design, were performed on quantitative data obtained from Groups 1, 2, and 3 in order to determine if any difference existed in the rates of upward mobility between blacks and similarly qualified whites employed in the corporate arena. The second approach involved an empirical analysis of qualitative data obtained from black senior corporate executives (Group 5) to obtain a better understanding of the factors which enhance and inhibit the corporate upward mobility of black employees, and the implications and impact of these factors.

The data collected from the study groups permitted some level of direct comparison between these groups. In addition, simultaneous inferences were drawn from the results of both the quantitative and qualitative analyses about the influence of key factors on rates of upward mobility of qualified black employees of corporations.

NOTES

1. This term refers to individuals who have met the requisite skills and qualification standards for employment and upward mobility in the corporate arena.

2. This program was deemed to provide the required training that corporate executives and researchers believe blacks need to complement their educational and professional backgrounds.

3. Since all respondents were guaranteed anonymity, salary questions were solicited in the context of a variety of other demographic questions. It was not apparent to the respondent that salary was one of the main measures of the study.

4. No vertical moves imply no vertical or only lateral moves.

5. Preliminary analysis of study data using chi-square yielded X^2=3.2526; df.=4; p >.7765 at the time of their initial employment and X^2=4.9890; df.=4; p >.5452 at the time of the study.

6. Preliminary analysis of study data using ANOVA yielded F=1.9866, df.=2,189; p >.1400.

7. Preliminary analysis of study data using chi-square yielded X^2=12.8673; df.=4; p >.5802 at the time of their initial employment and X^2=3.975, df.=4; p >.6084 at the time of the study.

8. See Appendix B for a description of the special training program.

9. Three of the subjects who participated in the special corporate training program ran their own businesses at the time that this study was conducted. In spite of this, the three entrepreneurs were included in the study because they had previously worked in corporate America over an extended period of time. Five years was the longest time period any of the three entrepreneurs had been running

his own business. In fact, one was working for his own company for five years, another for three years, while another for one year. The current salaries of the three entrepreneurs were also comparable to those of the group of trained black managers who were at the time of the study working within corporate America. These three entrepreneurs' background characteristics were, on average, similar to those of the trained black managers and the other two matched study groups. Exclusion of the three entrepreneurs from statistical analyses did not change study findings and thus the three entrepreneurs were retained in the sample groups of trained blacks managers for data analysis purposes.

10. Information as to the selection criteria, group characteristics, and data collection process for this group of supervisory personnel can be found in Appendix F.

11. The three entrepreneurs in Group 1 were unable to identify a black entrepreneurial counterpart in a similar business and industry within the same city as them.

12. The three entrepreneurs in Group 1 were unable to identify a white entrepreneurial counterpart in a similar business and industry within the same city as them.

Factors Predicting Black Upward Mobility: A Quantitative Analysis

To determine the relative influence of individual characteristics or personal background factors (demographic characteristics, academic credentials, and professional experience) on the upward mobility of qualified black employees, statistical analysis was applied. Two measures of corporate upward mobility were used in the study: average compound annual growth rate (CAGR) in salaries and average rate of vertical promotion. These measures were predicted by the respondents' personal background characteristics, and other factors such as company size and industry type of the three matched groups contrasted in the study—trained black managers, black managers, and white managers. Using two complementary statistical techniques of predicting the upward mobility measures, comparisons were made of the dependent and independent variables across the three study groups.

First, preliminary statistical analyses using one-way ANOVA were performed on the two dependent variables, salary growth rates and rates of vertical promotion, without controlling for any factors identified as having an impact on the corporate upward mobility of employees in general to mid- and upper levels of management. These analyses were performed to determine whether any differences existed across the three study groups for each variable[1].

Second, using one-way ANOVA and chi-square, the key factors that constituted the requisite skills and qualifications needed for black upward mobility were analyzed. This analysis was conducted to verify the degree to which each of the study groups had achieved the requisite skills and qualifications and to identify the differences and similarities between these groups along each of the variables.

Third, multiple regression analysis was introduced to determine whether differential rates of upward mobility existed between the white, black, and trained black study groups when controlling for the influence of factors identified as predictors of upward mobility for all employees. Fourth and finally, the statistical procedure Chi-Square Automatic Interaction Detector (CHAID) was also employed. This statistical procedure assessed the strongest predictors of the dependent variables. Based on these analyses, answers to research questions raised in Chapter III were sought.

DIFFERENCES IN UPWARD MOBILITY MEASURES ACROSS THE THREE MATCHED STUDY GROUPS

To determine differences in upward mobility measures across the three study groups, one-way ANOVA statistical procedure was applied.

Rate of Salary Growth

Rate of salary growth was one of the measures of upward mobility used in this study. In this preliminary analysis, an attempt to understand the rate of salary growth was made by comparing the initial and ending salaries (earned at the time of the study) across the three study groups.

One-way Analysis of Variance (ANOVA) revealed statistically significant differences among the three study groups in their salaries (adjusted for inflation[2]) at the time of their initial employment ($F=3.1025$; df.$=2,195$; $p <.0472$). Table 4-1 reveals that the two black study groups, especially the black managers, earned higher average initial salaries (a difference of $5,535) than the white managers. In fact, the black managers, at an average of $30,277 per year, earned statistically significantly higher beginning salaries than their white peers.

Table 4-1: Salaries at Initial Employment and at the Time of the Study for the Three Matched Study Groups

	Trained Black Managers (N=117)	Black Managers (N=28)	White Managers (N=51)
Mean Beginning Salary	$27,195	$30,277	$24,742
(Std. Dev.)	($9,276)	($14,267)	($6,484)
Mean Ending Salary	$33,897	$35,586	$39,922
(Std. Dev.)	($13,037)	($9,783)	($15,376)

The ending salaries (salaries at the time of the study) of the three matched study groups are listed in Table 4-1. With regard to ending salaries, the two black study groups, especially the trained black managers, earned lower average salaries than the white managers' group. One-way ANOVA revealed that statistically significant differences did exist between the three study groups in terms of their average ending salaries—adjusted for inflation[3] (F=3.6464; df.=2,195; p <.0279). In addition, Scheffe comparisons revealed that the trained black managers earned, on average, statistically significantly lower salaries at the time of the study than the white managers (a difference of $6,025). Scheffe comparisons also revealed that black managers earned, on average, lower salaries at the time of the study than the white managers (a difference of $4,336). However, although the white managers earned, on average, higher ending salaries than the black managers, this difference was not found to be statistically significant.

A question emerges: Why did the two groups of black managers, who began their corporate careers with higher average salaries than the white managers, have ending salaries that were typically $4,336 and $6,025 lower than the white managers whose beginning salaries had been the lowest among the three study groups? Since the analysis of beginning and ending salaries did not take into account differing lengths of time between the two job periods of the members of the three study groups or the cumulative effects of salary growth rates, the average compound annual growth rates (CAGR) in salaries was used to measure salary growth and was expressed as:

$$\text{CAGR in Salaries} = \sqrt[\text{years employed}]{\dfrac{\text{Ending Salary}}{\text{Beginning Salary}}} - 1$$

In this formula, beginning and ending salaries were adjusted for the effects of inflation on external economic factors, using 1988 as the base year.

Based on these data, the average CAGR in salaries for white managers was 12.1%, for black managers it was 9.0%, and for trained black managers it was 7.9% (see Table 4-2). One-way ANOVA of average CAGR in salaries revealed that the differences in salary growth between the three groups were indeed statistically significant (F=10.2342; df.=2,193; p <.0001). In addition, Scheffe comparisons showed the average CAGR in salaries for the white managers to be significantly higher than that for the trained black managers, while no significant differences existed between the black managers and the white managers or between the trained black managers and the black managers.

Though the annual salary growth rate differences between study groups (illustrated in Table 4-2) appear small, these differences can compound to large levels over the course of a person's working career. Table 4-3 depicts the calculated differential mean salary between the three study groups based on each group's mean CAGR in salaries. Assuming equal starting salaries for each group, the average shortfall of either the trained black managers' salaries or the black managers' salaries, relative to the white managers' salaries, progressively increases across the individual's working career. For instance, projected over 40 years, a trained black manager will earn salaries on average 21.2% of

Table 4-2: Average Number of Years Worked and Salary Growth Rates for the Three Matched Study Groups

	Trained Black Managers (N=117)	Black Managers (N=28)	White Managers (N=51)
Mean no. of yrs. worked	6.8	6.9	6.5
Mean CAGR (Std. Dev.)	7.9% (5.37)	9.0% (5.42)	12.1% (5.56)

what his or her white counterpart would earn. To understand what factors account for such differences in CAGR in salaries between the white and the two black study groups, this question will be addressed in the section of this chapter entitled "Multiple Regression Analysis of Upward Mobility."

Rate of Vertical Promotion

Members of the three matched groups used for this study experienced one or more of the following kinds of movement within the corporate arena: no promotion, lateral promotion, or vertical promotion. The trained black managers (9.4%) and black managers (3.5%), however, had a higher percentage of their members who made no moves at all in comparison to white managers. All of the white managers had made at least one vertical or lateral move. A one-way ANOVA revealed that the difference in the percentages of those members in the two black study groups and those in

TABLE 4-3

IMPACT OF AVERAGE ANNUAL SALARY GROWTH RATES*
(Assuming All Variables Constant)

	Trained Black Managers	Black Managers	White Managers
Average CAGR in Salaries	7.85%	8.97	12.11%
Assume Equal Starting Salaries	1.0	1.0	1.0
Salary at: [1]			
5 Years	1.46	1.54	1.77
10 Years	2.13	2.36	3.14
15 Years	3.11	3.63	5.55
40 Years	20.55	31.07	96.78
Percentage of White Managers Earnings: [2]			
5 Years	82.5%	87.0%	-------
10 Years	67.8%	75.2%	-------
15 Years	56.0%	65.4%	-------
40 Years	21.2%	32.1%	-------

[1] Ending Salary = Beginning Salary x $(1+CAGR)^{\text{years employed}}$

[2] Percentage of White Managers'
Earnings = $\dfrac{\text{Salary for Whites at X years} - \text{Salary for Blacks at X years}}{\text{Salary for Whites at X Years}}$

* Salary growth is defined as CAGR in salaries between first and last jobs for each subject. Growth rates were found to be distributed normally.

the white group who did not receive any promotions was not statistically significant (F=2.9595; df.=2,195; p >.0542).

One-way ANOVA also revealed that of the members of the three study groups who made only lateral promotions, no statistically significant differences were found (F=.1036; df.=2,193; p >.9017). Among the people who made vertical promotions, one-way ANOVA showed statistically significant differences in the average number of vertical promotions made between the three study groups (F=6.0716; df.=2,162; p <.0029). Scheffe comparisons revealed that the trained black managers' group (1.5 vertical promotions) and the black managers' group (1.7 vertical promotions) received significantly fewer vertical promotions than the white managers' group (2.4 vertical promotions) up to the time of this study.

To measure the average rate of vertical promotions for the three study groups the following formula was used:

$$\text{Rate of Vertical Promotion} = \frac{\text{Number of Years Worked}}{\text{Number of Vertical Moves}}$$

Over the employment histories of the three study groups, the white managers took, on average, 3.1 years to make each vertical promotion. Over the same period, the black managers took, on average, 4.6 years to made each vertical promotion and the trained black managers took, on average, 4.4 years. Statistically significant differences between the three groups were found in the average rates of vertical promotion (F=6.0716; df.=2,162; p <.0029). Scheffe comparisons revealed that both the trained black managers and the black managers experienced, on average, significantly slower rates of vertical promotion than the white managers' group. The results of these analyses suggest that the white managers experienced, on average, the fastest rate of vertical promotion, followed by the trained black managers, and finally by the black managers.

As Table 4-4 suggests, the larger standard deviations for the trained black managers and black managers as compared to the white managers indicate that the white managers experienced, as a group, similar rates of vertical promotion due to the smaller variance. However, unlike the white managers, the two black managers' groups experienced more variation in their rates of vertical promotion within groups, due to larger variances.

Table 4-4: Average Rate of Vertical Promotion for the Three Matched Study Groups

	Trained black Managers (N=117)	Black Managers (N=28)	White Managers (N=51)
Mean no. of years worked	6.8	6.9	6.5
Mean yrs. per vertical promotion	4.4	4.6	3.1
(Std. Dev.)	(2.3)	(3.3)	(1.5)

In summary, statistically significant differences were found within the three matched groups across the two measures of upward mobility. However, since these findings were only preliminary and did not involve the use of advanced statistical procedures, systematic analyses of the potential predictors of the two dependent variables using controls were conducted and will be discussed later in this chapter. The next section examines the identified predictors of upward mobility (independent variables) to determine whether the three study groups were similar with regard to these variables.

COMPARISON OF IDENTIFIED FACTORS PREDICTING UPWARD MOBILITY ACROSS MATCHED STUDY GROUPS

To validate that the sampling method used in this study resulted in groups that met the minimum requisite skills and qualification standards set by corporations and were similar across academic, professional, and demographic backgrounds, statistical analyses on identified factors predicting upward mobility were performed across study groups. The three matched study groups consisted of one group of 117 trained black managers, another group of 28 black managers who did not receive special training, and a third group of 51 white managers.

Demographic Background Variable
Gender

Among the three study groups, the black managers' groups and the white managers' group had more male than female respondents. The group of trained black managers had more females than males (see Table 4-5). However, no significant differences in the distribution of gender were found between the three groups ($X^2=3.3768$; df.=2; p >.1848).

Academic Background Variables
Academic Credentials[4]

As noted in Table 4-6, when individual levels of academic credentials at the time of the respondents' initial employment were analyzed, no statistically significant differences were found between the three study groups ($X^2=9.5033$; df.=6; p >.1472). When academic credentials at the time of the study were analyzed, statistically significant differences existed between the three study groups ($X^2=14.9591$; df.=6; p <.0206).

If the level of academic credentials is indeed a key determinant of upward mobility, the higher levels of academic degrees not achieved by the group of trained black managers at the time of the study may have influenced their rate of upward mobility. The trained black managers had lower levels of advanced degrees than both the black managers and the white managers (see Table 4-6). Also, it should be noted that no statistically significant differences were found across study groups in the variable "change in degree level," which measures the change in level of degree from the time of initial employment to the time of the study.

TABLE 4-5

RACE AND GENDER COMPOSITION OF GROUPS **

	MALE		FEMALE		TOTAL	
Group (1) Trained Black Managers	56	(48%)	61	(52%)	117	(100%)
Group (2) Black Managers	16	(57%)	12	(43%)	28	(100%)
Group (3) White Managers	32	(63%)	19	(52%)	51	(100%)
	104	(53%)	92	(47%)	196	(100%)

** Post Adjustment data -- Persons employed less than 15 years who have a college education.

TABLE 4-6
HIGHEST LEVELS OF ACADEMIC CREDENTIALS
AT TWO EMPLOYMENT PERIODS *

Academic Degree	AT INITIAL EMPLOYMENT			AT TIME OF STUDY		
	Trained Black Managers	Black Managers	White Managers	Trained Black Managers	Black Managers	White Managers
Associate Degree	0.0%	3.6%	0.0%	0.0%	3.6%	0.0%
Undergraduate	94.0	82.2	92.1	79.5	57.1	62.8
Master's Degree	1.7	7.1	2.0	2.6	10.7	7.8
Professional Master's Degree	4.3	7.1	5.9	17.9	28.6	29.4
	100%	100%	100%	100%	100%	100%
CPA	3.4%	0.0%	3.9%	10.3%	7.1%	7.8%

* The table shows movement from highest degree at time of initial employment to highest degree at time of the study.

School Prestige Rating

One-way ANOVA revealed no significant differences between the three study groups in the mean prestige ratings of the schools[5] where study participants obtained their highest degree at the time of either their initial employment (F=.2876; df.=2,195; p > .7504) or at the time of the study (F=1.4364; df.=2,195; p >.2403) (see Table 4-7).

Academic Major

The majority of respondents had majored in a business related subject area, both at the time of their initial employment and at the time of the study (see Table 4-8). The next most common major was in the engineering area. At the time of their initial employment and at the time of the study, on average, the trained black managers had the highest percentage of respondents with business majors (77.8%, 82.1% respectively), followed by the white managers (66.7%, 74.5% respectively), and then followed by the black managers (53.6%, 71.4% respectively). The black managers' group had the highest percentage of members with engineering majors at both points in time (28.6%, 17.9% respectively). Chi-square analysis revealed no statistically significant differences between the three study groups in the distribution of their academic majors at the time of their initial employment (X^2=7.7953; df.=4; p >.0994) and at the time of the study (X^2=2.1922; df=4; p >.7005).

Professional Experience Variables

Type of Position: Line or Staff

At the time of the respondents' initial jobs and current positions ("current" meaning at the time of the study), the trained black managers had the lowest percentage of respondents holding line positions, while the black managers had the highest (see Table 4-9). However, no statistically significant differences existed among the three groups with regard to type of position held at the time of their initial employment

TABLE 4-7
SCHOOL RATINGS
LOVEJOY'S RATINGS OF SCHOOLS ATTENDED FOR HIGHEST DEGREE

Lovejoy's Rating	AT INITIAL EMPLOYMENT			AT TIME OF STUDY		
	Trained Black Managers	Black Managers	White Managers	Trained Black Managers	Black Managers	White Managers
*	24.8%	32.1%	15.7%	27.4%	35.7%	11.8%
1	15.4	21.4	27.5	17.1	25.0	31.4
2	17.1	10.7	17.6	14.5	7.1	15.7
3	35.0	28.6	25.5	34.2	21.4	31.4
4	7.7	7.1	9.8	6.8	10.7	5.9
5	0.0	0.0	3.9	0.0	0.0	3.9
	100%	100%	100%	100%	100%	100%
Mean Score	1.85	1.57	1.98	1.76	1.46	2.00
Std. Dev.	1.34	1.40	1.39	1.36	1.45	1.31

* Represents schools not listed or rated in the *Lovejoy's College Guide* and not included in the mean score.

TABLE 4-8
DISTRIBUTION OF SCHOLASTIC CONCENTRATION

Scholastic Concentration	AT INITIAL EMPLOYMENT			AT TIME OF STUDY		
	Trained Black Managers	Black Managers	White Managers	Trained Black Managers	Black Managers	White Managers
Engineering [1]	15.4%	28.6%	19.6%	11.1%	17.9%	15.7%
Business [2]	77.8	53.6	66.7	82.1	71.4	74.5
Other [3]	6.8	17.9	13.7	6.8	10.7	9.8
	100%	100%	100%	100%	100%	100%

[1] Engineering Concentrations include: All engineering disciplines.
[2] Business Concentrations include: Accounting, MIS-Computers, Marketing, Business Management, Economics, Finance, Corporate Law.
[3] Other concentrations include: Social Sciences, Pure-Hard Sciences, Education, Medical-Health Care.

TABLE 4-9

DISTRIBUTION OF POSITION TYPE (Staff vs. Line)

Position Type	AT INITIAL EMPLOYMENT			AT TIME OF STUDY		
	Trained Black Managers	Black Managers	White Managers	Trained Black Managers	Black Managers	White Managers
Staff	65.0%	53.6%	58.8%	67.5%	50.0%	54.1%
Line	35.0	46.4	41.2	32.5	50.0	45.1
	100%	100%	100%	100%	100%	100%

(X^2=1.4872, df.=2; p >.4754) or at the time of the study (X^2=4.2986; df.=2; p >.1166).

Hierarchical Position Level

Most of the initial positions of members of the three study groups were at the "professional entry" level (see Table 4-10). Chi-square analysis revealed no statistically significant differences in the positional level among the three study groups at the time of their initial employment (X^2=2.8673; df=4 ; p > .5802).

The positions of the three matched study groups during the time of the study were mostly at the middle management level. No statistically significant differences were found between the three groups in terms of their position levels at the time of the study—the criterion used for matching the trained black managers with the black and the white managers' groups—(X^2=4.1651; df.=4; p >.3841).

Industry Type

Table 4-11 presents a breakdown of the industries in which the study respondents worked at the time of their initial employment and at the time of the study. Chi-square analysis revealed no statistically significant differences among the three study groups with regard to the distribution of industry type at the time of their initial employment (X^2=3.2526; df.=6; p >.7765) and at time of the study (X_2=4.9890; df.=6; p >.5452).

Company Size

One-way ANOVA revealed no significant differences among the study groups with regard to size of company for which respondents worked at the time of the study (F=1.9866, df=2,189, p >.1400).

Summary of Background Factors

The above analyses have shown no substantial differences in key academic, professional, and demographic background characteristics

TABLE 4-10

DISTRIBUTION OF HIERARCHICAL POSITION LEVEL

Position	AT INITIAL EMPLOYMENT			AT TIME OF STUDY		
	Trained Black Managers	Black Managers	White Managers	Trained Black Managers	Black Managers	White Managers
Upper Management	0.0%	0.0%	0.0%	2.0%	0.0%	4.3%
Middle Management	19.7	25.5	25.0	84.4	92.9	89.5
Professional Entry	77.8	72.5	67.9	13.6	7.1	6.2
Clerical	2.6	2.0	7.10	0.0	0.0	0.0
	100%	100%	100%	100%	100%	100%

TABLE 4-11
TYPES OF INDUSTRY

	AT INITIAL EMPLOYMENT			AT TIME OF STUDY		
	Trained Black Managers	Black Managers	White Managers	Trained Black Managers	Black Managers	White Managers
Manufacturing [1]	2.6%	7.4%	2.1%	2.6%	7.1%	3.9%
Services [2]	69.3	63.0	76.6	61.5	60.7	70.6
Financial Services [3]	20.2	18.5	14.9	24.8	17.9	21.6
Transportation [4]	7.9	11.1	6.4	11.1	14.3	3.9

[1] Manufacturing category includes Construction.
[2] Services category includes Consulting, Legal, Computer-MIS, Medical-Health, Government, and Education.
[3] Financial Services category includes Banking and Insurance.
[4] Transportation category includes Utilities and Communication.

among the three study groups. With regards to demographic factors, the groups did not differ by gender.

One difference arising between the three study groups pertained to their academic credentials at the time of the study. The trained black managers' group had a statistically higher percentage of members (79.5%) with undergraduate degrees only as compared to the black managers' group (57.1%) and the white managers' group (62.8%). However, the variable "change in degree level," which measures the change in level of degree from the time of initial employment to the time of the study, was not found to be significantly different across the study groups.

Looking at the study groups' professional background, no statistically significant differences were found between the three study groups with respect to the mean distribution of any of the professional background factors—position type, position level, type of industry, and company size—either at the time of their initial employment, at the time of the study, or in the change from their initial job positions to the positions they held at the time of the study. Thus, based on the literature reviewed and the section "Quantifiable Factors Contributing to Upward Mobility" of Chapter III, it appears that the three study groups not only met the corporate objective criteria standards for upward mobility with regard to their academic qualifications and professional experience but also were similar in terms of these characteristics.

MULTIPLE REGRESSION ANALYSIS OF UPWARD MOBILITY

Multiple regression analysis was used to determine the combined relative effect of the academic, professional, and demographic variables on corporate upward mobility along with the three study group variables: black, trained black, and white managers. Two sets of analyses were performed: one on the average CAGR in salaries measure and the other on the average rate of vertical promotion measure.

Predicting Average CAGR in Salaries

Comparing the differences in average CAGR in salaries among the three study groups, the black managers had an average CAGR in salaries that was 3.3% lower than their white peers (T=-2.575, df=190; p <.011). The trained black managers were found to have an average CAGR in salaries that was 4.3% lower than their white peers (T=-4.618; df=190; p <.000). However, while statistically significant differences existed between the white managers and the two black study groups, no statistically significant differences were found in average CAGR in salaries between the trained black managers and the black managers (T=0.868; df.=190; p >.387).

The effect of the independent variables along with the group dummy variables on average CAGR in salaries was found to be statistically significant (F=3.3836; df=17,174; p <.00001), as shown in Table 4-12. When controlling for all other background factors, the one demographic variable tested in the regression analysis (gender) was not found to be a significant predictor of average CAGR in salaries at the .05 level of significance (Beta=-.039; T=-.540; df.=190; p >.590).

Of the five educational background variables tested in the regression model, only one variable was a significant predictor of average CAGR in salaries at the .05 level of significance. Controlling for all other background factors, the independent variable "business major at the time of initial employment" (Beta=.232; T=2.678; df.=190; p <.008) was found to be significantly related to average CAGR in salaries. Looking at the regression coefficient (Table 4-12) for the "business major" variable, managers who majored in a business related area had average CAGR in salaries that was 2.9% higher than non-business majors[6].

Of the five professional experience variables tested in the regression model, only one variable was a significant predictor of average CAGR in salaries at the .05 level of significance. Controlling for all other background factors, the independent variable "position level at the time of initial employment" (Beta=-323; T=-4.595, df.=190; p <.000) was found to be significantly related to average CAGR in salaries. Looking at the regression coefficients for the "position level" variable, managers who occupied middle management positions at the time of initial

TABLE 4-12

COMBINED VARIABLES
(ACADEMIC, PROFESSIONAL, DEMOGRAPHIC, & GROUP)
as determinants of
AVERAGE SALARY GROWTH *
(trained black managers vs. White managers)
(black managers vs. White managers)

Variables	B	Beta	T Value	Sig. T
EDUCATION				
Master's Degree	.029	.082	1.152	.251
Professional Master's Degree	.008	.032	.467	.641
Degree Change	.009	.063	.708	.480
CPA	.011	.033	.456	.649
Business Major	.029	.232	2.678	.008
Change in Major	.007	.032	.341	.733
School	.002	.029	.422	.674
PROFESSIONAL				
Position Type (Line)	.012	.101	1.471	.143
Company Size	-1.352E-04	-.005	-.071	.943
Hierarchical Position	-.052	-.323	-4.595	.000
Finance	-9.312E-04	-.006	-.087	.931
Manufacture	.032	.098	1.308	.193
Transportation	.010	.047	.672	.502
Change in Industry	-.006	-.039	-.566	.572

TABLE 4-12 (Cont'd)

COMBINED VARIABLES
(ACADEMIC, PROFESSIONAL, DEMOGRAPHIC, & GROUP)
as determinants of
AVERAGE SALARY GROWTH *
(trained black managers vs. White managers)
(black managers vs. White managers)

Variables	B	Beta	T Value	Sig. T
DEMOGRAPHIC				
Gender	-.004	-.039	-.540	.590
Trained Black Managers	-.043	-.366	-4.618	.000
Black Managers	-.033	-.201	-2.575	.011
Constant	.054			

Average Salary Growth (std. dev.)	.047 (.057)
F Ratio	3.383
Sig. F	.00001

* Salary growth is defined as CAGR in salaries between first and last jobs for each subject. Growth rates were found to be distributed normally.

employment had an average CAGR in salaries of 5.2% lower than those employees who held lower professional entry management positions. This finding is consistent with what one would expect since middle level managers, being higher in the corporate pyramid, compete for fewer positions and thus their potential for salary growth will be lower than professional entry level managers who have more possible positions into which to advance (Mincer 1974; Landau 1995).

Among all the independent variables entered in the regression analysis, the group dummy variables were the strongest predictors of CAGR in salaries, above and beyond the effects due to the educational, professional, and demographic variables. The Beta coefficient for the "black managers vs. white managers" dummy variables was -.201 and the Beta coefficient for the "trained black managers vs. white managers" dummy variables was -.366. These two variables when combined accounted for 9.3% of the variance in the dependent variable.

Predicting Average Rate of Vertical Promotion

Comparing the differences in average rate of vertical promotion among the three study groups, the black managers took, on average, 1.6 years longer than their white peers to make each vertical promotion (T=2.898; df=160; p <.004). The trained black managers also took, on average, 1.6 years longer than their white peers to make each vertical promotion (T=3.861; df=160; p <.001). However, while statistically significant differences existed between the white managers and the two black groups, no statistically significant differences in average rate of vertical promotion were found between the trained black managers and the black managers' groups (T=0.000; df.=160; p >.999).

The effect of the independent variables along with the group dummy variables on the average rate of vertical promotion was found to be statistically significant (F=2.5855; df=17,144; p <.001), as shown in Table 4-13. When controlling for all other background factors, the one demographic variable tested in the regression analysis (gender) was not found to be a significant predictor of average rate of vertical promotion at the .05 level of significance (Beta=.117; T=1.466; df.=160; p >.145).

TABLE 4-13

COMBINED VARIABLES
(ACADEMIC, PROFESSIONAL, DEMOGRAPHIC, & GROUP)
as determinants of
AVERAGE RATE OF VERTICAL PROMOTION *
(trained black managers vs. White managers)
(black managers vs. White managers)

Variables	B	Beta	T Value	Sig. T
EDUCATION				
Master's Degree	2.793	.159	1.986	.149
Professional Master's Degree	.450	.041	.534	.594
Degree Change	.152	.026	.263	.793
CPA	-.382	-.031	-.363	.717
Business Major	-1.602	-.301	-3.169	.002
Change in Major	-.748	-.083	-.786	.433
School	.174	.070	.883	.379
PROFESSIONAL				
Position Type (Line)	.275	.056	.746	.457
Company Size (Log $_e$)	-.059	-.055	-.686	.494
Hierarchical Position	1.680	.224	2.763	.007
Finance	.183	.028	.362	.718
Manufacture	-1.873	-.150	-1.736	.085
Transportation	-1.138	-.121	-1.582	.116
Change in Industry	.492	.074	.972	.333

TABLE 4-13 (Cont'd)

COMBINED VARIABLES
(ACADEMIC, PROFESSIONAL, DEMOGRAPHIC, & GROUP)
as determinants of
AVERAGE RATE OF VERTICAL PROMOTION *
(trained black managers vs. White managers)
(black managers vs. White managers)

Variables	B	Beta	T Value	Sig. T
DEMOGRAPHIC				
Gender (Male)	.552	.117	1.466	.145
Trained Black Managers	1.619	.341	3.861	.000
Black Managers	1.619	.248	2.898	.004
Constant	3.573			

Average Rate of Vertical
   Promotion (std. dev.)   4.023 (2.367)
F Ratio   2.5855
Sig. F   .0012

* Rate of vertical promotion is defined as the number of years taken to
make each vertical move.

Of the five educational background variables tested in the regression model, two variables were significant predictors of the average rate of vertical promotion at the .05 level of significance. Controlling for all other background factors, the independent variable "business major at the time of initial employment" (Beta=-.301; T=-3.169; df.=160; p <.002) was found to be significantly related to the average rate of vertical promotion. Looking at the regression coefficient for this variable, managers who majored in a business-related area at the time of their initial jobs took, on average, 1.6 years less to obtain each of their vertical promotions than non-business majors.

Another independent variable "master's degree at time of initial employment" (Beta=.159; T=1.986; df.=160; p <.049) was found to be significantly related to the average rate of vertical promotion. Looking at the regression coefficient for this variable, managers who had master's degrees at the time of their initial employment took, on average, 2.8 years longer to obtain each of their vertical promotions than managers who had for their highest degree (at time of initial employment) either an undergraduate degree, professional master's degree, or CPA certification.

Of the five professional experience variables tested in the regression model, only one variable was a significant predictor of the average rate of vertical promotion at the .05 level of significance. Controlling for all other background factors, the independent variable "position level at the time of initial employment" (Beta=.224; T=2.763; df.=160; p <.007) was found to be significantly related to the average rate of vertical promotion. Looking at the regression coefficients for this variable, managers who occupied middle management positions at the time of initial employment took, on average, 1.7 years longer to obtain each of their vertical promotions than employees who held lower professional entry positions. Again, this finding is consistent with what one would expect since middle level managers, being higher in the corporate pyramid, compete for fewer positions and thus their potential rate of vertical movement will be lower than professional entry level managers who have more possible positions into which to advance (Mincer 1974; Landau 1995).

Among all the independent variables entered in the regression analysis, the group variable was the strongest predictor of the average rate of vertical promotion, above and beyond the effects due to the educational, professional, and demographic variables. The Beta coefficient for the "black managers vs. white managers" dummy variables was .247 and the Beta for "trained black managers vs. white managers" dummy variables was .341. These two variables, when combined, accounted for 8.7% of the variance in the dependent variable.

Summary of Multiple Regression Analysis

The black managers and the trained black managers were found, on average, to experience significantly lower CAGR in salaries and slower rates of vertical promotion than their similarly qualified white peers. When controlling for all other background factors, the regression analysis of average CAGR in salaries found only one statistically significant educational background predictor ("business major at the time of initial employment") and only one statistically significant professional background predictor ("hierarchical position at the time of initial employment"). When controlling for all other background factors, the regression analysis of the average rate of vertical promotion revealed two statistically significant educational background predictors ("business major" and "master's degree"—both at the time of initial employment) and only one statistically significant professional background predictor ("hierarchical position" at the time of initial employment). The group dummy variables, on the other hand, were found to be the strongest predictors of both average CAGR in salaries and average rate of vertical promotion, even after all other control variables were entered into the regression equations.

CHAID ANALYSIS OF UPWARD MOBILITY

Since this statistical procedure is particularly suited to analyzing categorical variables and is presently used in the business industry to analyze data when categorical variables exist, analysis of data using this procedure was performed in this study for comparative purposes. Similarly to the regression analysis, CHAID was used to test the relationships between independent variables and the two dependent variables, average CAGR in salaries (adjusted for inflation) and average rate of vertical promotion. Since the two dependent variables are continuous measures, they were first made categorical for use in CHAID.

The findings from the CHAID statistical procedure paralleled the findings from the multiple regression analysis. As in the regression analysis, CHAID found that the group dummy variable was the strongest predictor of either of the two measures of upward mobility. For the average CAGR in salaries, the significance level was less than .0004, and for the average rate of vertical promotion the significance level was less than .006. Furthermore, for the average CAGR in salaries measures, CHAID indicated that the variables "position level" and "business major" both at the time of the respondents' initial employment were significant predictors, consistent with the regression analysis findings.

Regarding the average rate of vertical promotion measure, the regression analysis identified the group variable and the "business major" variable at the time of the respondents' initial jobs as strong predictors of this dependent measure, whereas CHAID found no significant predictors other than the group variable. See Appendix G for a more detailed analysis of study data using CHAID.

CONCLUSION

The main purpose of this chapter was to investigate whether qualified black managers did indeed experience slower rates of upward mobility in the corporate arena as compared to their similarly qualified white peers. Secondarily, the influence of educational, professional, and demographic background characteristics of the three matched study groups on corporate upward mobility was assessed statistically.

The question this chapter sought to answer was whether being black significantly limited a manager's corporate upward mobility, taking into account the nature of the individual's academic, professional, and demographic backgrounds. Even though the three matched study groups had similar academic, professional, and demographic backgrounds at the times of both their initial employment and the jobs held at the time of the study, the trained black managers and the black managers tended to experience significantly slower rates of mobility than their white peers.

The regression analysis identified a few key predictors of the two measures of upward mobility. With regard to academic background factors, the study found that "business major" at the time of initial employment was significantly related to both CAGR in salaries and rate of vertical promotion. Individuals with business majors, according to Salmon (1979), are more likely to possess those skills, expertise, and experiences that are deemed important for higher levels of management by virtue of their specialization and training. Thus, it stands to reason that the extent to which an individual's academic major is important to a company's functioning determines the level to which that company is willing to compensate the individual either monetarily or through advancement.

The variable "master's degree" at time of initial employment was also found to be significantly related to rate of vertical promotion. Study findings revealed that, at the time of initial employment, a person holding a master's degree moved up slower than a person holding a professional master's degree. According to Salmon (1979), possessing business-related majors becomes more important at higher levels of the corporate hierarchy as opposed to lower levels where management and other related skills become more important. As a result, it would appear that a person with a professional master's degree (business-related) would tend to move up faster than a person with the non-business master's as his or her highest degree.

Study findings also revealed that a person holding a master's degree (and thus having more years of schooling) also moved up slower than a person holding an undergraduate degree or CPA certification[7] as his or her highest degree. Preliminary analysis of study data showed that most managers who had master's degrees for their highest degree had non-business majors for their master's as well as their undergraduate degrees. On the other hand, most managers who had only undergraduate degrees had majors in business. Thus, although people with master's degrees had more years of schooling, they had less years of schooling in a relevant business-related area. Therefore, study findings corroborate

Salmon (1979) who contended that corporations place more value on business related skills and qualifications, especially as one moves into higher level positions, rather than greater amounts of education in non-business related areas.

With regard to professional background factors, the "position level at the time of initial employment" variable was found to be significantly related to CAGR in salaries and rate of vertical promotion. It is understandable that managers in professional entry level positions are more likely to experience higher rates of vertical promotion and salary growth when compared to managers in middle management level positions. The most obvious reason for this assertion is that the professional entry level managers have more possible positions to advance into, whereas middle level managers, being higher in the corporate pyramid, compete for fewer jobs at higher level positions.

The study also examined whether being in line positions provided blacks with more opportunity for career advancement in the corporate arena. Many researchers argue that opportunities for corporate advancement generally are enhanced if one occupies a line position; and opportunities generally are limited if one is in a staff position (see Chapter II). Thus, one would assume that if one group occupied more line positions than another, then the former group should experience greater upward mobility rates than the latter group. Although the findings of this study indicated that more black managers occupied line positions than their white peers, no significant differences were found in the distribution of staff and line positions between the three study groups. Additionally, when controlling for all other background variables, the variable "position type" was not significantly related to either measure of upward mobility. Thus, based on these findings, it appears that for black managers and trained black managers other factors exist, other than occupying line positions, that must be explored in order to bring their rates of upward mobility to the level comparable to those of their white peers.

Some researchers and corporate leaders have indicated that for blacks to acquire the appropriate skills and qualifications required by corporations for the employment and upward mobility of a typical employee, blacks must also receive special corporate training (see Chapter

II). Consequently, as part of the study's efforts to understand the determinants of black upward mobility, it attempted to answer two questions:

1. Was special corporate training specifically geared toward enhancing black employment and upward mobility associated with raising the rates of black upward mobility within corporate settings to the point where they were comparable to those of their similarly qualified whites?

2. Did a special training program geared specifically toward enhancing black employability and upward mobility provide the black respondents in Group 1 with a mobility advantage over similarly qualified blacks (such as those in Group 2) who did not attend such types of training?

To answer the first question, the trained black managers and the white managers were compared on the two mobility measures, controlling for the possibility that white managers may have higher levels of requisite skills and qualifications beyond that which the trained black managers possessed. In addition, based on supervisor ratings (from those in Group 4), all the trained black managers met corporate mobility standards with 86% of these managers reportedly performing above average in comparison to their corporate peers (both black and white). The findings indicate that although Groups 1 and 3, on average, had similar academic and professional backgrounds both at the times of their initial employment and of the study, the group of trained black managers tended to experience statistically significantly slower rates of upward mobility than their similarly qualified white peers. In general, it appears that the targeted corporate preparation received by the trained black managers in and of itself was not enough to increase the rates of blacks' upward corporate mobility to the point where they were comparable to their white peers.

To answer the second question, comparisons were made between the group of trained black managers and the group of black managers with respect to the two measures of upward mobility. These comparisons were made presuming that blacks with special training acquired additional skills and experiences that made them more qualified than blacks without special training. In fact, the two study groups had similar academic, professional, and demographic backgrounds at the time of their initial employment and the time of the study.

The resulting analysis revealed no significant differences in the rates of mobility between Groups 1 and 2. However, no definite conclusions could be drawn as to the effectiveness of the training with respect to increasing black mobility, because it could not be determined how the trained black managers would have fared without such training.

It is important to note that this quantitative analysis did not assess the spectrum of qualitative benefits of the training received by the trained black managers. These included such benefits as increased awareness of the norms, values, and dynamics of the corporate culture, increased ability to "fit" into the corporate culture, greater knowledge of how to access mentors and informal networks, and so on. In fact, many of the members of Group 1 claimed on their questionnaires that their training experiences had enhanced their abilities in these areas.

When asked to assess their training experiences, 70% of the group of trained black managers asserted that the training program was instrumental in providing them with the skills needed to fulfill their career goals and professional needs. Respondents maintained that the training program helped prepare them to function effectively in American corporations. They said they had a better understanding of effective inter-cultural communication within corporate settings and as a result of the training they knew the norms, values, and dynamics of corporate culture and corporate environments. Because of the training program, they understood the process of accessing mentors and networking systems in the corporate arena, the nature of office politics, and the process of implementing clear and effective career goals and the appropriate strategies for achieving these goals. Also, 59% of the trained blacks agreed that their training assisted them in addressing some of the race-specific challenges—stereotypes and discrimination—which they might have to confront in the corporate arena.

More than half of the trained black managers indicated that the training program had provided them with skills and experiences that they could not have received without the benefits of the training. About 75% of the trained black managers contended that the training enhanced their chances for achieving upward mobility in their respective corporate arenas. In summary, though the quantitative comparison revealed no significant differences in the rates of mobility between the trained and non-trained blacks, the trained black managers' perception was that the training they received provided them with benefits that aided their career advancement.

The study's findings strongly suggest that race-related differences remain a salient factor in explaining differences in the average CAGR in salaries and average rate of vertical promotion, even when accounting for the academic, professional, and demographic background variables. The two black study groups received significantly lower CAGR in salaries and experienced significantly slower rates of vertical promotion than their similarly qualified white peers.

Interestingly, approximately 80% of the variance in the upward mobility measures was unexplained by a combination of all the identified factors controlled for in the regression model. One can conclude that there must be other factors, beyond demographic background, education, and professional qualifications, that influence corporate upward mobility.

In an attempt to explain some of the key variables accounting for the difference in the rates of mobility between similarly qualified black and white employees, the next chapter will examine the perceptions of black senior corporate executives. These executives were also asked to discuss the major factors influencing the upward mobility of blacks, beyond education and professional qualifications.

NOTES

1. These preliminary analyses only served to give the reader some insight into the relative differences in upward mobility rates between the three study groups before controls were introduced.

2. Base year 1988

3. Base year 1988

4. This variable denotes highest level of academic degree obtained at the time of initial employment and at the time of the study.

5. *The Lovejoy's College Guide* (1987), the source used in obtaining prestige ratings of schools in this study, did not list prestige ratings for schools attended by 48 of the 196 respondents. These schools, though not necessarily low prestige schools, failed to supply all the necessary data for the calculation of the rating. Thus, the mean substitution procedure was used in statistical analysis procedures.

6. Interpretation of this predictor variable in this analysis in relation to the dependent variables is independent of study group membership.

7. To be a Certified Public Accountant (CPA) one has to have acquired an undergraduate degree.

CHAPTER V

Enhancers and Inhibitors of Black Corporate Upward Mobility: A Qualitative Analysis

One explanation for the underrepresentation of blacks in upper level management is that they move up the corporate ladder more slowly than whites (see Chapters I and II). Do blacks lack the requisite skills and qualifications for career advancement in the corporate arena, or do they experience barriers in the workplace that inhibit their mobility because of their race? This chapter identifies key factors that are thought to enhance and inhibit blacks' rates of upward mobility in American corporations with the hope of determining the factors that may account for differences in rates of mobility experienced between white and black employees. To explore the range of factors, 50 black senior corporate executives[1] were interviewed on issues pertaining to the career advancement of blacks in the corporate arena. In addition, an earlier questionnaire collected information on these respondents regarding the nature and quality of their academic and professional backgrounds.

Black corporate executives comprised less than one percent of all executives holding senior level management positions within corporate

America (Korn/Ferry 1990; Federal Glass Ceiling Commission 1995). These executives are a valuable source of information regarding black upward mobility because they have succeeded to some degree in achieving upper level management positions. As their stories show, these executives have encountered many of the challenges blacks experience in their climb to higher levels of the corporate hierarchy. To place their stories in perspective, here is a brief outline of the backgrounds of the 50 black senior executives (Group 5) who participated in this study.

In terms of academic credentials at the time of the study, 72% of the black senior corporate executives held advanced degrees (13% had master's degrees, 46% had professional master's degrees, and 13% had both professional master's and juris doctor degrees), and the remainder (28%) had only undergraduate degrees. While 59% of black senior corporate executives held degrees in business related areas[2], 11% majored in engineering related areas and the remaining 30% majored in areas such as the social sciences, hard sciences, education, or medical-health care. Approximately 66% of these executives received their highest academic credentials from universities that were rated either 1, 2, or 3 on the Lovejoy rating scale (where 5.0 is the lowest and 1.0 is the highest score). Approximately 20% of these executives attended schools that were not rated in the *Lovejoy's College Guide* (1987)[3].

The black senior corporate executives' professional experience, which ranged from 8 to 40 years, was broad and varied. Ranging in ages from 30 to 66 (mean age of 48), the members of Group 5 had an average of 24 years working in corporate America. At the time of this study, the majority of these executives (85% of whom were male) were employed in prominent companies, predominantly in industries such as consulting, communications, banking, manufacturing, construction, and retailing. Sixty-eight percent of these executives held upper management positions, 15% held upper-middle management positions, and the remaining 17% owned their own businesses. It is from this diverse experience that the members of Groups 5 were asked for their insights into the critical factors that influence blacks' upward mobility.

This chapter outlines what the black executives considered to be the major enhancers of and inhibitors to black upward mobility. First to be explored are those requisite skills and qualifications that the interviewed black executives considered to be *enhancers* of black corporate upward mobility and characteristics these executives stated blacks must possess in order to be qualified for career advancement opportunities. Second, factors that the black corporate executives indicated were key *inhibitors* to black corporate upward mobility will be discussed. The chapter concludes with a summary of these findings.

To identify enhancing and inhibiting mobility factors perceived by black senior corporate executives, all interview transcripts were analyzed to obtain a sense of the major themes common to the interviews. Once a list of common factors was developed, every occurrence of these factors was noted for each person interviewed and supporting quotations were also extracted. Because perceptions and opinions of individuals tend to be regarded as subjective in nature, only those particular factors that were mentioned by a majority of these executives were used in the analysis of interview data.

REQUISITE CORPORATE QUALIFICATIONS (ENHANCERS)

The black corporate executives interviewed in this study were asked to indicate the attributes that they believed blacks needed in order to achieve success in the corporate arena. One of the most frequent responses was that blacks needed to obtain a sound academic and professional background. In fact, 80% of the black senior executives indicated that blacks must acquire requisite academic qualifications for career advancement in corporate settings. With respect to the academic background of blacks, these executives indicated that blacks needed to graduate from the "right" schools and major in the subjects areas in demand by corporations, such as business, finance, and accounting. They also stressed the importance of blacks obtaining advanced degrees in business related areas as a preparation for career advancement opportunities.

Fifty-six percent of the black senior executives indicated that blacks must accumulate strong professional backgrounds in order to achieve corporate success. The needed professional experience, according to these executives, comes from the variety and nature of work one encounters while on the job. Also, respondents from Group 5 explained that as blacks seek to acquire higher level positions in the corporate hierarchy, they must be viewed to a higher degree as competent performers who contribute added value to their companies with respect to managerial and leadership ability rather than merely technical expertise. These executives contended that managerial and leadership skills become increasingly important relative to technical competence as an employee obtains higher level corporate positions. It is assumed that by the time an employee is being considered for a management level position, he or she would have mastered the technical skills required to do the job. Thus, these executives recommended that blacks acquire experience in areas such as decision making, strategic planning, negotiation, interpersonal relations, and selling. Respondents indicated that all of these requisite skills can be acquired through education, professional work experience, and training.

These executives maintained that the acquisition and demonstration of these requisite skills, abilities, and experiences (referred to as "human capital" by Becker 1964; Mincer 1974) are key to the progress of blacks in the corporate arena, as illustrated in the following excerpts from interviews[4]:

To me, preparation is essential and that means having a solid undergraduate degree from an outstanding institution that challenges you. It means having the necessary professional degree for that field [into which one is hired or promoted]. And it can also mean getting a technical degree as an undergrad and then getting an MBA.

Again we have talked about the things blacks need, the analytical ability and education. Also, most companies have a certain kind of prejudice for people coming out of topnotch schools—Harvard, Yale, Cornell. If you look at the ideal white Protestant males, some or all have been trained and educated about corporate America. For instance, in the case of [this company], the people who have done the best have a tendency to be the whites who have been trained in the East or in some of the big name colleges in the Midwest. If you can get that kind of education it helps.

Three black senior corporate executives offered their personal experiences in relation to avenues they pursued to ensure that they had acquired what they believed corporations were looking for when judging whether a black employee or potential black employee is qualified to be hired or promoted.

> I went to good schools, I was a bright kid, and I have a lot of skills. I read a lot of books and provide advice and I do that fairly well. I understand the business that I work in. I went to superior schools such as Brown and Harvard, which is an important grading factor for blacks. If you look at the black people on this floor who are professionals and semi-professionals, you will find that they all attended Ivy League schools.

> I think the school from which one graduates is important. For example, an MBA from Indiana University had a hell of a lot to do with me being in [this company] because it just so happened that it was one of the schools [this company] did a lot recruiting from. If I'd gotten an MBA from Florida A&M University, for example, I don't think I would have gotten the job. Even if I had an MBA from Howard University, which is a well respected black university, I don't think I would have gotten the job. I think the school has a lot to do with it.

> I'm getting my Ph.D., from an Ivy League school and it is very important because nobody could say, "Look, she's got a Ph.D. , but look where she got it from." You have to make sure that if you are going for those kinds of degrees you get them from a competitive environment.

In addition to possessing the proper academic qualifications and attending the "right" schools, these executives indicated that as part of the requisite corporate qualifications black employees must be professionally credible and demonstrate outstanding performance levels. The following comments provide some insight into the views of many study respondents:

> We should understand the business our companies are in and we should acquire as many skills as possible to support our companies' success. If we do all of that very, very well and if we outperform our competition, then we should move into upper management.

> To be successful as a black you have to be highly competent, you have to be well prepared.

> Blacks must establish themselves as professionally credible. If a black is hired as an accountant, he or she must demonstrate that he or she can do accounting. If a black is hired as an engineer, then he or she has to show that he or she can do engineering. We must establish that we are professional within the disciplines in which we are trained.

In explaining their own success, the respondents in Group 5 talked about the acquisition of advanced academic qualifications, broad and varied professional experiences, and the countless hours of not only related on-the-job training but also formal corporate training received both on-site and off-the-job during their corporate tenure. These corporate executives pointed out that obtaining these skills, expertise, and experience—factors within their control—aided them in achieving a certain level of success in the corporate arena.

The following responses from these black executives, each with many years of corporate experience, help to shed some light on this issue.

> It was important that I presented myself as favorably as I could in terms of being prepared, having the necessary education, having a broad base of knowledge, having an understanding of the corporate culture and American society, and having good communication skills and interpersonal skills.

> Because corporate America wants only the best black talent, it's important that they perceived me as having a wide and useful variety of experiences and knowledge of the corporate world. Therefore, we [blacks] must acquire a wide variety of work experiences and excel in each one.

In order for a black person to move up within corporate America, it takes hard work and winning each and every day, winning by event, by event, by event. I had to work extra hard and win when everyone else would give up.

I tried to do every job so well . . . that they have had to promote me to another level. I still approach the job the same way. So success is doing the best kind of job I can do in numbers and results. Whatever else is the measurement of corporate objectives, I'm going to give them my best and then say now take it and do whatever you want to do with it because I'm going to be as effective and successful as anyone else around here.

I had to be much better in every way and in every respect. I could not be "as good"; I had to be "much better than" my peers.

One black senior corporate executive encapsulated the profile of a qualified black employee as follows:

In order to be successful within the corporate world, blacks must have the requisite skills, expertise, and experience that will enable them to perform the job in an outstanding manner.

The views expressed by these black senior corporate executives, regarding the need for blacks to come to the work world fully prepared and well qualified and be outstanding performers in order to succeed, are in accordance with the views expressed by researchers and theorists in the literature reviewed in Chapter II.

However, it is important to recognize that the literature reviewed on this subject indicated that *any individual* seeking to move into the upper levels of American corporations must have the skills and experience required to be highly productive and competitive. In fact, human capital theory explains that individuals increase their productivity and competitive edge through such personal investments as formal education, training, and on-the-job experiences. Therefore, the skills, abilities, experience, and performance levels that study participants in Group 5 indicated blacks must acquire to be considered qualified are also indeed needed by *all* employees seeking corporate success. However, employees expect to be rewarded through promotions when they demonstrate superior performance (Freedman 1995).

When the black senior executives were asked to identify the highest position in their corporations they believed they could reach, despite their academic qualifications, broad and varied professional experience, training, and motivation, only eight out of 41 of the responding black senior executives believed that they had a chance of reaching the pinnacle of their respective corporations. Also, 42% of the black senior corporate executives believed that they were, at the time of the study, at their "ceiling" level in their particular companies. In expressing their reasons for believing they could not reach the pinnacles of their companies, four black senior executives summed up the feelings expressed by most of the respondents in Group 5.

> I would have to say that I could not reach the top of this company. Both the odds and history are against me. First of all, this company has never had a black partner before. Second, the question becomes, "Is there enough support from the present partners to make me a partner and do they feel that there is a need to make me a partner?" I'm not sure that their answer would be yes.

> In our society and in this company, many feel that in order for a company to be successful it has to have a figure at the top that is identifiable with the masses. Here and in society people don't see a black person as being able to identify with the masses of people, particularly those people comprising the corporate world. In order for someone to be successful he or she has to be accepted by the customer. The majority of the customers are firms run by whites, or the majority group in this country. Therefore, I or any other black will not be successful in reaching the top because the corporation feels that it will not be successful with a black as its chief representative.

I don't think I will reach the top of this corporation because business, and I mean major corporations, are not ready for blacks to make real and significant achievement. There is still a reluctancy on the part of business. They recognize that some of us are good but they keep us at a certain point. It is subtle and it's nothing that I can really pinpoint. When I say it is subtle, I mean [there are] instances when you know you should be promoted but you are not or instances when you should be given some experience in one area but you are not. I see whites come in who are not as experienced but something about their being white makes them seem more credible in the eyes of the company controllers.

Majority members say that if you come into a company with good credentials, if you work hard, if you establish contacts, if you become a team player, if you outperform your white peers, and if you stay in a company long enough, you will move up the corporate ladder. These things apply generally to whites but not to blacks.

Apparently, requisite corporate qualifications, even when achieved to a high degree, have a limited ability to enhance blacks' upward mobility. It is clear from the responses of the black corporate executives that many of them believed their mobility is inhibited by a "glass ceiling," or a point in the corporate hierarchy beyond which very few, if any, blacks advance. These black executives believed that their race was a major factor inhibiting them from obtaining the top positions at their companies. In fact, 80% of the black corporate executives indicated that they themselves had experienced difficulty due to their race in moving up the corporate ladder. These black senior executives indicated that despite their credentials, motivation, hard work, training, and experience, they believed that "glass ceilings" exist within corporations which prevent them from attaining the top positions on the corporate ladder. This sentiment has been expressed by many researchers such as Wernick (1994) who contends that despite comparable educational background and professional experience, white men move more quickly in mid and upper levels of management.

Indeed, the significance of these remarks becomes more apparent upon comparing the responses of the group of trained black managers with those of their similarly qualified white peers. Both groups were asked about their chances of reaching the pinnacles of their corporations. Only 20% of the trained black managers believed they could reach the pinnacles of their respective companies. Yet, 96% of the white managers believed they could reach the pinnacle of their respective corporations. Evidently, at early stages of their careers, blacks begin to express doubt over their chances of becoming the top leaders of corporate America.

The next fundamental question that remains to be answered is: Beyond requisite corporate qualifications, what additional factors exist that impact significantly on the upward mobility of blacks in the corporate arena? The following sections review data obtained from black senior executives in search of an answer to this question.

FACTORS BEYOND REQUISITE CORPORATE QUALIFICATIONS THAT INFLUENCE BLACK UPWARD MOBILITY (INHIBITORS)

The black senior corporate executives identified two key groups of factors that can retard the upward mobility of black employees who have met requisite corporate qualifications. These inhibitors pertain to:

- differences in the socioeconomic and cultural backgrounds between blacks (and other minorities) and members of the majority group, and;
- beliefs, values, norms, and assumptions based on racial stereotypes within the larger societal culture that permeate the smaller cultures of America's corporations.

These two inhibiting factors raise cause for concern over the nature and extent of their influence on blacks' upward mobility and the extent to which these factors help to explain the differential rates of upward mobility between the similarly qualified white and black study groups. To address this concern, black executives' responses to questions pertaining to blacks' corporate mobility were analyzed.

Nature of the Differences in the Socioeconomic and Cultural Backgrounds Between Blacks and White

Twenty-one out of the 50 black corporate executives indicated that they believed, based on their experiences and the experiences of other blacks, that many blacks face difficulties in corporate America because of the differences in the socioeconomic and cultural backgrounds between blacks and majority group members.

Surveys have shown that a large proportion of the black population in the United States exists in the economically deprived, poorly educated, and socially isolated neighborhoods of this country's major cities (*The Economist* 1991). Research shows that many blacks entering the corporate arena have had little exposure to the majority culture and consequently have had limited exposure to the culture of white corporations (DiTomaso and Thompson 1988). It must be acknowledged "forthrightly" that cultural barriers make it unlikely for people who are of a different race (not white) to achieve advancement to upper management positions (Butler 1995).

The black corporate executives contended that business has not been traditionally viewed by blacks as a viable career option since careers at management levels were not accessible to blacks. In addition, they stated that historically blacks who obtained a high level of academic qualifications or credentials were steered into career areas other than those in the corporate arena. These non-corporate job areas included teaching, law, medicine, social work, and the ministry. The executives maintained that as a result of blacks' lack of exposure to and experience in corporate environments, they encounter difficulties in understanding many of the dynamics (norms, values, rituals, modes of operation) of that environment. One black senior executive explains:

> We're raised in very confined areas of inner city or rural areas, so we don't have a broad base. We don't have the cultural scope or experience. You don't get that in four years of college. Too often people do not realize how limited our exposure has been in this country and globally. Because we work very narrowly on things and we compare ourselves with the top 5% in corporate America who have

spent their time getting a much broader experience and exposure, it affects our judgments and perspectives. We have a lot of catching up to do.

Careful analysis of survey responses revealed three major areas critical to upward mobility which respondents believed were directly affected by the different socioeconomic and cultural backgrounds of blacks and whites. These areas include: a) the ability of blacks to communicate with members of the majority population in the corporate arena, b) the ability of blacks to plan and devise sound career goals and strategies for achieving these goals, and c) the ability of blacks to fit into the corporate arena through effective socialization.

A. Ability of Blacks to Meet Communication Standards of Corporate Culture

Respondents indicated that, in general, blacks coming from poor inner city neighborhoods are going to be at a disadvantage when attempting to communicate with members of the majority population in the corporate arena. These respondents argued that blacks from the inner city are disadvantaged when competing with their white corporate peers since the culture of the corporate arena is established and dictated by majority members. In respondents' opinion, most blacks from poor neighborhoods are not raised speaking the standard English that is spoken in the white culture or in corporate America, and that four years of college is not long enough for blacks to adjust completely to the language and standards of the corporate world. They contended that while a good college education helps to increase blacks' ability to compete in the corporate arena, it cannot overcome *all* of the deficiencies in communication skills that blacks from deprived backgrounds may possess. Comments made by three black senior corporate executives reflect these views:

> When I first came into the corporate arena I was really raw material. I had done well in my books but I believed I had to work harder than most people because my English wasn't good. I was bred in the housing projects. My mother and father are from the South and neither finished

grammar school. These are the conditions under which I had to learn to communicate. I really could not communicate on the level that is required within the corporate arena.

They always complain about our communication skills when they want to exclude minorities, particularly inner city blacks, from particular events or positions. If you grow up in a neighborhood like mine where we spoke "black English" then you have something that you must overcome to be successful within the corporate environment.

The problem with blacks is that we come out of our poor and isolated inner city neighborhoods, homes, and schools with poor written and verbal communication skills and, unfortunately, four years of college cannot correct this. An individual can learn to take tests. But one must be unique in that he or she can write. I, myself, have had to take some additional writing courses. I'm 49 years old and last year I took a course in grammar because that is an area in which I have a weakness. I am able to write good reports; but it's grunts and groans all the way through. Generally, blacks need to acquire these skills.

In pointing out aspects of their backgrounds that they had to adapt or change to meet the standards of corporate America, these respondents acknowledged that their white peers had an advantage over them. They also maintained that their white peers, products of the majority culture, grew up hearing and using standard English and as a result were familiar with and more versed in the standard English used in the corporate arena. Thus, 37 out of the 50 black senior corporate executives emphasized that for blacks to be successful in the corporate arena, they must become effective communicators (both oral and written). They argued that blacks must understand that the level and nature of skills obtained in this area are determined by standards set by the majority culture, and that these are the standards to which blacks must strictly adhere.

The following comments reflect the views of five black senior corporate executives regarding the importance of blacks having good communication skills as defined by corporate culture:

To succeed, we [blacks] need to get a better command of the English language. We need to become effective communicators.

In striving for success, oral and written skills are absolutely essential. If you cannot explain anything in "good English," in any particular meeting at any particular time, people peg you and they just pass over you at the next meeting. They'll say, "We don't need to hear from you." Also, if you can write in a coherent way, when someone reads your memos at least they could say, "This is a wonderfully done memo. I don't necessarily agree with it, but I understand it." These are the things which blacks must overcome in order to achieve success within the corporate arena.

I believe that one of the main things that blacks and other minorities need to do to succeed is to obtain or acquire excellent communications skills. The problem with a lot of minorities is that we think that all we have to do is get our degree. We go to school, get our degree or degrees and believe that once we have our credentials that this is it—"I'm ready for success." But this, along with some hard work, is just the starting point. We must address a myriad of intangibles and one of the biggest intangibles is the ability to communicate within the corporate world. And this is something that many of us neglect to address satisfactorily.

[Blacks need to be] good communicators by the standards of that company. You need to start working on that because technical competence has to get parlayed through oral and written communication. It doesn't do any good to develop new concepts if you can't relay them to other people who need them.

The language of corporate America is standard English, not "black English" or slang. To succeed within the corporate arena, minorities have to become both bilingual and bi-cultural because we don't normally come from that "strictly traditional white family system."

The concerns and needs emphasized by respondents regarding the ability of black employees, particularly those from poor socioeconomic backgrounds, to communicate effectively in the corporate arena by using a certain acceptable standard of English appear to be legitimate ones. These views coincide with those of the theorists and researchers discussed in Chapter II who also stressed the value of good communication skills. As a result, the ability of blacks to communicate effectively with majority group members should be considered as one possible source of explanation for the differences in rates of upward mobility experienced between blacks and whites in the corporate arena.

B. Ability of Blacks to Set Sound Goals and Develop Effective Strategies

When asked to identify characteristics or factors that differentiate successful blacks employed in the corporate arena from non-successful blacks, 34 out of the 50 study respondents in Group 5 asserted that a key factor was the ability to develop clear, succinct, and focused career goals and systematically implement strategies for accomplishing them. In fact, many study participants stressed that though it is important for *all* employees seeking upward mobility to develop such abilities, it is particularly important for blacks since the corporate arena is very different from the environment in which they were raised.

The comments of two black senior executives employed by major Fortune 500 American corporations emphasized the importance of goal setting and strategizing:

> Blacks seeking success must set goals and objectives for themselves. Successful blacks guide themselves towards that end and give the very best of what they are capable of giving. Any successful person, even if they do not achieve all of their objectives, must put forth an honest effort, and maintain maturity and insight in making the necessary sacrifices and plans that go into achieving an objective. The "goal" is part of the overall thrust of being successful. Blacks have to know what specifically it is that they want to do.

> I believe in career planning. I believe that a person has to look at what he would like to do and achieve. If he says that "I would like to be CEO of a corporation," then he has to realize that there are 10 or 12 steps to

get there. He has to figure out what he needs to do to prepare himself to obtain this position. He needs to figure out: Is it education? Do I like this kind of company? Is this the proper company for me to thrive in? Then he or she must go out and begin to find out what things he or she needs to do to prepare himself [or herself] for accomplishing his [or her] goals.

These respondents also emphasized the need, on the part of blacks, to pursue their established goals with tenacity and purpose. In the following comment, one black senior corporate executive of a Fortune 500 company explained the formula for his personal success:

I strongly believe in a structured approach to success. By that I mean the establishment of goals and the strategizing for the attainment of those goals. I still structure my goals, even my personal goals. These personal goals tend to be focused along education. A long time ago I established that I would get a college education and go beyond that. I have done just that. In pursuing my personal goals I still stress education and I continue to learn every day. In most cases I learn in informal settings. Now as far as my work is concerned, that is even more structured. I believe in establishing goals for career development and in setting a time schedule for that development. I believe in communicating with my superiors and to some extent even my peers in developing ways to accomplish my goals. Then with all of my energy I work towards attaining my goals.

Other black senior corporate executives explained the persistence and confidence with which blacks must pursue goal setting and career planning.

The thing that got me started very early was my home life, my parents. Growing up in the country there were never any limits put upon us by my mother. My mother always taught us that we could be anything that we wanted to be. If we were discouraged by anything, she would tell us not to worry and to go ahead to achieve our goals. In her vocabulary there was no such word as can't. My mother truly believed that an individual can accomplish any goal once he understands what has to be done to achieve these goals.

The difference between some successful people and the ones that are not, are people who continue to pursue a goal at any costs—meaning there's got to be a way to accomplish your goal rather than throwing up your hands saying "Well, we can't accomplish it so we might as well stop trying." Those are individuals that are usually the ones that end up at the top, because they pursued their goals with tenacity and perseverance.

In discussing the importance of having sound career goals and strategies, one black vice president of a major U.S. corporation captured concisely the nature, purpose, and value of goal setting and strategic planning. He explains:

Goals give direction, provide a means of gaining perspective and a way of discerning what is and is not important. If some structure is not imposed upon these goals, one can easily lose sight of them. [I recommend that] to keep one's goals in focus a detailed strategic plan is needed to develop a course of action for accomplishing them.

The black corporate executives believed that it is especially important for blacks to develop career goals and strategies since the corporate environment is an arena with which blacks are unfamiliar. The following comment made by a black senior executive offers an explanation as to why it is critical for blacks in particular to develop career goals and strategies.

I believe it helps to know what kinds of obstacles you are going to run into. It helps to know what types of roadblocks are going to be encountered when I go into a job. How can I anticipate what I am going to be up against? Maybe all job seekers need to know this, but blacks need to know the uniqueness of the types of roadblocks that are going to be placed in their way. Clearly defined career goals and well thought out strategies are keys to identifying some of these roadblocks.

Some black senior corporate executives surveyed spoke of being raised in poor neighborhoods, most often located in the inner cities of this country. These respondents spoke of being reared in environments in which neither their parents nor any immediate role models could have provided information about the corporate arena or how it functioned. This phenomenon was seen by some respondents as a deficiency that prevented them from charting accurate career paths and strategies, because they simply did not have the information to go about such a task. Respondents believed that many whites, because they have had family or friends who were or are employed in the corporate arena, are surrounded by people who provided them with information on the mores, customs, norms, and expectations of corporate culture. As a result, their white peers tended to have a better initial understanding of the nature and dynamics of the cultures existing within corporate America. One executive explains:

> The white male or female who comes from an affluent family has an advantage over us because their real training begins at the dinner table. These people have parents who are professionals or business people and they see this world every day. Their uncles, aunts, and neighbors all were a part of this world. The values that exist in the corporate world become a part of these people long before they have reached business school or college. They instinctively know what the corporate world is about. Blacks who were deprived of this type of background are naive to believe that once they have their educational credentials all they have to do is to work hard to reach the top of their corporations. This is simply not true.

These study participants indicated that normally blacks with the requisite academic and professional backgrounds who nonetheless are unable to obtain career planning information from family or friends should seek the help of individuals in the corporate arena. However, one top executive believed that because blacks are unable to fully assimilate into or effectively socialize within a corporation's culture, it is difficult for them to obtain assistance from individuals or access corporate networks.

The thing that frustrates many black managers is that they cannot map out career paths, because they don't know what's going on inside the business. Networks allow you to tap into sources of valuable information that may not be available any other way. Let's assume that you are new to a finance organization. You may feel threatened to ask your boss for information, because he might assume that you don't know anything. You may feel uncomfortable asking any majority member, because they may also believe that you don't know anything at all. It is a valuable asset to informally acquire information through networks. In planning career paths, networks provide such information as what kind of background is needed to pursue a particular career path and how you should go about preparing for a particular path. This type of information is very difficult to obtain outside of networks . . . in corporate America. Unfortunately, blacks tend to lack such access.

The general theme provided by the black corporate executives is that regardless of one's qualifications or capabilities, if a black employee has not developed clear career goals and plotted a path for achieving these goals, then he or she reduces the chances of obtaining advancement opportunities. Thus, it appears that blacks who have been deprived of the information needed to develop sound career goals and strategies—either because of the nature of their backgrounds or upbringing or because of their exclusion from informal networks and mentoring systems and developmental opportunities—must find creative methods and avenues to obtain the information required of them. Wernick (1994) supports this viewpoint. These executives warned that blacks who do not adhere to this approach, regardless of their credentials and qualifications, face a disadvantage in their attempts to move up in the corporate hierarchy in relation to their similarly qualified white peers. Thus, difficulties encountered by blacks in developing clear career goals and effective strategies for achieving these goals should be considered as a viable explanation for some of the differences in the rates of upward mobility experienced between similarly qualified black and white employees.

C. Ability of Blacks to "Fit" into Corporate Culture

Another factor raised by corporate executives and supported by researchers such as Baker (1995) and Butler (1995) as influencing black upward mobility is the ability of blacks to "fit" into the mainstream of American corporate culture. When questioned about the characteristics that distinguish a non-successful black person employed in the corporate arena from a successful black person, 39 out of 50 respondents identified the ability to adapt to the norms and standards dictated by the corporate culture. This factor has also been identified in the literature reviewed in Chapter II as being positively associated with career mobility.

Black corporate executives explained that if blacks are to experience increased rates of upward corporate mobility, it is essential for them to adapt to a corporation's culture and to be viewed by their white co-workers as part of the "team". These executives argued that teamwork is essential to the effective functioning of a corporation. They maintained that to work cooperatively as a team, the individuals involved must feel comfortable with each other and fit into the team structure. These individuals must be able not only to conform to the norms or codes that govern the team, they must also feel at ease in their conformity if they are to operate efficiently and effectively within the group. This view is supported by researchers such as Baker (1995) and Loden (1996).

These executives maintained that without this ability to adapt successfully and be accepted into the culture of America's white-run corporations, employees would find it difficult to achieve higher levels within the corporate hierarchy. They argued that without this ability, an employee's efficiency is reduced; thus his or her capacity to compete with other qualified employees is reduced. This, in turn, prevents these individuals from ascending the corporate ladder.

The following remarks by black corporate executives represent the views of many of the study participants and demonstrate the contribution that they believed successful adaptation into corporate culture can make to the success of blacks in corporate America:

I believe that those blacks who succeed within the corporate arena are those blacks who can interact with the cultures of the corporations they are working in. They are able to go beyond the barriers caused by diversity and really communicate with their non-black peers and supervisors and fit into the culture to accomplish things. Successful blacks are able to interface and communicate with their peers across racial lines, . . . and thus become part of the business team, management team, and the corporate culture.

What is needed by blacks to be successful is acceptance by peers, learning to work with white people, making them feel comfortable with us, showing them that we belong, and showing them that we are indeed a part of the solution and not a part of the problem. Blacks must function within corporations in such a way that they don't isolate themselves. They must constantly be viewed by whites as "one of the boys." Blacks must do this even if it means doing something you don't like to do every once in a while like having a drink with someone who may have a crew cut [i.e., a white man] after work, going to tennis matches, golf tournaments, and doing other social activities with your white peers. Blacks have to go to the country clubs. They have to go to the boss' house if he invites you. They must socialize. If senior management is not comfortable with you, regardless of how good you are, they'll never allow you to have access to their inner circle. If a black person does not make the extra attempt to socialize, he or she will never be accepted in their eyes. Management has to be comfortable with black employees before we can move up.

To succeed within the corporate arena blacks need to have an awareness of the culture more so than a white person because the black individual is a lot more unfamiliar with that environment than a white person who has been exposed to it through family and friends.

Respondents indicated that to successfully socialize into any corporation's culture, an array of skills is needed. Most often noted by black corporate executives as being critical to the socialization process were strong interpersonal skills or the ability to integrate successfully within the corporate culture. The following comments illustrate this view:

To be successful within the corporate arena, we have to not only be academically prepared but we also have to have good interpersonal skills.

I have all kinds of managers who are technically qualified yet the one who wins the promotion is the one who is technically qualified and who possesses good people skills. You can fake people skills for about two weeks, but when real life situations begin to occur, the real person comes out. If you are generally disagreeable and used to being difficult with people, this will surface at about the third week into your managerial role. This type of individual has a hard time getting people to work for him day in and day out. I think that good managers have the personality and the ability to work with people and these are the individuals who succeed.

Blacks need to recognize that part of survival and success means that one has to be skilled in human relations and that one has to be skilled in being able to read or judge people. We must also recognize that people come from different backgrounds and can have different experiences.

These comments illustrate the views expressed by many study respondents that the ability to fit into corporate culture is so critical to blacks' career advancement that they must be willing to conform to corporate norms.

The black corporate executives suggested that those blacks who grew up in areas similar to those of the majority culture are more familiar with that culture and as a result tended to experience less difficulty with the corporate socialization process. The following comments illustrate this point:

I grew up in a small town out . . . West which had very few blacks. Because of my experiences with whites I have a very comfortable feeling dealing with them. This is a primarily white company and culture which does not make it very easy on blacks. However, I have had it a little easier than many blacks, because of my background. I think that because I grew up in a community with thousands of whites, I'm comfortable with them.

I grew up around whites and went to superior white schools. So, I am not so distant from the prevailing culture that I have problems communicating or understanding the motivations of my co-workers. However, I understand that this is often a lot more difficult for a lot of other blacks. I am more assimilated than a lot of other blacks who, as a result, are less successful. One has to be totally assimilated into the corporate environment in order to be successful.

Respondents contended that since the assimilation process is a function of corporate culture, the assimilation of black employees into corporate work environments is contingent upon the corporate culture's acceptance of them as an equal, integral, and important part of that culture. Researchers such as Carnevale and Stone (1994), South (1994) and Baker (1995) support this view and contend that decision makers who tend to be Euro-Americans often hire and promote based on subjective factors as chemistry, ability to fit, and similarity to them in terms of attitudes, beliefs and values.

However, despite the great emphasis on blacks successfully socializing into their particular corporations, the majority of black survey participants, both upper middle level managers and senior level executives, indicated that they experienced difficulty in this area. Thirty-four out of 46 responding black corporate executives expressed some form of discomfort when attempting to find a niche in the cultural structure of many of America's white-dominated corporations. They stated that they harbored feelings of isolation and separation while at work. These respondents expressed concern that many of the discomforts felt by whites toward blacks and the discomforts felt by blacks toward whites serve only to harm the progress of blacks, since it is blacks who must adjust to a white-run culture and not vice versa.

The difficulty that blacks experience fitting into corporate culture may have a great deal to do with their unfamiliarity with the nature and dynamics of the cultures of America's white-run corporations. This unfamiliarity appears to result from the differences in socioeconomic backgrounds between blacks and majority group members which ultimately impact black advancement. This sentiment is shared by Carnavale and Stone (1994) who contend that "cultural differences are at the core of the obstacles to opportunity in the workplace" (25).

The claims of these black senior corporate executives regarding the difficulties that qualified blacks experience in adjusting fully to corporate culture were consistent with the views expressed by many researchers and theorists. In Chapter II, many researchers maintained that individuals who are unable to adapt to corporate culture and "fit" into the corporate structure often have a hard time functioning efficiently at work and as a result, they often find their mobility inhibited. Researchers such as Butler (1995) and Baker (1995) support these views and emphasize that ability and fit is a two-way street. Thus, it appears that to be successful, validation must be a two-way process. Additionally, because such large percentages of blacks expressed that they experienced difficulty in fitting into corporate culture, this factor must be considered to have the potential to influence the rates of upward mobility of black employees.

The Nature of Stereotypes about Blacks Existing in the Corporate Arena

One of the most frequently occurring concerns expressed by black senior executives was the presence of stereotypes about blacks in the corporate arena which results in the practice of racial discrimination in the workplace. Eighty-two percent of the black senior corporate executives in the study argued that blacks experience some form of stereotyping and prejudice from white co-workers and that this practice inhibits not only their progress but also the progress of all minority group members employed at America's corporations. Respondents explained that the racial prejudice and stereotypes existing in American society permeate the culture of American corporations, manifesting itself in the form of discrimination aimed at blacks and other minorities. The following range of comments represents the views expressed by a number of black senior executives concerning the issues of racial biases, stereotypes, and discrimination occurring in the corporate arena.

> Yes, racial discrimination is alive and well within the corporate arena. It is different now than 30 years ago, because now it is more subtle. Today, it is very difficult to exactly pinpoint racial discrimination. But it is there working against us.

> Blacks must understand that they are different and that whites have expectations and stereotypes about us. They have formulated prejudices which they bring to work with them every day. These prejudices and stereotypes held by whites hinder our progress. It is such a hindrance to have to consistently fight against these stereotypes.

> One of the biggest obstacles I have faced in attempting to move up the corporate ladder is racial discrimination. The whole racist environment cultivates and propagates a whole range of actions that are traceable back to basic racial prejudice. Racial discrimination is insidious and blacks within the corporate arena must always be cognizant of its presence.

> I always have to prove myself over and over again. Every time there is a supervisor change, it appears as if I'm starting all over again from ground zero. I must constantly dispel or disprove the stereotypes that exist about black people.

> I don't believe that this company is prepared to let a black achieve the highest position. The reason is because of the presence of racial prejudices and discrimination. These racial prejudices are the final analysis. It is an irrational phenomenon that prevents blacks and other minorities from fully demonstrating to white people that we are capable of performing and making a contribution.

These respondents argued that, within society as a whole and within the corporate arena in particular, a number of stereotypes and biases exist about blacks that act as barriers that can hinder the upward mobility process of black employees. In their opinion, because whites often perceive blacks to be poorly qualified and have poor work habits, white employees often devalue blacks' credentials, performance, and value to the corporation.

Respondents most often attributed the stereotypes and sources of prejudice and discrimination to the unfamiliarity whites have with blacks. These black executives argued that because most whites have little contact with blacks, blacks fall prey to the many stereotypes existing about them. Respondents believed that whites in the corporate arena, more often than not, base their judgments about blacks not on experience but on popular, negative beliefs and stereotypes existing in American society and thus within American corporate culture.

These black respondents believed that as a result, their white peers, supervisors, and employers often were suspicious about their competence, loyalty, and their ability to engage in sound decision making. The following statements by two black senior corporate executives represent the opinions expressed by many black survey respondents:

> Basically, we [blacks] have to constantly work against those major stereotypes and prejudices that white America has about us that manage to seep into the corporate arena. These stereotypes often lead to racial discrimination and we, as black people, must constantly prove to whites that we are capable, and that we are qualified. For instance, many whites believe the stereotype that black people are not analytical problem solvers. We, as blacks, must work hard to overcome this stereotype and demonstrate that we do indeed have the ability to solve problems.

> I think that there are some subtle distrusts of black people by whites within the corporate arena and it occurs in four major areas: (1) Distrust of *our competence*—regardless of our credentials; (2) A distrust of *our judgment*. They (whites) always believe that our judgment might be flawed. They believe that we generally come from another side of the track than whites and that a lot of us have been raised culturally deprived. Because [of] these differences in background and the fact that the typical white may have had very little experience with our

judgments, we can naturally expect to see some suspicion on their part; (3) Distrust of *our loyalty*—it's very important to a senior executive to have people who are loyal to the company, and; (4) Distrust of *our leadership ability*—it's very interesting that whites don't see us in leadership roles.

One black female senior corporate executive hypothesizes a reason behind white stereotyping of blacks and provides an example based on her experiences in the corporate arena.

It's just that we stand out more because there are fewer of us in corporate America. And we're always suspect because there are so many stereotypes that whites have of us. We walk into a room with so many strikes against us no matter what type of suit you have on or how your hair is, or how professionally you look. The stereotypes still stand in the way. They are roadblocks. The same thing with black men. They think that all black men have a gun in their pockets, etc. They believe that I, as a black woman, have double strikes although people say you have a double opportunity.

Another senior executive shares his personal experience with racial stereotyping:

In investment sales, the typical investor was a 50-year-old white Caucasian male, had a wife, two to three children in college, made over $100,000 per year. Here comes this 25-year-old black kid to sell him some investments, but I was not one of his peers. Because of age and color they would go to another stockbroker or somewhere else. Over the phone things were okay, but when they saw me, color became the issue. No matter how bad things got, I knew I would come out on top, somehow, even though they categorize me and put me into a stereotype slot. They tried more to disqualify. They didn't look at my accomplishments because it doesn't matter how significant my accomplishments. They had already made up their minds in the beginning how my performance would be evaluated.

Study respondents argued that as a result of the stereotypes about blacks existing in the workplace, black employees continue to be under greater scrutiny by their supervisors than their white peers. One black senior executive captures this sentiment:

> What happens is that a black employee receives much more scrutiny than the normal population. I think that their credentials have to be more in order. There's more consideration about education and where they went to school and factors like previous experience or situations like that. I believe that blacks are under much more scrutiny and consequently they have to be superior candidates in order to be weighed against an average white candidate.

These and other similar comments expressed by black executives demonstrate their definite concern regarding the practice of stereotyping and racial discrimination by majority group members. Many scholars have discovered that racial prejudice and stereotyping by whites can, indeed, exclude blacks from the mainstream of corporate culture. Prior studies, some of which were mentioned in the literature reviewed in Chapter II, substantiate and strengthen the validity of the black executives' contention that racial prejudice and stereotyping in the corporate arena inhibit their chances at upward mobility.

Sufficient evidence exists from survey respondents and the research literature to suggest the strong possibility that stereotyping, which can lead to the practice of racial discrimination, does account for some of the differences in the rates of upward mobility experienced between qualified white and black employees. A careful analysis of the survey responses of the black corporate executives revealed four major areas or processes critical to upward mobility in which racial prejudice and stereotypes manifest themselves and as a result inhibit the career advancement of qualified black employees. These are: a) the process of having a positive influence on the corporate bottom line, b) the corporate appraisal process, c) the process of gaining access to networks within the corporate arena, and d) the process of accessing corporate mentors.

A. The Process of Positively Influencing the Corporate Bottom Line

Twenty-six of the 50 black senior corporate executives stressed the importance of blacks being able to have a positive influence on a company's bottom line. They claimed that having a significant influence on a company's profits, the main reason for a company's functioning, contributes to a company's success and thus makes one an asset. According to respondents, these high contributing employees are promoted to the upper corporate ranks where they can have an even greater positive impact on profit and loss. The following comments made by respondents represent the attitudes of many blacks about the importance of being able to impact their corporations' bottom line:

> That's the important thing that you've got to do. I think that you have to develop a way to have the organization believe that you're adding something important to it—an expertise that, hopefully, isn't interchangeable with someone else's.

> You have to show that you can, in fact, have a positive influence on the bottom line, that you are bringing some added value. I think that if you are bringing added value you could survive and do okay. But if you really want to achieve the top positions, you have to convey or demonstrate to the organization that you are bringing in added value beyond the normal expectation and that it positively influences the company's bottom line.

> I had to be damn good at what I did. I had to be seen as an added value in my attempt to overcome the barriers that prejudice and stereotyping present—then we begin to observe a whole different phenomenon. I began to move up because I was viewed as an added value to the corporation. Suddenly, it is no longer an issue of race but one of economics in which corporations value the work and input of the black employee.

> Be very good or be an expert at what you do. You must have a great impact on the corporation's bottom line.

We [blacks] must indeed affect the bottom line. I think we all should begin doing something to affect the bottom line in a way that corporations know through the feedback that they get. Then they will say, "That's a valued employee who is an asset and we don't want to lose you." This will get you rewards in the form of salary increases and vertical promotions.

You have to be in a position that's important to the business. By that I mean that you must be in a position to score a goal or make a significant contribution towards your company's success. You must position yourself in such a way that you can say, "I negotiated this contract to save this amount of money, or made this sale and made this amount of money, etc." You must realize that your organization counts goals or measures individual success, and thus you must place yourself in the position to score goals or to make contributions to the company's success.

Essentially, employees are more likely to reach the upper rungs of the corporate ladder if they hold certain types of positions that lead more directly to revenue and profit generation for the corporation. The black executives contend that these positions are more directly involved with the main functions of the corporation and thus are viewed as more valuable, from a corporate perspective.

However, many of the black executives were quick to point out that most blacks tend to be located in less valuable positions (e.g., staff positions) from a corporate perspective. They believed that corporations tend to channel blacks into these positions and away from the more important job functions, because of the existing stereotypes about blacks regarding their loyalty, abilities, and competence. Butler (1995) and Collins (1997) support the views of these back executives. These black executives also believed that many leaders of America's corporations feel uncomfortable working with blacks, and as a result are unwilling to promote them into positions that have a large amount of influence on their company's bottom line. Many felt that white corporate executives secretly believe that blacks are unable to meet the demands of influential positions. The following comments by black senior executives sum up what they felt were the many problems blacks face in their attempts to impact significantly the corporation's bottom line.

> I have had difficulties moving up the corporate ladder because of the stereotype which says that minorities belong in certain positions. Blacks and other minorities are placed in jobs which are thought to be fairly easy, marshmallow jobs where nothing is really accomplished. Once you have been categorized in this manner, it is very difficult to get into an operating or line position. Companies allow you to do urban affairs and community relations but not much else. It's a "Catch 22" position.

> If you haven't been given an opportunity to do anything else, you become typecast. Once a minority is typecast into a particular type of position, he or she tends to stay there.

> I have experienced many more obstacles as a black person than as a woman. What constantly angers me is that no matter how many times I prove my competence and my ability to white people, they simply do not believe it. They don't believe the results of my efforts. They rationalize it in such a way as to convince themselves that it was luck or that I was good at mimicking other people's ideas and work. They don't believe that I really own the intelligence to come up with excellent results on my own.

The literature reviewed in Chapter II supports these executives' claims by stressing the importance and effectiveness of performance in positions that can more readily impact a company's bottom line results. The literature also showed that because of the impact of these types of corporate positions on a company's success, corporations promote those individuals who perform well in those roles. Some blacks believe that because of existing stereotypes about the abilities and competence of black employees, many of them tend to be channeled into jobs that greatly reduce their chances of significantly impacting a corporation's bottom line. Cox Jr. and Smolinski (1994) and the Federal Glass Ceiling Report (1995) support these assertions and indicate that minorities and women tend to be steered into "staff" positions that provide limited visibility to key decision makers and direct connection to strategic business decisions. Fernandez (1993) contends that minorities who are promoted into these less powerful and non-operational departments develop feelings of powerlessness unlike their white male counterparts who tend to be steered into line positions. Butler (1995) adds "unacknowledged are the roadblocks that guarantee that African Americans will fail to have essential background and experience for upper level posts!" (246). Because of the importance placed on influencing a company's bottom line and because a majority of respondents argued that the opportunity for blacks to do this is denied them, this factor should be considered as having the potential to negatively influence the rates of upward mobility experienced by blacks in the corporate arena.

B. The Corporate Appraisal Process

In answering questions about the mobility of blacks in the corporate arena, only 16% of the respondents in Group 5 specifically identified the appraisal process as directly influencing the upward mobility of black employees. However, this area warrants some discussion , because of the importance researchers place on the appraisal process and how it affects the mobility of employees (see Chapter II). Literature exists that identifies the subjective nature of the appraisal process as an inhibitor to the upward corporate mobility of blacks and other minorities (Work 1984; Jones 1986; Clarke 1987; Wernick 1994). For this reason the remarks made by respondents on the nature of the appraisal process as it relates to black employees will be briefly discussed.

Some black executives argued that the corporate appraisal process significantly reflects the biases and stereotypes about blacks that exist in corporate culture. Even the evaluations of work performed by employees in line positions, which can be more objectively measured than the work output of staff positions, contain some degree of subjectivity—if only because the work output is being evaluated by human beings.

These study respondents indicated that because of the subjective nature of the appraisal process, any amount of negative bias which seeps into this process is an inhibitor to an employee's potential advancement.

They argued that biases which factor into the appraisal process as a result of stereotypes about blacks have the potential to act as an inhibitor to their upward mobility.

The following responses by black executives employed at major U.S. corporations illustrate the subjectivity of the appraisal process and the negative results that can occur from this process:

> One of the things I tell young managers coming into the corporation is that it is important to be liked. If you want to succeed within this arena, it is important that someone, preferably your supervisor, likes you. Look, how else do you think supervisors make decisions on who gets promoted when you have a number of equally capable individuals? It comes down to who likes who. Those who are liked get promoted. Those who are not liked don't get promoted.

> White managers tend to give promotions based on the "old boy" system. In other words, they tend to promote those individuals who they perceive to be most like them. As a minority, no matter how much they like you, white managers are reluctant to promote you because they don't perceive you to be like them.

> Whites always try to categorize blacks and put us into stereotyped slots. During evaluations they try to disqualify us and they ignore our accomplishments. It doesn't matter how significant your accomplishments are, they have already made up their minds how the evaluation will come out, even before the evaluation process has begun. This has happened to me on a number of occasions and each time it has inhibited my progress up the corporate ladder.

According to these respondents, racial prejudice, biases, and stereotypes about blacks' abilities, qualifications, and competence can enter the appraisal process. Respondents contended that blacks generally are evaluated by a majority member who has usually been raised to believe certain stereotypes about blacks and has brought these stereotypes into the work force. They explained that every time a majority member evaluates a black person or any minority member and allows stereotypes and prejudices based on race to factor negatively into the process, the appraisal then serves as a mechanism that impedes a minority employee's efforts to successfully achieve higher levels in the corporate hierarchy. These views are reinforced by Igbaria and Wormely in their 1995 study "Race Differences in Job Performance and Career Success." These researchers contend that because of evaluation bias against minorities, they are assessed more negatively than the actual performance warrants. Somerick (1993) warns that ineffective appraisals also lead to decreased employee productivity.

Thus, it is important to consider the nature of appraisal processes when attempting to account for some of the differences in the upward mobility rates between similarly qualified black and white employees.

C. The Process of Accessing Corporate Network Systems

Thirty-nine out of the 50 black senior corporate executives indicated that having access to informal networking systems in the corporate arena is very important to any employee wanting to reach the upper levels of the corporate ladder. Respondents argued that a great deal of information is exchanged within these networks, and that being a participant provides you with useful and important information on how to perform a job efficiently and effectively.

Some survey respondents indicated that if they had greater access to informal corporate networks, this would have allowed them to acquire information that would have been much more difficult, if not impossible, to obtain outside those networks. Others pointed to the emotional support that employees receive as members of informal networks and its significance to their survivability and success in the corporate arena. A few explained the comfort and ease that informal networks bring to all members.

The following comments made by a few black executives express the value of these informal networks which are considered central to a corporation's effective functioning. The influence of these networks on their career advancement is also highlighted.

You really need access to the power brokers within the company. You get the confidence of the majority population. There is a unique thing of acquiring the confidence of upper management. It is very critical for blacks. It's very hard for them to get a job assignment that shows that they're competent. Finding those opportunities to show that they're trustworthy and capable is difficult to get. There's a mental toughness that goes along with getting important assignments. You have to have the opportunity to demonstrate your capability and competence.

To succeed within a corporation one has to have an awareness of what's going on in the organization at all times and this comes with having an understanding of the more informal organizational structures. In organizations there are the formal power structures and there are the informal power structures. The informal power structures have a great deal of influence as to what happens in organizations. Being aware of the informal structures and how they function is important. It is very difficult for us [blacks] to become a part of these informal structures. I was fortunate enough to make friends with some people who were tied into networks and as a result of these friendships, I was able to learn from them and be exposed to things that I might not have otherwise been exposed to.

You have to find a way to understand the very social nature of the business environment. By that I mean you have to tap into the informal structure or networks that exist within the corporations. I think that lack of access to these type of networks is one of the main problems that black managers face. Black managers have to understand that the power of the enterprise is not vested solely in the formal mechanisms for running the enterprise, but that the informal mechanisms are very powerful also. Whether you golf, go out for a couple of drinks, or whatever, you have to find a way to be sure that you're not excluded from these networks.

Another experience from a black senior corporate executive illustrates how his tapping into these informal networking systems has allowed him to have access to information pertinent to his job and be viewed as part of the team.

At this company we have what we call an early shop. All of the key managers are at this informal social meeting between 7:00 a.m. and 8:30 a..m. I found out about 10 years ago that most of the decisions were made between 7:00 and 8:30 and then implemented from 8:30 a.m. to 5:00 p.m. I came into work at about 8:30 a.m. and didn't have a clue as to when all the decisions had been made. So, what I started to do was to come in earlier and participate in these early shops. I slowly began to find myself having access to important information and being part of the crew as opposed to an outsider.

In the literature reviewed in Chapter II, it was shown that researchers and theorists alike place great value on the informal network systems in corporations and the advantages of participation in these networks for an individual seeking upward mobility. Naisbitt, in his 1982 study predicting ten megatrends of the 1980s and 1990s, went as far as to say that anyone not having access to these networks would almost certainly be at a serious disadvantage. Therefore, the assertions expressed by a large percentage of respondents on the value of gaining access to informal corporate networks are substantiated by the works and findings of researchers and should be considered an important influence on the mobility process.

However, in light of the significant role that these networks play in an individual's success in the corporate arena and implicit in comments made by study respondents, it appears that most blacks face disadvantages to their corporate mobility because they perceive that they have limited access to informal networks. Twenty-three out of 50 black executives asserted that they experienced a number of difficulties in accessing the informal network systems in their white-run corporations. They attribute most of their difficulty to the deleterious effect of stereotypes about blacks existing in the corporate arena.

These black executives also reported experiences of isolation and exclusion as they attempted to fit into the corporate culture and thus gain access to informal networks. Many argued that their exclusion from these networks at their particular companies prevented them from acquiring important information and excluded them from having input in the decision making that occurred during informal meetings.

The following comments by black senior corporate executives outline the difficulties that many blacks indicated they experienced in attempting to access and become an accepted member of the informal networks within their respective corporations.

At the level at which I am and above, it is very stressful on blacks. It is mostly due to the nature of the corporate culture. There is a lot of isolation and blacks quickly begin to realize that they really don't fit in anywhere at these levels. Your white peers don't want you around because they feel very uneasy around you. It can get very lonesome and difficult to survive.

The problem with isolation is that it ends up causing you to not have access to the informal networks. That is the price one pays when they are isolated from networks within the corporate culture.

The old saying is that "you have to be a team player." But how can you play the game if you are not allowed on the field? We [blacks] are excluded from social groupings and environments. We are not invited to the social clubs, the lunches, and the dinners. In those kinds of events, decisions are made that are not made during the regular work hours and you are left out.

These respondents argued that the disadvantages they faced when excluded from informal networks undermined their upward mobility by depriving them of information that would have enabled them to compete more effectively with their white peers who have access to these networks. Respondents also explained that the emotional support provided by informal networks was lost to them because of the mutual discomfort they and their white peers faced when interacting with each other. As one executive explains:

Blacks have to go a long way to make majority members feel more comfortable with them, because a lot of whites are still very uncomfortable around a black face.

The claims made by survey participants that stereotypes about blacks prevent them from gaining access to important information from corporate networks is substantiated by literature discussed in Chapter II. In Chapter II, several researchers indicated that employees do indeed bring their prejudices and stereotyping (racial and otherwise) into the workplace. These researchers contend that racial prejudice provides a barrier between blacks and whites, who view blacks in stereotypical ways, and this inhibits blacks when they try to access systems traditionally open only to white male employees.

When it comes to informal networks, it has been shown that: a) access is considered extremely important to any employee seeking to move up the corporate ladder, and b) the difficulties blacks experience in accessing informal corporate networks may be due, in part, to the existence of racial stereotypes in the corporate arena which results in their inability to "fit" into the predominantly white corporate culture.

Due to the number of black executives who expressed difficulty in accessing informal networks and due to the importance researchers place on such networks, this phenomenon should be considered a viable factor that can account for some of the differences in the rates of upward mobility between similarly qualified black and white employees.

D. The Process of Accessing Corporate Mentors

In response to a series of questions focusing on the keys to corporate success, 38 out of the 50 black senior corporate executives indicated that mentors play an important role in enhancing the rates of upward mobility of all individuals in the corporate arena. These sentiments are supported by researchers such as Forbes and Piercy (1991), Shea (1994), and Bell (1996). Respondents did not go so far as to say that it would be impossible to move up the corporate hierarchy without the assistance of a mentor or mentors. They simply asserted that access to mentors aids the mobility process, thereby enhancing one's chances for corporate advancement.

Participating black executives indicated that mentors assist individuals with the mobility process by providing valuable information on the corporation: how it operates, the protege's role and function within the company, and the company's culture. This information allows the protege to understand and adjust to the norms, values, expectations, and dynamics of the corporation which, in turn, aids the protege in functioning better in his or her role within the particular company. The following comment reflects the views of many black executives surveyed about the importance of mentoring relationships:

> To be successful, blacks must have mentors within their companies. We must have someone who takes an interest in us, who helps us, and whom we can consult.

A few of the black senior executives, who had the opportunity to be mentored at certain times in their career, explain the influence their mentors had on their career advancement.

> In my case mentoring did play a part in my career success. Mentors are individuals you must feel comfortable with (and vice versa) and whose advice and counsel you can trust. The mentor must keep your confidence when you share with them problems and difficulties you have while on the job. There are at least two or three times in my career where it is clear that someone had literally moved me into a job I might not otherwise have had. Each time I was mentored into a very demanding job.

> I'm sitting here today because of a man who was the president and CEO of the previous corporation I worked in. When I met him he hired me as vice president of claims. I am here today because when he came here to turn it [the company] around he asked me to come with him. He's the first person, a white man, who told me I could achieve my dreams.

> In my early years at this company I had a mentor. He was a fairly stern taskmaster. He would take me to his apartment and we would sit and talk for hours. We would talk about what kinds of things he had to do to get ahead. We talked about the organization and who the key people were in the organization. He gave me a perspective that I wouldn't have

had otherwise. That was important; understanding the corporate environment and learning how to function in [it] is critical to one's success.

These respondents reported that while at certain periods of their careers they had the opportunity to be mentored, for blacks in general in the corporate arena, this is a rare phenomenon.

As was the case with informal networks, a great deal of literature discussed in Chapter II addressed the importance of employees gaining access to mentors at corporations. Researchers and theorists such as Baker (1995), Pfleeger and Mertz (1995), and Bell (1996), like the respondents in this survey, concur that mentors are important and vital components of the mobility process. Both of these groups contend that mentors are vital resources because they are an emotional support system, role models, information sources, and sponsors or promoters.

The respondents believed that despite the importance mentors can play in an employee's career advancement, a great number of black employees find it very difficult, if not impossible, to identify and gain access to corporate mentors. In fact, 24 out of the 46 responding black executives argued that they had experienced difficulties in gaining access to mentors within their respective work environments. The influence of stereotypes about blacks in the workplace is the reason most often given by the black executives for why blacks experience difficulty in accessing networks. Survey participants pointed out similar problems with finding and accessing corporate mentors:

> To be successful within the corporate arena you must have a mentor. The problem with blacks is that most times a mentor or sponsor wants a protege that is in his own image, one he perceives to be like him. I cannot think of one instance when a minority has been selected and groomed by a superior officer and brought up the ranks in my company. Minorities lack mentors and this is a hindrance to us.

> Blacks rarely get mentored. If you are an extraordinary type, if you have great personality skills, and if you have great academic credentials,

you might be lucky enough to find a mentor. But most often blacks
don't get mentored.

Blacks don't have mentors. At least they don't have them here in this
company. As a result, many times we are put in situations where we
don't have all the information about a certain issue. That's a problem
we face and which tends to hinder our progress. We are excluded from
developing mentoring relationships.

This is a very important concern for black employees. Respondents
argued that qualified blacks within the corporate arena who are unable to
find mentors, because of the stereotypical perception that whites usually
have of blacks, experience a form of exclusion that whites do not
experience. One black senior executive sums up the feelings expressed by
many blacks:

Every time a black within the corporate arena experiences difficulty
acquiring a mentor or someone who can aid that person in learning how
to survive and succeed within the corporate arena, because of
stereotyping and differences in blacks and the dominant white culture
of American corporations, blacks face a disadvantage most whites do
not face.

These corporate executives believed that gaining access to corporate
mentors enhances an employee's success. However, they contended that
blacks often had trouble gaining access to these mentors. The views
expressed by these executives are corroborated by the works of
researchers, discussed in Chapter II, who also stressed the importance of
mentors, the benefits derived, and the difficulties blacks experience in
accessing them (Chao 1988; Thomas 1986; Fernandez 1988; DiTomaso
et al. 1988; Wernick 1994; Butler 1995; Baker 1995). Thus, any exclusion
of blacks from establishing mentoring relationships within their work
environments should be considered as a factor that can influence the
mobility of blacks. As a result, this factor can possibly account for some
of the differences in the rates of upward mobility experienced between
similarly qualified black and white employees.

IMPLICATIONS OF ENHANCERS AND INHIBITORS

As was said earlier, in explaining the factors which contributed to their achieving upper management level positions, the black executives surveyed spoke about attaining superior academic qualifications and excellent professional experiences, investing in numerous hours of training, and putting forth large amounts of hard work and perseverance. They argued that their preparation and hard work helped them to overcome some aspects of the factors negatively influencing black mobility (e.g., stereotypes and different socioeconomic and cultural backgrounds), which in turn aided them in achieving certain levels of corporate advancement. However, a large percentage (48%) of these executives said that in spite of their efforts to meet a company's requisite skills and qualifications and assimilate into the white dominant corporate culture, they had either reached or would soon reach the highest level in their companies that a black could attain, with no hopes for further career advancement. In other words, many of these black senior executives felt the proximity of the "glass ceiling" at their respective companies beyond which they believed they could not advance because of their race.

When examining the mobility of blacks in the corporate arena and considering the inhibitors that they face, it is important to keep in mind that the success of the black executives in this study represents the rare exception. Evidence suggests that many qualified blacks simply opt to leave the corporate arena, citing limited opportunities and race related inhibitors to their mobility. Literature reviewed in Chapter I indicated that when blacks sense they have reached an arbitrary "ceiling" in terms of their corporate advancement, they seek other less uncomfortable arenas in which they perceive greater opportunities to utilize their skills and abilities and fewer limits to their career advancement caused by their race. The following quotes of black senior corporate executives express the plight of many blacks in the corporate arena who perceive limited opportunities for upward mobility.

> There was this black guy who had been in this company for 25 years. He had an MBA from a prestigious university and was generally well qualified. About eight or nine years ago the chairman promised him that

if he went out and acquired the additional necessary qualifications and performed the necessary tasks, he would be promoted to a higher position. Well, he did all the things that he was supposed to do but after a long period of time nothing had happened. In other words, he had not received his promotion. He ended up leaving the corporate arena.

I think that of those blacks who are frustrated and perceive no opportunities . . . they do two things. Some scrap their dreams, find a level within the hierarchy that they can tolerate and live with and remain there until they retire. However, a lot of them have gone out on their own and formed their own businesses and have tried to realize their dreams by being entrepreneurs.

Many blacks who feel that they can't advance leave the corporate arena and start their own businesses. Some leave and go to work for black companies where they feel more comfortable and [where] their chances for success are better.

In fact, all of the black senior corporate executives indicated that they knew blacks who left the corporate arena because they felt that certain inhibitors removed any additional opportunities for career advancement. Seventy-eight percent of the respondents indicated that they knew of competent blacks who left the corporate arena to start their own businesses and became successful entrepreneurs. Thirty-four percent indicated they knew of qualified blacks who left to work for black corporations. Twenty-two percent of the respondents indicated they knew of qualified blacks who left the corporate arena out of frustration and dismay over perceived mobility barriers and were unemployed at the time of the study.

A few of the black senior executives who participated in this study expressed concern over competent blacks leaving the corporate arena. They emphasized that corporations need to maximize the use of all of their human resources if they want to compete successfully on a global scale. The following insightful remark by a black corporate executive helps to demonstrate this view:

Well, I think that some of the more enlightened companies are beginning to recognize that they need all the minority brain power, talent, and person-power that is available. A few have begun to realize that, in the long run, it is in their best interest to have a society in which all groups are equal participants and not to have large segments which are underutilized. Therefore, a very few are forthright and progressive in what they do to bring minorities in and make them a part of their institutions. However, all corporations need to reach out to minorities and create environments in which equal opportunities are given for them to grow and flourish. They need to take steps to make sure that minorities are truly welcomed and that their [corporations'] gestures are not just a facade.

Some of the black corporate executives who participated in this study felt that in addition to the efforts of blacks to meet their responsibility for becoming qualified and competent employees, corporations also must meet certain responsibilities. If corporations are to fully utilize their available work force, they must provide environments in which equal opportunity is given to *all* employees, as is the opinion evident in the following statements:

Corporate culture has never incorporated blacks into the culture. When steps are taken to allow blacks to become part of the culture, only then will the atmosphere change to be a more wholesome place for blacks to grow and develop.

There has to be a commitment on the part of the corporation to support the black managers and to give them the opportunities for advancement. It is not enough just to make them managers. They must have the opportunities to advance. Otherwise, I think that they will peak out at a level within the company that is far below their true capabilities.

The corporate structure has to create an atmosphere that we [blacks] can trust. We can't be expected to just work to death and not be rewarded. Corporations must do something to make sure that all employees are equally rewarded.

These black executives believe that if corporations make an effort to create work environments in which blacks are given equal opportunities and just rewards based on their qualifications, abilities, and performance, then blacks will be more inclined to stay within the corporate arena and have a positive influence on the growth and productivity of American corporations. The following statement by a black corporate executive summarizes this view:

> Those blacks that I know who perceived no opportunity to advance have gone into business for themselves. However, I believe that if they had been provided with better opportunities to compete and move up, they would not have left. It must be understood that at certain times blacks get to a certain plateau in a company that is far short of their goals and see no opportunity for movement. So the other recourse is to go into business for themselves. I think that if blacks were not to experience so many inhibitors and were to continue to have equal access up the corporate ladder, they would not go into business for themselves. I had one good friend who was well qualified and who was viewed by his white peers and superiors in a very stereotypical way. He wasn't going any place within the corporate arena. So, he opted to go into business for himself—and he's doing very well now. But, if the company had provided a fairer environment, he never would have made the decision to leave the company.

CONCLUSION

This chapter discussed the views of black senior corporate executives regarding several factors which enhance and inhibit the upward mobility of black employees in the corporate arena. These executives stressed the acquisition of requisite skills, academic credentials, professional experience, and training as enhancing the upward mobility of all employees. However, these executives argued that acquiring the requisite qualifications and demonstrating the desired behaviors allowed blacks to achieve only certain levels in their work environments. In addition, interviews of black executives revealed that they perceived several major factors that inhibited the progress of qualified black employees:

A. differences in socioeconomic and cultural backgrounds between blacks and majority group members. This, in turn, influences the ability of blacks to:

- meet communication standards of corporate culture;
- set sound goals and develop effective strategies; and
- "fit" into the corporate culture.

B. beliefs based on stereotypes about the ability, competence, and performance levels of blacks. This, in turn, influences:

- the placement into job positions and functions that have a positive influence on the corporate bottom line;
- the corporate appraisal process;
- the process of accessing corporate network systems; and
- the process of accessing corporate mentors.

The analysis of the interviews with the black corporate executives revealed that each of these factors is a possible source of explanation for the differences in the rates of upward mobility between similarly qualified black and white employees. It is not the intention of the researcher to claim that these are the only factors that can explain the difference in the rates of upward mobility between similarly qualified black and white employees. The researcher can only claim that these factors are the salient ones which black senior corporate executives perceived to have a significant impact, not only on their own career advancement but also on those of black employees in general.

These executives offered additional viewpoints regarding an approach that can be employed to address these inhibitors. They contended that if the identified inhibitors to blacks' upward mobility are to be removed, one intervention by corporations is to institute various types of training programs for all employees. They pointed out that because of socioeconomic and cultural differences between blacks and whites, various strategies may need to be implemented during training initiatives to service diversified needs. These black executives argued that unless some level of corporate in-house special intervention is offered to all employees, including the perpetuators of discrimination, blacks and other minorities will continue to be singled out as incapable of succeeding. However, these executives maintained that offering special assistance only to blacks and other minorities can potentially lead to even more racial stereotyping and discriminatory practices since this type of intervention serves to further stereotypically classify, label, and isolate these groups.

Members of the black senior executive group argued that special training and interventions can assist both blacks and whites in dealing more effectively with differences in their socioeconomic and cultural backgrounds and practices of racial stereotyping and discrimination. However, these black executives believed that ultimately blacks will not experience rates of upward mobility comparable to those of their white peers until all the inhibitors to black corporate upward mobility are effectively addressed and eradicated.

NOTES

1. Similar questions were asked of all of these black senior corporate executives. Appendix H outlines some of the pertinent questions from which information was gleaned for use in discussing the various issues addressed in this chapter.

2. Accounting, MIS-computers, marketing, business management, economics, finance, and corporate law.

3. Schools that were not rated in the Lovejoy's College guide are not necessarily low prestige schools. However, they failed to supply all the necessary data for the calculation of the rating.

4. Respondents from Group 5 were promised anonymity; hence, there are no names attached to any of their statements.

CHAPTER VI

Conclusions, Recommendations, and Implications of the Study

The primary goal of this study was to further the understanding of why qualified blacks perceived their opportunities for upward mobility in the corporate arena to be limited despite their having the requisite skills and experience for advancement. To accomplish this end, a model of corporate upward mobility (Chart 3-1) was developed from a review of the literature. This review revealed two sets of factors influencing blacks' career advancement: 1) those factors influencing the mobility of employees in general, and 2) those factors influencing the mobility of blacks in particular. The model shows how the factors generally influencing mobility as well as those specifically influencing black upward mobility could actually lead to slower rates of advancement for blacks in the corporate arena.

BACKGROUND

Researchers such as Salmon (1979), Arthur, Hall, and Lawrence (1989), Francis and Woodcock (1990), Fernandez (1993) and President Clinton's Economic Report (1997) consistently noted the requisites needed for a typical employee to achieve upward mobility: he or she must have acquired specific academic qualifications and professional experience, and must have met specified performance standards set by corporations for movement into a particular position. Many corporate leaders and some researchers, including Zweigenhaft (1984), DiTomaso et al. (1988) and U.S. Department of Commerce (1997), contend that the main reason blacks are underrepresented at upper levels of the corporate hierarchy is because there are not enough blacks with the requisite skills and qualifications to compete at higher levels in U.S. corporations (Path 1, Chart 3-2).

On the other hand, other researchers, corporate leaders, and many blacks believe that additional factors influence the mobility of blacks in the corporate arena. Researchers such as Jones (1986), Clarke (1987), Fernandez (1988, 1993), America and Anderson (1996), and the Department of Labor (1996), who studied the career advancement of blacks and their perceptions, consistently reported that most blacks believed that despite having met the requisite skills and qualification standards set by corporations for employability and upward mobility, they were still not being afforded the same opportunities for career advancement as their similarly qualified white peers. Path 2 (Chart 3-3) of the mobility model reflects this belief—that there exist additional factors, specific to blacks, that influence their rates of upward corporate mobility. The previous chapter, Chapter V, provides an in-depth discussion of this issue.

These two main paths reflect the two dominant points of view that emerge from the literature. However, since the focus of the study is on the mobility of qualified black employees (blacks who overcame the obstacles of the first path), only Path 2 (Chart 3-3) of the mobility model was tested.

STUDY DESIGN

It was important to take into account potential methodological biases inherent in designs of the nature employed in this study (Stanley and Campbell 1967). Design biases included such possibilities as: a) the inability to generalize from a single case to the larger population of interest, and b) the failure to control adequately for key factors which might influence the dependent variables under study.

Prior studies of the upward mobility of blacks and other minorities in the corporate arena have been particularly criticized for one or more design defects that make generalizability difficult. These prior studies have been challenged by researchers for the following alleged design deficiencies: a) they were based solely on "soft" (anecdotal) descriptive data (i.e., they relied exclusively on surveys of perceptions and opinions of minorities or corporate leaders); and b) there were no comparative experiences across control groups (e.g., minority versus non-minority, or trained versus untrained minorities). Because of these types of criticisms of earlier research, every attempt was made to avoid many of the design shortcomings of prior studies.

Thus, qualitative as well as quantitative data were obtained and analyzed from five groups of corporate managers (three of which were matched on position level, company, and industry) in 153 companies, representing 16 different industries and located in 16 cities in the United States. In looking at the potential impact of race on upward corporate mobility, this study controlled for key academic, professional, and demographic characteristics attested to in the literature, and viewed as critical to the employability and upward mobility of all employees. Additionally, the study obtained the perceptions of a nationwide sample of qualified black corporate executives (Group 5) who succeeded in achieving certain upper level management positions at their respective companies. The findings from both the qualitative and quantitative analyses have added to the field of research on black upward mobility in corporate work environments.

CONCLUSIONS

Many researchers and corporate leaders have maintained that once blacks acquire the requisite skills and qualifications and become as qualified as their corporate white peers, they then will experience comparable rates of upward mobility (Chapter II). However, in this study's statistical analyses of the mobility rates of specially trained black managers, black managers, and white managers—each of whom shared similar qualifications[1]—the two black groups experienced significantly slower mobility rates than the white group, even when controlling for demographic, academic, and professional experience background factors. Beyond these traditional predictors of a typical employee's corporate upward mobility (identified in Chapter II), other factors must exist to explain the differences in the rates of upward mobility between the black employees and their similarly qualified white peers.

Other researchers and some corporate leaders (Chapter II) have argued that in order for blacks to meet the requisite skills and qualification standards set by corporations for employability and upward mobility, blacks must receive special corporate training. As a result, attempts were made in this study to observe the influence of special training on black upward mobility. The trained group of black managers (Group 1) who received special training as well as the black managers' (Group 2) were found to experience significantly slower rates of upward mobility than a similarly qualified white group even when controlling for demographic, academic, and professional experience background factors. Additionally, this group of trained black managers experienced no significant differences in the rates of upward mobility as compared to the similarly qualified black group without such training. It appears that this special training, in and of itself, has no significant impact on the corporate upward mobility of qualified blacks.

It is important to note here that many of the trained black managers (more than 75%) maintained that the special training they received had provided them with skills and experiences that enhanced their career advancement. For instance, many of the trained blacks stated that their training addressed areas such as meeting corporate communication standards, developing goals and strategies, understanding and "fitting" into the corporate culture, accessing corporate mentors and networks, and addressing racial stereotyping and discrimination. However, the fact that the trained black managers experienced significantly slower rates of upward mobility than their white peers, despite the additional training, suggests that other factors may influence black mobility. These other factors go beyond the requisite skills and qualification standards set by corporations, which the special training did not or could not fully address. Thus, one can conclude that special training, by itself, beyond the acquisition of requisite skills and qualifications, is not enough to have an appreciable positive impact on the rates of upward mobility of blacks in the corporate arena.

An empirical analysis of qualitative data obtained from black senior corporate executives (Chapter V) confirms this assertion and similar findings of some researchers, including (Salmon (1979), Forbes and Piercy (1991), Fernandez (1993), Wernick (1994), Cross et al. (1994) and the U. S. Department of Labor (1997), who suggest that certain influencing factors specific to black upward mobility exist, other than academic and professional qualifications. The analysis of qualitative data from these black executives revealed the following key factors with the potential to inhibit substantially the upward mobility of blacks in the corporate arena:

A. differences in socioeconomic and cultural backgrounds between blacks and majority group members. This, in turn, influences the ability of blacks to:

- meet communication standards of corporate culture—demonstrate oral and written command of standard English;
- set sound goals and develop effective strategies—prepare and pursue career plans;
- "fit" into the corporate culture—adapt to norms and standards and assimilate and feel comfortable within the corporate structure.

B. beliefs based on stereotypes about blacks' ability, competence, and performance levels. This, in turn, influences:

- blacks' placement into job positions and functions that have little or no impact on the corporate bottom line;
- a tendency toward racial bias during the corporate appraisal process;
- the process of accessing corporate network systems—leading toward isolation and limited access to pertinent information on promotion opportunities, and the like;
- the process of accessing corporate mentors—without whom an employee lacks critical support, on-the-job "training," and career guidance.

RECOMMENDATIONS

To provide some understanding of the context in which the process of addressing blacks' corporate upward mobility must be conducted to be effective, a brief review of some of the literature concerning systemic and holistic change is given.

A Comprehensive Approach to Change

Kanter (1977) argues that in order to facilitate systemic/holistic change, comprehensive and integrated approaches encompassing all contributing factors are needed to bring about real change, since no one innovation by itself is likely to improve significantly the quality of work life or equity for disadvantaged groups. In their study on the evaluation of organizations and interventions that bring about organizational change, Thomas and Kramm (1988) support Kanter's approach. They described an "organizational change approach" that systematically identifies and addresses all possible factors that impede or enhance organizational development. The comprehensiveness of this approach avoids the shortcomings of other approaches, in which programmatic interventions may become undermined by inconsistencies that occur from not taking into account all factors relative to the problem. Cummings and Worley (1997) support the above positions and recommend that change agents should stop interpreting organizational problems as requiring the favored technique but should instead recognize the systemic nature of change which requires holistic and cross-functional collaboration and interventions.

To fully address the issue of black upward mobility, an integrated and holistic approach is needed, such as those purported by the above experts. The nature of factors integral to the mobility process is complex. To focus merely on one or two key factors critical to black mobility will provide an insufficient and flawed approach to addressing the discrepancy in the rates of upward mobility between similarly qualified black and white employees. For example, companies that set up mentoring programs for qualified blacks and other minority group members to provide them with increased opportunities for career advancement will fail to achieve this goal, if at the same time these proteges are not given the types of assignments where they can demonstrate their ability and competence. Wernick (1994) reinforces this viewpoint and adds that the informal selection processes (e.g., assignment, distribution, and accessing mentors) support the need for executives and managers to know, trust, and to feel comfortable with those they choose. Unfortunately, the informal selection process tends to be subjective and biased. As a result, minorities are less likely to be selected for developmental opportunities or special assignments in key areas.

Thus, once all factors that influence blacks' upward mobility have been identified, interventionists or change agents must deal with every identifiable barrier that can impede blacks' progress. Any method attempting to increase the upward mobility rates of blacks in the corporate arena must follow the guidelines of an approach that integrates all significant factors impacting that mobility and any other barriers (institutional or otherwise) that can derail the change process. If these guidelines are not employed fully, the probability is substantially decreased that the discrepancy in the rates of upward mobility between comparably qualified black and white employees will be eradicated.

An abundance of literature exists on various types of interventions that can be used to remove the barriers to black upward mobility in the workplace. Although the recommendations that follow are not necessarily unique, they are designed to get at the root causes. It is the coming together of these interventions that is essential to addressing effectively the problems blacks face in the corporate arena. No one recommendation in and of itself can be expected to be effective in solving the pervasive barriers to black corporate upward mobility. It is important to note that these recommendations go beyond the data and are based on the author's experience and knowledge, the literature reviewed, and the analyses of data (quantitative and qualitative) conducted in this study.

Furthermore, the implementation of a holistic approach employing the following recommendations does not guarantee that all qualified blacks in every corporate setting will experience rates of upward mobility comparable to those of their similarly qualified white peers. One reason might be that all factors impacting black upward mobility may not have been identified specific to a particular company. These recommendations address only the key enhancers and inhibitors identified in this study as impacting black corporate upward mobility. Corporate leaders will still have to take the initiative to identify any factors beyond those identified in this study and those particular to their work environments.

Enhancers to Black Upward Mobility
Requisite Skills and Qualifications

Addressing the corporate upward mobility of blacks requires, first, that blacks who enter the corporate arena are qualified. It is essential that blacks, like any other employee—irrespective of the backgrounds and environments in which they grew up and the difficulties and blocked opportunities they face in the larger society—meet the academic, professional, and performance standards set by corporations for all employees. In fact, blacks have to have the skills to function effectively in two worlds—that of corporate culture as well as their own reality (Howard 1996).

Blacks must seek out avenues that enable them to obtain the basic requirements needed to qualify for employment opportunities and to perform in ways that meet corporate advancement standards. Blacks and other interested groups must place pressure on their neighborhood schools, their local and state boards of education, and their state and federal legislatures to make certain that all the nation's children are obtaining the basic skills necessary for success in the larger society and in any work environment. Quality education should be available to all students from as early as kindergarten and throughout their academic career. Because of the nation's poor educational system (particularly in the inner cities), ensuring quality education for all the nation's children poses some serious questions. Who is responsible for:

- providing the nation's children with information that will broaden their perspectives and knowledge about a range of career related opportunities?

- insisting that the education of the nation's children in inner city public schools is egalitarian and globally oriented and that the curriculum in these schools is universal and oriented toward success?

- communicating to our nation's children about the diverse cultural systems existing in society and in the various work environments?

- ensuring that there is equal funding for education in all locations, including inner city neighborhoods?

- offering multicultural education to all students so that they can effectively function in any type of work environment and among culturally diverse peoples?

- providing students with opportunities to practice goal setting and strategizing?

Though some blacks have the opportunity to go to good schools, the majority do not (*The Economist* 1991). Thus, another question arises: How do blacks acquire the requisite skills and qualifications needed for success in the world of work if, in fact, they have unequal access to a high quality of education? Certainly, this process should begin in the home, with the black family assuming the primary responsibility for the education of their children. Family values about education must be reinforced in children to strengthen their interest and commitment to learning and acquiring skills that will lead to growth and development opportunities. If blacks do not get all of the requisite skills and qualifications from the family or the school, one option is to provide them with access to special training programs geared toward providing blacks and those similarly situated with the skills and expertise needed for employment and career advancement. In addition to providing blacks and other minorities with requisite skills and expertise, these programs often prove to be of further help by providing these groups with firsthand exposure to corporate environments and relevant on-the-job experience. Appendix B provides a description of such a program. Based on the results of this study, we see that these interventions even when available are not sufficient, by themselves, to successfully address corporate barriers to higher levels of career advancement for black employees.

In recent years, there has been a change in emphasis away from government being the sole provider of all services and solutions to the nation's ills. The private sector is being challenged to take more responsibility for helping to address some of the nation's problems. This effort is evidenced by the trends toward corporate involvement in school-business partnerships, mentorship programs, and adopt-a-school programs. Corporations can have some level of input into school curricula, since it is from the schools that their employees originate. Through corporate interventions, students can have access to business publications and state-of-the-art equipment, and obtain relevant professional experience through corporate internships. Other interventions take the form of school based, business related projects in collaboration with corporations and community groups.

Furthermore, blacks must pursue positions and opportunities that provide the necessary experiences needed for developing skills and abilities (such as management, leadership, problem solving, and decision making) that are considered important to function at upper levels of management and for running America's corporations. Irrespective of their academic and professional backgrounds, blacks have been traditionally relegated to positions less directly related to the central functioning and profitability of a company (e.g., staff positions), and thus are less likely to be provided with experiences that develop the skills critical to leading large corporations. Wernick (1994), Baker (1995), Butler (1995), and Collins (1997) support this assertion. However, to what extent are blacks not pursuing these critical assignments because of the unwritten rules that are integral to corporate culture and the implications and repercussions associated with actions that go against the status quo?

A challenge, then, is posed: Blacks must aggressively pursue positions that play a substantial role in a company's operation. And corporations must, in turn, take an active and decisive part in providing equal opportunity to blacks and others similarly situated who seek such positions.

Inhibitors to Black Upward Mobility

A) Differences in Socioeconomic and Cultural Backgrounds

Different cultural backgrounds can bring different strengths to a team's effort. Thus, removing from the workplace the practice of stereotyping different cultural groups will help lead to greater equality of opportunity, a more equitable income distribution, greater access to development and career advancement opportunities, and increased access to areas and processes critical to upward mobility. The Glass Ceiling Initiative Report (1997) quoted some revealing findings from a study of the Standard and Poors 500 by Covenant Investment Management. This study revealed that those companies committed to the career advancement of minorities achieved an average annualized return on their investment of 18.3% over a five-year period, as compared with 7.9% for those companies whose "glass ceilings" were impermeable. Based on these and other benefits, corporations and individual employees must begin to value and respect the different cultural backgrounds which minority groups bring to the corporate setting. Another by-product of these changes is that blacks and other minorities over time will be able to achieve a higher standard of living and have greater access to educational opportunities and a wider variety of experiences—leading to further opportunities and growth for themselves and their offspring.

In the meantime, blacks must realize that they are, in fact, part of society and that in present day corporate America, it is necessary for them to adapt at some level to, and function appropriately in, various corporate settings. Blacks must not only meet performance standards set by their particular corporations, they must also acquire an in-depth understanding of the less obvious rules, values, mores, biases, assumptions, and modus operandi of their particular corporate environments. In present day America, for qualified blacks to be effective and achieve certain levels of career advancement, they will sometimes have to take on many of the trappings of the dominant culture or modify their personal cultural behavior to conform to the corporations' norms. This is the reality of present day corporate life which black and other minority groups must acknowledge, despite perceived unfairness or actual restrictions.

However, in no way does this author imply that blacks should completely isolate themselves from their cultural ties or abandon or deny their personal identity or mores. Blacks must continue to be proud and celebrate the richness of their culture. But they must also be willing to adapt to corporate culture to the extent that it enables them to be viewed as team players and as "fitting" into corporate life. Although this author recommends that blacks should attempt to adapt to corporate culture, successful integration of blacks and other minorities into corporate life will not occur fully unless senior management: a) trusts and is comfortable with the abilities and contributions of diverse groups, and b) creates environments that accept and appreciate diverse cultural groups and their contributions.

The challenge, then, is for blacks *and* corporations to make the adjustments needed that will result in an environment where diversity works harmoniously and empowers, rather than opposes corporate norms.

B)   Stereotypes About Blacks

Of the factors found to influence the upward mobility of blacks in the corporate arena, probably the most difficult factor to address is the stereotyping of blacks that exists in corporate culture. Removal of these stereotypes from corporate culture is difficult because it encompasses individuals' feelings, biases, values, and learned attitudes and behaviors. Consequently, because it is difficult to change these attitudes and behaviors, more questions are raised than answers proposed:

- How does one remove hundreds of years of reinforced stereotypes about blacks that are perpetuated in the larger society and, as a result, exist in the corporate arena?
- How does one make the corporate performance appraisal process fair for all employees, when the performance of blacks is generally evaluated by members of the majority population who learned their values, attitudes, and behaviors from a society that still implicitly condones racial stereotypes?
- How does one develop effective networking systems and mentoring relationships free of racial distinctions, when networking and mentoring normally occur on a voluntary and selective basis?
- How does one promote expectations of top notch performance for all employees, when a segment of the work force is viewed as being incapable of reaching the highest standards of efficiency and effectiveness?
- How does one shape a corporate culture that promotes and actually pursues the maximization of all human resources irrespective of race, gender, national origin, and other non-work related factors?

In examining the issue of removing the practice of stereotyping in the corporate arena, of the important interventions that can be implemented, only two will be discussed here:

a) special training for blacks and other minorities and diversity programs that facilitate corporations in maximizing the use of their human capital. These initiatives must be tied to the achievement of bottom line business results; and

b)   commitment and active participation by senior management in addressing issues related to stereotyping that negatively impact the performance and advancement of black employees and other groups who encounter similar stereotyping.

a) *Special Corporate Training and Diversity Programs*

Based on the results of this study and findings of other researchers, corporations need to recognize that special corporate training programs geared strictly toward blacks and other minorities, conducted in-house or outsourced, have significant limitations and are destined to be less than fully effective. These programs usually focus all their training efforts on ensuring that these groups have the requisite skills and qualifications and familiarizing them with the dynamics of the existing corporate culture. However, study findings suggest that there are limitations to what this kind of approach can accomplish. Quantitative comparisons between similarly qualified trained black managers (Group 1) and white managers (Group 3) revealed that the trained blacks experienced slower rates of upward mobility than their white peers. Furthermore, there was no significant difference in the rates of upward mobility between Groups 1 and 2 (trained and untrained blacks), despite Group 1s belief that their special training had enhanced their mobility. Clearly, the type of special training similar to many such programs used at corporations failed to do enough to eliminate the differences in mobility rates between similarly qualified white and black employees.

Where does the failure lie? These inhibitors cannot be fully dealt with in the context of most special corporate training programs. This type of training approach or intervention process places the responsibility for improving blacks' upward mobility squarely and solely on blacks' shoulders. The perception is that the burden for subsequent career success belongs exclusively to blacks. In fact, blacks have little or no control over:

- the practice of anti-black stereotyping in the workplace;
- racially biased hiring and appraisal practices;

- accessing informal network systems which, for the most part, are closed to blacks' participation;
- job typecasting, in which blacks are channeled into positions and levels with minimal impact on a company's central functioning or profitability;
- unavailable or unwilling mentors;
- other policies, processes, and systems that support or are perceived to support or reward discriminatory behavior.

While traditional corporate training programs for minorities have usually been helpful with those areas over which blacks and other minorities can exert some control—goal setting and strategizing, improving communication skills, and pursuing more in-depth or specialized academic experience—these areas by no means represent the totality of factors influencing their corporate advancement. Corporations must join blacks and other minorities in claiming responsibility for change and be held accountable. Loden (1996) raises an alert to corporate leaders. She contends that "biased behavior can and does impact the bottom line" (95).

Other initiatives that are being used to address the underrepresentation of blacks and other groups similarly underutilized include diversity training and related programs. These initiatives grew out of a proactive response to the changing U.S. work force and the limited ability of employment laws to assure inclusion, respect, and fair treatment (Loden 1996). To maximize the use of all human capital and thereby impact the bottom line positively, corporations must develop and provide, as a first step, diversity programs with teeth for all employees and, especially, executives and managers at all levels. Since it is crucial that all groups support their companies' diversity initiatives, it is important to get support from each group. Each group must perceive that diversity change agents recognize its individual and collective issues as important and, in turn, change agents must see to it that each group understands the benefits that will accrue to them as well as to the corporation as a result of supporting such an initiative.

The focus of diversity training and other diversity initiatives should be on assessing and altering stereotypes in the corporate environment that create barriers to the upward mobility of any qualified employee. Also, integral to these programs should be a comprehensive approach, targeting corporate systems and processes. Since corporate systems and processes shape and mold desired behaviors, corporate leaders and managers must ensure that diversity initiatives are linked to the corporate business strategy and include the implementation or strengthening of systems and processes that would eradicate stereotypical and discriminatory behavior within their respective corporations. These kinds of systems and processes should be established as a critical part of their diversity programs. These views are reinforced by Swanger (1994).

Unfortunately, these initiatives are beginning to be derailed and lose favor. This derailment seems to stem from the myopic way that many of these programs are currently being implemented (as human resource programs) with no discernable, visible link to the corporate business strategy or bottom line. The term "diversity" is so loosely used and is such a catchall phrase in corporate America that it loses its meaning in the light of corporate racism (America and Anderson 1996). As a result, corporate leaders find that it is difficult to fully embrace and give visible commitment especially in light of the perceived risks associated with these programs' successful implementation (Loden 1996). An important question needs to be raised and answered by corporate leaders and diversity change agents: How can a company truly reap the full benefits of its diversity initiatives when there is not true representation throughout all levels of the corporate hierarchy?

Loden (1996) contends that if corporations do not have a specific plan focused on hiring, training, and promotion of underrepresented groups, they undermine the power and effectiveness of these programs and fall short of achieving their desired goals. Carnevale and Stone (1994) contend that this plan must be developed within the context of particular and unique organizational realities and not be generic in nature.

A critical aspect of any cultural diversity training should be to provide corporate managers, white and black, with the tools for analyzing and understanding the unique personality and attributes of the person being managed, rather than the perceived stereotypes of the group to which the individual belongs. Thus, these programs also should avoid reinforcing corporate cultural norms of a discriminatory nature, since traditionally special training programs and some diversity awareness programs have tended to unwittingly affirm cultural stereotypes. To avoid this reinforcement, corporations must methodically analyze existing systems to understand fully the nature of the systems and processes presently in place and to detect: a) areas where stereotyping and other inhibitors are occurring, and b) areas where enhancers are operative for the betterment of all employees.

Corporations must also begin to train their mid- to upper level employees to manage and evaluate each employee's work related characteristics, rather than basing appraisals on non-work related attributes such as racial stereotypes. Corporate leaders and managers must treat employees as individuals who bring unique and particular dynamics, skills, expertise, and experiences to the workplace.

The business case for valuing diversity intensifies, especially in light of shifting U.S. demographics, the spending power of ethnic groups, global competition, and other changes taking place in the global marketplace that directly impact business success. Thus, maximizing the use of a company's human resources is not an altruistic or moral gesture but a good business decision. It is a process, not an event.

b) *Commitment and Active Participation of Senior Management*

Corporations need to recognize that qualified blacks are not going to experience increased rates of upward mobility if biases based on stereotypes and discriminatory behaviors continue to exist in their work environments. Since senior management, for the most part, dictates the nature of corporate culture and its policies, change will occur faster and more effectively when it flows from the top down. Boards of Directors, CEOs, and other senior management personnel must actively initiate and participate in removing institutional barriers based on stereotypes and other race related inhibitors within their particular corporate arenas.

However, initiatives or efforts of this nature (e.g., diversity programs) get derailed because of perceived risks and repercussions associated with them and past experiences with unsuccessful diversity programs (Carnevale and Stone 1994). Corporate executives are constantly assessing the risk-reward factor. In reality, they are still being judged by the criteria derived from the current culture and status quo that they want, or have been asked, to change. The risk-reward factor is assessed by these executives in the context of a range of issues, including their:

- social conditioning
- level of discomfort with change;
- fear of retaliation, rejection, or hostility by peers, friends, or employees who have benefitted and are still thriving as a result of the nature of the status quo;
- lack of knowledge, information, and direct experience with diversity;
- lack of belief or guarantee that the initiatives will have a visible and measurable impact on the corporate bottom line results and competitive advantage;
- fear of not getting support for the initiative from key entities and players and being used as a scapegoat in the process, if the initiative does not achieve expected outcomes;
- fear of white male backlash—displacement of senior white males presumably because of downsizing but possibly attributable to diversity.

To address many of these challenges, outside consultants have been used to assist in leading the change effort and to help buffer the risks and repercussions that leaders or change agents may have to bear.

.Once senior executives have overcome these hurdles, in attempting to make any type of organizational change of this nature, they must understand and recognize the systemic/holistic nature of real change and must keep in mind certain inherent barriers to the change process. Thus, in developing and implementing strategies, programs, and policies to produce significant change in addressing differential treatment of blacks and others similarly situated based on non-work related factors, corporations must ensure that:

a. an adequate and comprehensive diagnosis is made of the actual state of the systems and processes to be changed. Then, the programs must be customized to meet the company's specific needs, challenges, and strategic business goals;

b. programs or initiatives focus not only on changing behavior but also on changing the policies, processes and systems (e.g., performance appraisal, selection, succession planning, mentoring, networking, etc.) that shaped and molded the old, no longer desired behavior. These policies, processes and systems should be formally structured, objective, measurable, and inclusive;

c. policies implemented to effect organizational change are designed in such a way that they provide equal opportunity based on qualifications, experience, demonstrated performance, and other work related factors. This approach should empower all workers without creating inefficiencies in the system;

d. built into the systems designed to produce organizational change are strategies to address the reality that there will be resistance to changes in real power by those individuals who have a stake in maintaining the status quo. Leaders of change initiatives must hold themselves accountable as well as the managers who are responsible for developmental and employment decisions for employees. Associated rewards and penalties should be factored into these systems for adherence and non-adherence;

e. actual and active support for the change is demonstrated not only by the top level (corporate leaders and senior management), but also by all levels (managers and employees in general) if it is to be effective. Since top management should be the drivers of the process, their involvement and support must be visible and extensive. They must walk the talk. Additionally, support is also needed and must be obtained from entities external to the organization, especially from those whom the proposed changes will affect;

f. sufficient time is allocated for implementation of the changes to take place;

g. adequate resources (human, financial and material) exist to successfully aid in bringing about agreed upon changes;

h. the people, areas, and organizations involved in or directly affected by the proposed changes understand the benefits to them and the corporations' bottom line, as a result of their active support for such changes;

i. leaders and managers are truthful in sharing the facts regarding the advancement of blacks as well as whites. They must cease reinforcing the entitlement posture ingrained in corporate cultures—the notion that success for whites at upper levels is naturally a factor of performance while for minorities it obviously is based on preferential treatment;

j. mentoring and feedback systems should be in place so that the skills, concepts, and tools reinforced in the formal training are practically applied in their particular work environments and that business goals and objectives are being achieved.

Numerous researchers offer one or a combination of these recommendations for leaders to be aware of in implementing effective initiatives (Wernick 1994; Federal Glass Ceiling Commission (1995); Cox Jr. and Smolinski 1994; Carnevale and Stone 1994; Butler 1995; U.S. Department of Labor 1997).

If stereotyping and its negative consequences are to be removed from the workplace, it is important that qualified blacks and other minorities be represented at all levels of the corporate hierarchy. The existing belief that blacks lack the ability to manage and lead will never be eliminated if qualified blacks are not provided the opportunity to demonstrate their individual talents. Only when everyone becomes accustomed to seeing more blacks and other minorities perform successfully and consistently in various roles at all corporate levels, will there be a realization and an internalization that these groups can truly have a positive impact on a company's productivity, profitability, and competitive advantage. Thus, corporate leaders must begin to place blacks and other minorities in positions for which they qualify that influence the central functioning and profitability of their companies. Blacks' successful performance in these roles will begin to erode existing perceptions and stereotypes.

The achievement and visibility of General Colin Powell is a case in point of how stereotypes, such as the supposed inability of blacks to hold leadership positions, can be addressed. Many people never thought that a black person could effectively fill the role of head of the Joint Chiefs of Staff. When Colin Powell, a black man, performed successfully in this capacity, surely he diminished concerns of whites as to whether a black individual could effectively function in a top level position. Accomplishing this end called for senior personnel at the White House and the Defense Department to take the risk of going against the majority's preconceived notions about blacks and make such an assignment.

Because of the changing nature of the work force, a dynamic global marketplace, and the need for corporations to develop productive management strategies by the year 2000 and beyond, corporations cannot wait until everyone is ready to accept blacks and other minorities in upper levels of management and leadership. In the long run, it is advantageous for corporations to take the lead and create a diverse yet effective work force, thereby acknowledging and reflecting the increasing proportion of blacks and other minorities in the population. If corporate leaders do not soon learn how to capitalize upon the skills and talents of minority workers in a fair and effective way, they will experience greater difficulty in meeting the needs of their growing diverse customer base, accessing markets traditionally untapped, and achieving or exceeding profitability goals (Federal Glass Ceiling Commission 1995).

Therefore, the future success of a company requires that senior executives establish a climate which strongly affirms that management based on biased perceptions and stereotypes about blacks, other minorities, or groups similarly situated will not be the way their companies do business. Corporate leaders must communicate to all employees that while individuals are entitled to their personal beliefs, they must conduct themselves according to the company's newly established culture, norms and practices when in the workplace. Systems and processes should also be put in place to support the newly desired behavior; for example, that it is incumbent on all employees to abide by the new norms of judging and managing all individuals based on merit and in an unbiased manner.

Leaders and senior management must be visibly and actively involved in the process of removing stereotypes from the workplace. Commitment to equal access and opportunities for all employees of an increasingly culturally diverse work force can be demonstrated through such activities as inclusion of blacks in corporate promotional materials, (e.g. brochures, annual reports, advancement of blacks to key positions, and vigorous recruitment of blacks at a variety of undergraduate and graduate schools). Additionally, as the Federal Glass Ceiling Commission Report (1995) states, all corporate materials must reflect that diversity is a core value for the organization. These modes of demonstration also hold true for other groups similarly underrepresented.

Senior executives and management are challenged to take the lead and mentor blacks and other members of underrepresented groups. These types of relationships influence increased productivity on the part of the mentee—ultimately having a positive impact on the corporate bottom line. These actions reinforce in the minds of employees, customers, and other audiences that corporations as well as their leaders are more than just verbally committed to equal opportunity; they are in fact actively promoting it.

STUDY IMPLICATIONS

In addition to the findings of this study and the conclusions and recommendations that have emerged, it is worthwhile to address certain implications for future research, training organizations, blacks and other minorities, and corporations that acknowledge their people as their greatest asset, their most precious resource, and thus their competitive advantage.

Implications for Future Research

This study has attempted to advance the debate as to the reasons for the underrepresentation of blacks in upper levels of the corporate hierarchy. Study findings suggest that other factors exist—beyond education, professional experience, and performance standards that must be met by all employees—that can limit the advancement opportunities for qualified blacks in the corporate arena.

It is important to note that in no way is this author arguing that the factors identified are the only possible inhibitors to the upward mobility of qualified blacks in corporate America.. The 80% of unexplained variance in the upward mobility measures from the quantitative analysis suggest that there are a number of factors other than those related to education and professional experience influencing black corporate upward mobility. Furthermore, the factors discussed in the qualitative analysis (Chapter V) may represent only a portion of those factors that account for the remaining 80% of the unexplained variance in the upward mobility measures.

Future studies should attempt to develop more precise quantitative measures of all key factors influencing upward mobility, in order to explain a larger percentage of the variance when analyzing mobility rates statistically. Although more quantitative measures may not change the direction of the results, the reality is that corporations tend to rely heavily upon hard data to guide their decision making. Thus, corporate leaders may tend to criticize the findings from qualitative data analyses on black upward mobility and question the methodological approaches used to analyze such data, because the data are often based on opinions and perceptions rather than statistical fact. In other words, although the qualitative measures may provide more insight into the nature of the influencing factors, quantitative measures provide more objective outcome indicators and more rigorous and systematic measures of influencing factors. Future research should provide leaders and other change agents with more definitive and quantitative factors accounting for the differential in the mobility rates this study found between qualified blacks and white employees.

Some other challenges exist regarding quantitative measures. Pertinent data are not as available, accessible, comprehensive, or consistent across certain categories and across similar time period as one would think for an issue as critical as race relations in corporate America. The manner in which statistical data have been collected and compiled on minorities and women in business make it difficult to demonstrate clearly where progress is being achieved and not achieved in these groups' attempts to shatter the barriers that prevent their progress to upper levels of management. The author concurs strongly with the recommendations made by the Federal Glass Ceiling Commission (1995), that governmental agencies and other entities assigned to compile these statistics must refine existing data categories, improve specificity of data (i.e., information on similar categories differ between EEOC Reports and the Statistical Abstracts), delineate racial categories, and stop the double counting of minority women, so that a true picture can be produced as to the realities of the situation these groups experience in the work force.

Additionally, a follow-up study on the same groups of participants could be conducted to determine any subsequent changes in their mobility rates and to probe more deeply into the specific ways in which race related factors continue to influence their mobility. This follow-up could also probe more deeply into aspects of the participants' socioeconomic and cultural backgrounds.

The nature of this study's findings is in consort with a preponderance of studies, research, and writings of others on the mobility of blacks and other minorities in the corporate arena.. While a more detailed investigation can be conducted, this author believes that we now need to move forward to more decisive action in developing and implementing strategies that will actually facilitate equal opportunity for all and thus maximize this nation's human capital and competitive advantage.

Implications for Special Training Programs—Outsourced or In-House

It is important that training organizations address their alumni's continuing difficulties in achieving corporate upward mobility. Otherwise, serious consequences will likely occur. Black alumni of corporate special training programs have not been shown to achieve the upward mobility that their qualifications, preparation, and experience warrant. The likelihood of these alumni's continuing disaffection with the corporate arena, as well as the possible loss of corporate sponsorship of training programs, can hardly be regarded as positive developments for traditional training organizations to anticipate. While corporate partnerships with training organizations for minorities may continue to reap the benefits of good public relations, this alone will not be sufficient to sustain enthusiastic support for these training organizations. Some training organizations may choose to focus their efforts on helping corporations with recruitment only. But this will not sustain the need for full access that a diverse work force demands. Furthermore, these training organizations will not be able to justify their existence if they assume responsibility for being able, by themselves, to impact significantly minority upward mobility in American corporations.

Another, very dangerous scenario could arise. When a corporation participates in an external or internal training program designed to aid blacks and other minorities, but ignores the program's inability, in and of itself, to address actual upward mobility, corporate leaders and other employees will become convinced of the stereotype—that blacks and other minorities are essentially inferior and lack something essential for success at higher levels of the corporate hierarchy. What else can corporate leaders be expected to conclude when minorities tend to lag behind in the competition for promotion, after being given every reasonable chance to succeed through special training and still fail to compete effectively? By their mere existence, these training programs will be viewed as ineffectual and will seem to validate that corporations have done everything on behalf of blacks' and other minorities' advancement. Additionally, failure of these training efforts to produce desired results will only serve to further reinforce the existing stereotypes and preconceived notions about blacks and other minorities. Lack of success of these internal and external programs to effectively address, by themselves, minority advancement could also result in their long-term diminution and possible demise.

Clearly, a two-pronged challenge is posed here. First, external training organizations need to offer corporations comprehensive diversity assistance (e.g., programs and initiatives) for *all* employees and particularly all managers who impact employee career advancement and the achievement of the company's productivity levels and profitability goals. Second, it is clear that these types of training programs cannot operate in isolation. While the initial focus of these diversity initiatives should be on people (diversity awareness), in order to eradicate stereotyping, biased hiring, and biased performance appraisals, an added emphasis must be placed on the systems, processes, policies, and implementation levels—since these factors shape and mold desired behavior. Furthermore, corporate executives and senior management must walk the talk. They must be actively and visibly involved and held accountable for making these systemic changes.

Implications for Blacks and Other Minorities

If blacks' upward mobility continues to crawl toward the infamous "glass ceiling," deleterious consequences will exist for them and other minority managers—especially graduates of special corporate training programs. Minority employees will continue to enter and operate within the corporate environment with concerns about the potentially negative implications of their race. Yet, despite of this concern, they also have high hopes and expectations of succeeding in their careers. Even if they find that they can achieve some initial upward mobility based on their qualifications, professional experience, training, and performance, they quickly come to realize the fallacy of "the myth"—their credentials do not generate the same rewards as their white counterparts.

For graduates of special training programs, this discovery can be particularly perplexing. During training, blacks and other minorities are told that they can compete and succeed. Every warning and preparatory effort designed to anticipate and address the unique inhibitors facing minority employees carries with it the implicit notion that special training will enable them to overcome these inhibitors to corporate success. Why else would a training program make the effort to prepare interns to deal with these barriers? For these graduates, with their confidence bolstered, completion of the training program brings with it the sense of self-worth and optimism that is intended to cushion their entrance into and functioning in the work force. What, then, are graduates or beneficiaries of these programs to think and how are they supposed to react when they discover that all their additional preparation has not enabled them to achieve rates of upward mobility that parallel those of their similarly qualified white peers?

By focusing the approach to limited mobility exclusively on blacks and other minorities, corporations and special training organizations mistakenly or erroneously suggest that the burden for subsequent success is exclusively the responsibility of minorities. The challenge is for minorities as well as corporations to shoulder the responsibility and accountability for eliminating minority immobility.

On the other hand, will blacks and other minorities take the necessary steps within their control—obtaining additional training and education, improving their communication skills, and gaining knowledge about corporate culture—so that their qualifications and exposure cannot be questioned and their corporate advancement can be unquestionably merited? Will corporate leaders embrace the value and benefits of a diverse work force and its unique capabilities, and therefore honestly and visibly demonstrate a commitment to equal opportunities for advancement?

Another area that is seldom addressed but that blacks and other minorities must pay close attention to is the denial or amnesia that tends to set in once success seems imminent or realized. In pursuing career advancement to the mid- and upper levels of the corporate hierarchy, corporate culture demands that blacks and other minorities "fit in"—adopt the norms, values, and beliefs of that culture. Attempting to "fit in" should not be at the expense of losing self and negating one's culture and history—thereby severely influencing what make blacks and other minorities unique: their diversity. Thus, blacks must make sure that they do not take on all of the trappings and disposition of the dominant group. They must not internalize the stereotypes about blacks and other minorities, so that their decisions and actions are reflective of those held by the dominant group with whom they have tried so hard to assimilate out of the need to achieve career success.

It is incumbent that blacks do not allow their acquired state of amnesia to allow them to forget that their successes are a result of the sacrifices and prices paid by others who have gone before them. Blacks must be honest with themselves and acknowledge that they are still reaping the positive effects, no matter how limited, of affirmative action, equal employment laws, and the civil rights movement. Their obligation is to repair, strengthen or build new bridges upon which others like themselves can walk. This should not be viewed as a burden or imposed responsibility, but as the right and fair thing to do. We all must do our part in building bridges of success for present and future generations.

Implications for Corporations

In recent years, efforts to produce a culturally diverse work force have been met with varying reactions. Some see it as preferential, undeserved treatment, a way of handing out jobs to minorities who are not as qualified as their white peers. Others see it as a welcomed change which will help American businesses.

In the past, a few changes in the complexion of the American work force have been brought about by legal efforts, special training programs, moralistic and ethical considerations, social pressure, and altruistic considerations—undoing the wrongs of the past. More recently, the emphasis on creating a culturally diverse work force where all employees have equal access to opportunities for career advancement has been in response to demographic and technological changes and heightened competition on the domestic and international fronts. Seen in this light, it is to a corporation's advantage to make substantive adjustments that acknowledge the increasing proportion of blacks, women, and other minorities entering the work force and the increase in the proportion of these groups comprising the diverse customer base.

If corporations develop and use all available qualified workers, irrespective of their racial or ethnic backgrounds, the outcome in the long run will be a work force that can make American corporations more competitive in the global marketplace and better able to meet the needs of a more diverse customer base. If America wants to maintain its position as a premier economic power in the global market, it is an economic imperative that U.S. corporations begin to develop and maximize the use of their human resources by providing opportunities for all employees, now and into the 21st century. The Federal Glass Ceiling Commission Report (1995) reinforces this viewpoint and adds that if the level of utilization does not occur and the glass ceiling continues to exist for qualified minorities, the economic problems that will be experienced will take a substantial financial toll on American business.

Though many of the factors revealed in this study were based on black employees' perceptions, as long as these perceptions persist there is the potential to influence negatively the motivation, productivity, and efficiency of these workers which, in turn, can influence corporate effectiveness and productivity. This dilemma holds true for other groups similarly impacted.

As a result of the continued unfair treatment of blacks and other minorities, a company's image will be tarnished and thus its ability to attract a significant number of qualified employees will be adversely affected. If no attempt is made to address barriers to upward mobility, stereotypes about blacks and other minorities will continue to be reinforced in corporate culture and, as a result, the progress of talented blacks and other minorities will continue to be stymied.

At this point pertinent questions need to be raised. How do we offer equal opportunity in an environment where the playing field is still not level (statistical data and findings of this study and of other researchers support the existence of this imbalance)? How was the unlevel playing field created? Was it the result of preferential treatment extended to one group over another? Is that what could be or is presently called "preferential treatment" or "quotas"? Or is it known by a more palatable term such as "the status quo" when it is in reference to a certain group? Does this practice (maintaining the status quo) lead to feelings of entitlement by the preferred group—white males? The implication here is that any effort to level the playing field will be met with serious resistance, as evidenced by what is taking place in corporate America, federal, state, and local governments, and society at large.

In this competitive global arena, U. S. corporations can no longer afford to allow valuable segments of its actual or potential work force to remain isolated from the mainstream of corporate structure and functioning. The Federal Glass Ceiling Commission (1995) recommends that current action by government and business is not sufficient to effect real change. Instead, "bias and discrimination must be banished from the board rooms and executives of corporate America" (6). Will corporations squarely and fully confront the challenge of maximizing their use of all available human capital? Will corporate executives take the leadership role and demonstrate that diversifying their work force and ensuring fairness in employees' advancement can have a positive impact on employee productivity and their company's economic power? Essential to long-term corporate productivity is the corporation's ability to fully utilize all of its resources, including blacks, other minorities, and women.

NOTES

1. These included comparable academic qualifications, position level, professional experience, etc.

Epilogue

The challenge of changing times demands creative and fundamentally different approaches. Resistance to change will detract from corporate America's ability to be "king of the global economic hill." The 1992 U.S. Department of Labor Report, "Pipelines of Progress," indicated that the bad news is that "surveys in the corporate world do not point to an optimistic future unless commitments to positive change are sustained and enhanced" (4). Evidently, as this study supports, corporations must seek solutions beyond special training and diversity awareness training and also be willing to actively and consistently undertake certain challenges and make system changes in order to effectively combat the obstacles/inhibitors to blacks and other minority success that ultimately impact bottom line results negatively. Some of these initiatives must center around promotion-related problems at particular levels or segments of the corporate hierarchy, which can eventually have a negative effect on productivity, innovation, turnover, attrition, and absenteeism rates. The initiatives which must take place within the context of a corporation's vision, mission, and values and must be linked to its business strategy include:

Performance appraisal process: Corporate leaders must see to it that appraisal processes are fair and that managers are held accountable for their decisions and the successful implementation of these processes. The measures used to evaluate employees should be tied to tangible and objective, performance related criteria.

Feedback processes: If employees do not understand where their deficiencies lie, how can they improve their performance? Thus, management needs to be able to:

- assess skills and identify strengths and deficiencies;
- make specific recommendations for improvement;
- implement interactive feedback processes which should emphasize employee deficiencies and use past accomplishments as a motivator for future improvement.

Reward and Recognition system: Managers need to learn how to recognize and reward the positive performance of others irrespective of their (managers') perspectives on race and gender. Since the managers' evaluation is critical to this process, they must be held responsible and accountable for their actions. Thus, their compensation, advancement, bonuses, and recognition should also be tied to the achievement of the company's diversity objectives.

Succession Planning: Succession planning can also effectively combat the traditional corporate practice of racial steering. Systems need to be established to tap the talents of those employees who can impact revenue generation and profitability, regardless of race, gender, religion, and other non-work related factors. Some of the factors that need to be considered are:

- job position and function;
- nature of assignment;
- access to networks;
- access to mentors.

The "glass ceiling": Firstly, corporate leaders must admit that the "glass ceiling" exists. Secondly, they must make certain that any decisions made concerning employees' ability to attain and perform successfully at certain corporate levels do not occur within the context of stereotyping and are free from preconceived notions. Diversity awareness training is but one of many steps in the process of combating the "glass ceiling."

Change processes: Management must establish change processes that are ongoing and holistic, and that are not isolated or transient events. They must be grounded in root causes and not just address symptoms of the problem. Leaders must understand and recognize the systemic nature of change.

Managing the change: Active, visible, and committed support of senior management is crucial in removing institutional barriers. Beyond this, there must be a committee established to manage the change process. This committee should consist of members with the skills, sensitivity, and understanding of the issues. They must also have decision making power, be held accountable for results, reflect a cross-section of the company, and have top management support.

Mentoring programs: Mentoring programs must be available to all employees since they can assist in career guidance and preparation of employees for senior positions. Because of the difficulties and implications associated with mentor-mentee relationships between different races, careful selection of pairs is essential. Thus, mentors chosen to coach blacks and other minorities must have a strong commitment to their advancement and an understanding of the perceived risks and rewards.

External assistance: Because of the possible risks and repercussions associated with these initiatives, and since the current corporate culture is still the evaluative force of employee performance, there needs to be a mechanism to reduce the risks. Here, assistance from external consultants can act as a buffer.

Addressing obstacles to change: Throughout any initiative to produce organizational change, there will be obstacles imposed by those who perceive this change as a threat to their power. Senior management, working in concert with their company's change agents and committee(s), must identify and acknowledge the existence and impact of these obstacles. Furthermore, they must adopt solutions that effectively address the obstacles in ways that are aligned with their particular desired corporate culture without diminishing the beneficial impact of enhancing upward mobility for all employees.

LOOKING TOWARD THE 21ST CENTURY

Special training organizations and internal special corporate training, blacks and other minorities, and corporations should be working in tandem to achieve mutually beneficial ends. In fact, if America's most precious resource is its people (Federal Glass Ceiling Commission 1995), then these groups all have a great deal at stake. All these partners must also realize that dealing exclusively with people related issues (the hiring and placing of qualified minorities in management positions), without these individuals realizing career advancement comparable to that of their similarly qualified white peers, could produce long-term deleterious effects for all concerned. More needs to be done by corporations in addressing the systemic elements that shape present discriminatory behavior in the workplace.

Unfortunately, as we move into the 21st century, the myths and stereotypes about blacks follow us. In the coming years, corporate America invariably will realize and be forced to take more decisive action in utilizing fully all segments of the work force, including minorities. Nathanial Thompkins, an executive at the time of the study (1992) with Baxter Healthcare, explains the situation best:

> The realities of the work force in the next decade are as multicultural as the reality of previous decades was monocultural. Corporations that fail to build a workplace that is attractive to the most talented segment of this emerging diverse work force will lose in talent, creativity, quality, productivity, and customer satisfaction. Business is what makes America run, but talent is what makes business run ... Our diverse and talented American society can't afford to let corporations off the hook when it comes to attracting, developing, and retaining their most precious resource, their people.

Some form of compromise, in which all parties move toward greater understanding and cooperation, is the economic challenge that, when tackled successfully, will provide greater productivity and subsequently greater prosperity for American business. To a certain extent, minorities must continue to play an "adaptability game" that will no doubt be revised in coming years. Yet, business must adopt a new strategy as well—that of accepting, respecting, and rewarding the contributions of those who may differ from traditional mid- to upper management. If this strategy is adopted, business will begin to remove the practice of stereotyping and the "glass ceiling" that apparently block the progress of so many talented and capable blacks and other minorities. The Federal Glass Ceiling Commission (1995) contends that "the permanent destruction of the glass ceiling will be a profound legacy we must leave for future generations" (6).

A new era will soon dawn and with its arrival will come the prospect of inevitable change. The possibility of corporations and people of color achieving mutually beneficial goals still exists. U.S. businesses can demonstrate to the world that they will face the future with a perspective bred not from anxiety and the shortsightedness of the past, but rather one that is determined to achieve greater productivity from a diverse labor pool whose full potential is being realized.

Questionnaires and Interview Questions

QUESTIONNAIRE - BLACK CORPORATE EXECUTIVES

1. Indicate your Academic/Professional qualifications.
    (Circle the ones that apply for each item and complete the table.)

Qualifications (circle one for each item)	G.P.A.	Major	Year Gained	School	Public/ Private
a) B.A./B.S./B.Ed.	_____	_____	_____	_____	_____
b) M.A./M.S./Ed.M.	_____	_____	_____	_____	_____
c) M.P.A./M.B.A./ M.F.A.	_____	_____	_____	_____	_____
d) Ph.D./Ed.D./ D.B.A./D.P.A.	_____	_____	_____	_____	_____
e) Other: Specify					
1._____	_____	_____	_____	_____	_____

2. Please list below in chronological order the jobs you have held.
    Note: Under Column 1 (position held) use titles such as:
        Technical, Professional, Supervisor, Manager, Senior Staff,
        Assistant Vice President, President, C.E.O., etc.

    Note: Also under Column 1 (position held) write"L" if the move from your
           previous position was a lateral one, write "V" if it was vertical.

Name of Company	** 1. Position Held	mth./yr. began mth./yr. left	Salary	Reason for Leaving
a)_____	_____	___|___	_____	_____
b)_____	_____	___|___	_____	_____
c)_____	_____	___|___	_____	_____
d)_____	_____	___|___	_____	_____
e)_____	_____	___|___	_____	_____
f)_____	_____	___|___	_____	_____
g)_____	_____	___|___	_____	_____
h)_____	_____	___|___	_____	_____
i)_____	_____	___|___	_____	_____
j)_____	_____	___|___	_____	_____

3. How valuable are the following training experiences with regard to facilitating the upward mobility and success of blacks within the corporate environment?
(Circle the most appropriate category for each item)

Note: Put a check in the space provided if you have ever attended any of these workshops.

TRAINING EXPERIENCES	Extremely Valuable	Very Valuable	Valuable	Not Valuable	Not Valuable At All	Check
a) Study Skills............	5	4	3	2	1	( )
b) Goal Setting/Life Planning..............	5	4	3	2	1	( )
) Corporate Etiquette.....	5	4	3	2	1	( )
) Money Management........	5	4	3	2	1	( )
) Assertiveness Training..	5	4	3	2	1	( )
) Career Assessment and Clarification.........	5	4	3	2	1	( )
) Time Management.........	5	4	3	2	1	( )
Orientation to the Business World/Self Development...........	5	4	3	2	1	( )
Interpersonal Relations.	5	4	3	2	1	( )
Selecting a Mentor......	5	4	3	2	1	( )
Management Skills.......	5	4	3	2	1	( )
Planning/Organizing.....	5	4	3	2	1	( )
Management by Objectives	5	4	3	2	1	( )
Communication Skills 1) Oral..............	5	4	3	2	1	( )
2) Writing............	5	4	3	2	1	( )
3) Listening..........	5	4	3	2	1	( )
Survival of Minority Professionals in Corporate America.....	5	4	3	2	1	( )
Problem Solving/Decision Making................	5	4	3	2	1	( )
Functioning in Corporate America..............	5	4	3	2	1	( )

3. (Cont'd): Circle the most appropriate category for each item.

Note: Put a check in the space provided if you have ever attended any
of these workshops.

TRAINING EXPERIENCES	Extremely Valuable	Very Valuable	Valuable	Not Valuable	Not Valuable At All	Check
r) Office Politics.......	5	4	3	2	1	( )
s) Leadership Skills.....	5	4	3	2	1	( )
t) Supervisory/Admin- istrative Skills....	5	4	3	2	1	( )
u) Technical Skills......	5	4	3	2	1	( )
v) Business Skills.......	5	4	3	2	1	( )
w) Stress Management.....	5	4	3	2	1	( )
x) Corporate Realities and Professionalism..	5	4	3	2	1	( )
y) Business Operations....	5	4	3	2	1	( )
z) Negotiation Skills.....	5	4	3	2	1	(
aa) Women in Business/ Balancing Career and Family..............	5	4	3	2	1	(
bb) Personal Financial Planning............	5	4	3	2	1	(
cc) Interviewing Skills....	5	4	3	2	1	(
dd) Resume Writing........	5	4	3	2	1	(
ee) Values Clarification...	5	4	3	2	1	(
ff) Economics.............	5	4	3	2	1	(
gg) Analysis of Financial Statements...........	5	4	3	2	1	(
hh) Evaluating the Job Offer...............	5	4	3	2	1	(
ii) Other(s): Specify 1)_____..	5	4	3	2	1	(
2)_____..	5	4	3	2	1	(
3)_____..	5	4	3	2	1	(

4. Using the scale immediately below, indicate the extent to which the following:

    Que. A) have been obstacles to achieving your career advancement within your work environment?

    Que. B) have been obstacles to your minority peers within your company?

    SCALE: Great   Large   Some   Little   Not at
             Extent   Extent   Extent   Extent   all
             (5)   (4)   (3)   (2)   (1)

	Que. A Your Experience	Que. B The Experience of your minority peers
1) race and ethnicity.....................	[＿＿]	[＿＿]
2) colorism (shades of color).............	[＿＿]	[＿＿]
3) gender (sex)...........................	[＿＿]	[＿＿]
4) age....................................	[＿＿]	[＿＿]
5) political views/attitudes..............	[＿＿]	[＿＿]
6) education:		
a) prestige of the university attended.	[＿＿]	[＿＿]
b) college performance.................	[＿＿]	[＿＿]
c) perception of ability...............	[＿＿]	[＿＿]
7) previous work experience...............	[＿＿]	[＿＿]
8) quality of job performance.............	[＿＿]	[＿＿]
9) supervisors...........................	[＿＿]	[＿＿]
10) lack of upward mobility opportunities..	[＿＿]	[＿＿]
11) lack of formal corporate networks......	[＿＿]	[＿＿]
12) political savvy/office politics........	[＿＿]	[＿＿]
13) lack of informal social networks.......	[＿＿]	[＿＿]

4. (Cont'd): Using the scale immediately below, indicate the extent to which
    the following:

    Q.1) have been obstacles to achieving your career advancement
         within your work environment?

    Q.2) have been obstacles to your minority peers within your
         company?

SCALE:	Great Extent (5)	Large Extent (4)	Some Extent (3)	Little Extent (2)	Not at all (1)

	Que. A Your Experience	Que. B The Experience of your minority peers
14) cronyism (not being part of the dominant group).....................	[_____]	[_____]
15) external social networks.............	[_____]	[_____]
16) difficulty in finding the following people with values similar to my own:		
a) peers...............................	[_____]	[_____]
b) supervisors........................	[_____]	[_____]
c) mentors............................	[_____]	[_____]
d) role models........................	[_____]	[_____]
17) other(s): specify:		
a)_____...	[_____]	[_____]
b)_____...	[_____]	[_____]

INTERVIEW - BLACK CORPORATE EXECUTIVES

CRITICAL QUESTIONS

5. a) Sex: M_____F_____   b) Date of Birth:_____/_____/____

6. a) Name of Current Employer/Own Business:_____

   b) Type of Industry:
        1) Banking.............[____]   6) Construction.............[____]
        2) Financial Services...[____]   7) Insurance................[____]
        3) Manufacturing........[____]   8) Retailing................[____]
        4) Transportation.......[____]   9) Communications...........[____]
        5) Utilities............[____]   10) Other: (Specify):
                                                 _____[____]

7. What differentiates those blacks who succeed from those who don't?

    a)_____

    b)_____

    c)_____

    d)_____

    e)_____

8A. What is your definition of success versus the corporate definition of
    success?

    1._____

    2._____

    3._____

    4._____

    5._____

8B. On a scale of 1 to 5 (5=most important, 1=least important) how would you
    rate the following based on your definition of success?
    [____] power
    [____] money
    [____] status
    [____] other (specify)_____

9A. How successful are you in terms of your career aspiration?

    5 - Extremely Successful   2 - Not so successful
    4 - Very Successful   3 - Not successful at all
    3 - Successful

9B. What occurrences have happened to you in your career that have led you to
     this conclusion?

     1._____

     2._____

     3._____

     4._____

     5._____

9C. How did you succeed/why did you not succeed and what plans do you have
     for the future that would enhance/continue to enhance your success within
     the corporate environment?

     1._____

     2._____

     3._____

     4._____

     5._____

10A. What are the characteristics of successful people in your corporate
     environment ?

     1._____

     2._____

     3._____

     4._____

     5._____

     6._____

     7._____

10B. Do you believe that there are characteristics of successful people in
     your corporate environment that no amount of training can develop?

              Yes [____]   No [____]

10C. If yes, what are they?

1._____

2._____

3._____

4._____

5._____

11A. When you graduated from college/graduate school did you have a career objective (ultimate position) that you wanted to achieve?

Yes [_____]   No [_____]

11B. If yes, what was this career objective (ultimate position)?

_____

_____

_____

11C. How did you decide on this particular career objective and who was instrumental in helping you?

1._____

2._____

3._____

4._____

5._____

11D. Why did you pursue this particular career objective and would you pursue the same one if you had to do it all over?

1._____

2._____

3._____

4._____

5._____

11E. If not, what career objective would you have chosen and how
     would you have pursued it?

1. _____

2. _____

3. _____

4. _____

5. _____

12A. Is your present position the one which you ultimately wanted when you
     first completed college/graduate school?
                    Yes [_____]   No [_____]

12B. If no, how many years do you think it will take you to achieve it?

1. _____

2. _____

3. _____

4. _____

5. _____

3A Have you experienced difficulty in moving up within your current company?

              Yes [____]   No [____]

3B. If yes, what type of difficulties have you experienced and what do you
    plan to do next?

1. _____

2. _____

3. _____

4. _____

5. _____

IMPORTANT QUESTIONS

13A. How important were the following in facilitating your upward mobility
     within your corporate environment?
     (Circle the most appropriate category for each item.)

	Extremely Important	Very Important	Important	Not Important	Not Important At All
a) mentors:					
1) formal corporate..	5	4	3	2	1
2) informal social...	5	4	3	2	1
b) networks:					
1) formal corporate..	5	4	3	2	1
2) informal social...	5	4	3	2	1

13B. To what degree have your most important mentors:

	Great Degree	Large Degree	Some Degree	Little Degree	Not at All
1) motivated you in meeting your desired goals................	5	4	3	2	1
2) been instrumental in your growth and development........	5	4	3	2	1
3) allowed you to develop your own individual identity.......	5	4	3	2	1
4) maintained their objectivity towards:					
a) your own ideas...............	5	4	3	2	1
b) your career goals...........	5	4	3	2	1
5) other(s): specify					
a)_____ ...	5	4	3	2	1
b)_____ ...	5	4	3	2	1

14. Indicate the following for your first job after graduating from college/
    graduate school and for your current job?

    a) How often do you participate in the policy making decisions of your
       company?

       (Policy decisions are those that establish-- rather than implement--
       the fundamental direction, major goals or orientation of the
       organization.)
                                                    FIRST JOB   CURRENT JOB

       1) frequently   [_____] [_____]

       2) occasionally   [_____] [_____]

       3) never   [_____] [_____]

    b) Staff or line positon   [_____] [_____]

15A. Is there a particular level in your company beyond which you believe
     minorities/blacks have little or no chance of achieving? EXPLAIN

     _____

15B. Explain why?

     1._____

     2._____

     3._____

     4._____

5C. How far are you from this level (number of promotions necessary)?
                      [_____] promotions

5D. Do you want to reach the very pinnacle of your organization?
    (e.g., President/C.E.O.)
              Yes [_____]   No [_____]

5E. Do you believe you can reach the very of your organization?
    (e.g., President/C.E.O.)
              Yes [_____]   No [_____]

5F. If yes, what factors and/or attributes would be necessary?

     1._____

     2._____

     3._____

     4._____

     5._____

15G. If no, what factors and/or attributes would inhibit you?

    1. _____

    2. _____

    3. _____

    4. _____

    5. _____

16. Based on your corporate experiences, what characteristics other than those required of a typical corporate employee do Blacks need?

    a) to gain employment in your corporate business:

      1) _____

      2) _____

      3) _____

      4) _____

      5) _____

    b) to survive within your corporate environment:

      1) _____

      2) _____

      3) _____

      4) _____

      5) _____

    c) to achieve upward mobility in your corporation:

      1) _____

      2) _____

      3) _____

      4) _____

      5) _____

17. Of the blacks you have known who felt that there was no opportunity for advancement within corporate America, what actions have they taken?

a) _____

b) _____

c) _____

d) _____

e) _____

18A. Is upward mobility for blacks easier today than it was 20 years ago within the corporate environment?

1. _____

2. _____

3. _____

4. _____

5. _____

18B. Have conditions changes from the 1960's to better facilitate the upward mobility of blacks with corporate environments?

Yes [____]   No [____]

18C. If yes, in which ways?

1. _____

2. _____

3. _____

4. _____

5. _____

8D. If no, why?

1. _____

2. _____

3. _____

4. _____

18E. What opportunities do you believe blacks have now that you did not have in
trying to suceed within corporate America?

1. _____

2. _____

3. _____

4. _____

5. _____

19A. Define Affirmation as it is now and also how you perceive it to be.

1. Affirmation Action Now: _____

_____

_____

2. Affirmation Action as it should be: _____

_____

_____

19B. Does affirmative action have a place in the corporate arena?

Yes [_____]   No [_____]

19C. If no, why?

1. _____

2. _____

3. _____

4. _____

5. _____

19D. If yes, in which ways?

1. _____

2. _____

3. _____

4. _____

19E. If yes, what impact, if any, did affirmative action have on your ability to move up within the corporate environment?

1._____

2._____

3._____

4._____

5._____

VERY IMPORTANT QUESTIONS

20. What key things, if any, must occur at the following strategic points to better facilitate the upward mobility of blacks within corporate environments?

a) at entry level:

1._____

2._____

3._____

4._____

5._____

b) at mid management level:

1._____

2._____

3._____

4._____

5._____

c) at upper management level

1._____

2._____

3._____

4._____

5._____

21A. Is the presence of a black network within your company important for upward mobility? What about outside your company.?

                    Yes [____]   No [____]

21B. If yes, in which ways?

    1._____

    2._____

    3._____

    4._____

    5._____

21C. If no, why?

    1._____

    2._____

    3._____

    4._____

22A. Is the presence of a black network outside your company important for upward mobility?

                    Yes [____]   No [____]

22B. If yes, in which ways?

    1._____

    2._____

    3._____

    4._____

    5._____

22C. If no, why?

    1._____

    2._____

    3._____

    4._____

23. At you present company location, indicate approximately how many people
    are at, below, and above your level?
    Also, for each level indicate the number of these that are black?

	TOTAL	BLACK	
a) at your level	[_____]	[_____]	[do not know____]
b) below your level	[_____]	[_____]	[do not know____]
c) above your level	[_____]	[_____]	[do not know____]
d) Company Total	[_____]	[_____]	[do not know----]

24. What aspects of corporate culture inhibit the upward mobility of blacks?

    1._____

    2._____

    3._____

    4._____

    5._____

QUESTIONNAIRE - WHITE MANAGERS

SECTION 1 - BIOGRAPHICAL DATA AND GENERAL INFORMATION

Instructions: Please fill in all of the blank spaces below.

1. a) ID : _____

    c) Date of Birth:_____/_____/_____
    d) Sex (circle): M_____ F_____

    e) Race: Black..........................[_____]
    Hispanic.............................[_____]
    Native..................................[_____]
    White...................................[_____]

2. a) 1) Name of Current Employer _____
            or
        2) Name of Own Business _____

    b) Type of Industry:
        1) Banking.......................................[_____]
        2) Financial Services.......................[_____]
        3) Manufacturing.............................[_____]
        4) Transportation.............................[_____]
        5) Utilities.......................................[_____]

    6) Construction............................[_____]
        7) Insurance...............................[_____]
        8) Retailing................................[_____]
        9) Communications....................[_____]
        10) Other: (Specify):
            _____ [_____]

3. Indicate your Academic/Professional qualifications.
    (Circle the ones that apply for each item and complete the table.)

Qualifications (circle one for each item)	G.P.A. (4 pt. scale)	Major	Month/ Year Gained	School	Public/ Private
a) B.A./B.S./B.Ed.	_____	_____	___/___	_____	_____
b) M.A./M.S./Ed.M.	_____	_____	___/___	_____	_____
c) M.P.A./M.B.A./ M.F.A.	_____	_____	___/___	_____	_____
d) Ph.D./Ed.D./ D.B.A./D.P.A.	_____	_____	___/___	_____	_____
e) Other: Specify					
_____	_____	_____	___/___	_____	_____

5. Indicate the following for your first job after graduating from college/graduate school and for your current job?

	First Job	Current Job
(a) Number of people you supervise(d) directly	_____	_____

(b) How often do you participate in the policy making decision of your company?

(Policy decisions are those that establish-- rather than implement--the fundamental direction, major goals or orientation of the organization.)

1) frequently	_____	_____
2) occasionally	_____	_____
3) never	_____	_____
c) Staff or Line Position	_____	_____

QUESTIONNAIRE - BLACK MANAGERS

INSTRUCTIONS: Please fill in all of the blank spaces below.

1. a) Date of Birth:____/____/____   b) Sex: M_____ F_____

2. a) Name of Current Employer/Own Business:_____

   b) Type of Industry:
   1) Banking..............[____]   6) Construction............[____]
   2) Financial Services...[____]   7) Insurance................[____]
   3) Manufacturing........[____]   8) Retailing................[____]
   4) Transportation.......[____]   9) Communications...........[____]
   5) Utilities............[____]   10) Other: (Specify):
                                         _____[____]

3. Indicate your Academic/Professional qualifications.
    (Circle the ones that apply for each item and complete the table.)

Qualifications (circle one for each item)	G.P.A.	Major	Year Gained	School	Public/ Private
a) B.A./B.S./B.Ed.	_____	_____	_____	_____	_____
b) M.A./M.S./Ed.M.	_____	_____	_____	_____	_____
c) M.P.A./M.B.A./ M.F.A.	_____	_____	_____	_____	_____
d) Ph.D./Ed.D./ D.B.A./D.P.A.	_____	_____	_____	_____	_____
e) Other: Specify 1._____	_____	_____	_____	_____	_____

4. Please list below in chronological order the jobs you have held.
    Note: Under Column 1 (position held) use titles such as:
            Technical, Professional, Supervisor, Manager, Senior Staff,
            Assistant Vice President, President, C.E.O., etc.

    Note: Also under Column 1 (position held) write"L" if the move from your
           previous position was a lateral one, write "V" if it was vertical.

Name of Company	1. Position Held **	Duration (in Months)	Salary	Reason for Leaving
a)				
b)				
c)				
d)				
e)				

5A. What differentiates those blacks who succeed from those who don't?

    1._____

    2._____

    3._____

B. What is your definition of success versus your corporation's definition
    of success?

    _____

    _____

    _____

.   On a scale of 1 to 5 (5=most important, 1=least important) rank the
    following based on your definition of success?
    [____] power
    [____] money
    [____] status
    [____] other (specify)_____

.   How successful are you in terms of your career aspiration?

    5) Extremely successful [____]   2) Not so successful   [____]
    4) Very successful   [____]   1) Not successful at all [____]
    3) Successful   [____]

5E. What occurrences have happened to you in your career that have led you to
this conclusion? (Specify a maximum of three occurrences.)

    1._____

    2._____

    3._____

5F. How did you succeed/why did you not succeed and what plans do you have
for the future that would enhance/continue to enhance your success within
the corporate environment?

    1._____

    2._____

    3._____

5G. Do you believe that there are characteristics of successful people in
your corporate environment that no amount of training can develop?
          Yes [____]   No [____]

5H. If yes, state the characteristics and explain? (Specify a maximum of four

    1._____

    2._____

    3._____

    4._____

6A. When you graduated from college/graduate school did you have a career
objective (ultimate position) that you wanted to achieve?
          Yes [____]   No [____]

6B. If yes, what was this career objective (ultimate position)?

_____

6C. Is your present position the one which you ultimately wanted when you
first completed college/graduate school?
          Yes [____]   No [____]

6D. If no, how many years do you think it will take you to achieve it?
          [_____ years]

6E. Are you experiencing difficulty in moving up within your current company

          Yes [____]   No [____]

F. If yes, what type of difficulties have you experienced?

1._____

2._____

3._____

G. If yes, what is your next move?
1) remain at present company.......................................[_____]
2) leave present company..[_____]
3) speak to supervisor..[_____]
4) other (specify):_____...[_____]

Indicate the following for your first job after graduating from college/
graduate school and for your current job?   FIRST JOB   CURRENT JOB

a) Number of people you supervise(d) directly   [_____]   [_____]

b) How often do you participate in the policy
   making decisions of your company?

   (Policy decisions are those that establish--
   rather than implement--the fundamental
   direction, major goals or orientation of
   the organization.)

   1) frequently................................ [_____]   [_____]

   2) occasionally.............................. [_____]   [_____]

   3) never..................................... [_____]   [_____]

c) Staff or Line Position.................... [_____]   [_____]

Is there a particular level in your company beyond which you believe
minorities/blacks have little or no chance of achieving? EXPLAIN
             Yes [_____]   No [_____]

EXPLAIN_____

_____

_____

How far are you from this level (number of promotions necessary)?
             [_____] promotions

Do you want to reach the very pinnacle of your organization?
(e.g., President/C.E.O.)
             Yes [_____]   No [_____]

Do you believe you can reach the very of your organization?
(e.g., President/C.E.O.)
             Yes [_____]   No [_____]

8E. If yes, what factors and/or attributes would be necessary?

1._____

2._____

3._____

8F. If no, what factors and/or attributes would inhibit you?

1._____

2._____

3._____

9.   Based on your corporate experiences, what characteristics other than those required of a typical corporate employee do Blacks need?

a) to gain employment in your corporate business:

1._____

2._____

3._____

b) to survive within your corporate environment:

1._____

2._____

3._____

c) to achieve upward mobility in your corporation:

1._____

2._____

3._____

10. Of the blacks you have known who felt that there was no opportunity for advancement within corporate America, what actions have they taken?

a)_____

b)_____

c)_____

11. How valuable are the following training experiences with regard to
    facilitating the upward mobility and success of blacks within your
    corporate environment?
    (Circle the most appropriate category for each item)

    Note: Put a check in the space provided if you have ever attended any
          of these workshops.

TRAINING EXPERIENCES	Extremely Valuable	Very Valuable	Valuable	Not Valuable	Not Valuable At All	Check
a) Study Skills............	5	4	3	2	1	( )
b) Goal Setting/Life Planning..............	5	4	3	2	1	( )
c) Corporate Etiquette.....	5	4	3	2	1	( )
d) Money Management........	5	4	3	2	1	( )
e) Assertiveness Training..	5	4	3	2	1	( )
f) Career Assessment and Clarification.........	5	4	3	2	1	( )
g) Time Management.........	5	4	3	2	1	( )
h) Orientation to the Business World/Self Development...........	5	4	3	2	1	( )
i) Interpersonal Relations.	5	4	3	2	1	( )
j) Selecting a Mentor......	5	4	3	2	1	( )
k) Management Skills.......	5	4	3	2	1	( )
l) Planning/Organizing.....	5	4	3	2	1	( )
m) Management by Objectives	5	4	3	2	1	( )
n) Communication Skills 1) Oral...............	5	4	3	2	1	( )
2) Writing............	5	4	3	2	1	( )
3) Listening..........	5	4	3	2	1	( )
o) Survival of Minority Professionals in Corporate America.....	5	4	3	2	1	( )
p) Problem Solving/Decision Making.................	5	4	3	2	1	( )
q) Functioning in Corporate America..............	5	4	3	2	1	( )

11. (Cont'd): Circle the most appropriate category for each item.

Note: Put a check in the space provided if you have ever attended any of these workshops.

TRAINING EXPERIENCES	Extremely Valuable	Very Valuable	Valuable	Not Valuable	Not Valuable At All	Check
r) Office Politics.......	5	4	3	2	1	( )
s) Leadership Skills.....	5	4	3	2	1	( )
t) Supervisory/Admin- istrative Skills....	5	4	3	2	1	( )
u) Technical Skills......	5	4	3	2	1	( )
v) Business Skills.......	5	4	3	2	1	( )
w) Stress Management.....	5	4	3	2	1	( )
x) Corporate Realities and Professionalism..	5	4	3	2	1	( )
y) Business Operations....	5	4	3	2	1	( )
z) Negotiation Skills.....	5	4	3	2	1	( )
aa) Women in Business/ Balancing Career and Family..............	5	4	3	2	1	( )
bb) Personal Financial Planning............	5	4	3	2	1	( )
cc) Interviewing Skills....	5	4	3	2	1	( )
dd) Resume Writing.........	5	4	3	2	1	( )
ee) Values Clarification...	5	4	3	2	1	( )
ff) Economics..............	5	4	3	2	1	( )
gg) Analysis of Financial Statements...........	5	4	3	2	1	( )
hh) Evaluating the Job Offer...............	5	4	3	2	1	( )
ii) Other(s): Specify 1)_____..	5	4	3	2	1	( )
2)_____..	5	4	3	2	1	( )
3)_____..	5	4	3	2	1	( )

12.   Using the scale immediately below, indicate the extent to which the
      following:

      Que. A) have been obstacles to achieving your career advancement
               within your work environment?

      Que. B) have been obstacles to your minority peers within your
               company?

      SCALE: Great   Large   Some   Little   Not at
               Extent   Extent   Extent   Extent   all
               (5)   (4)   (3)   (2)   (1)

		Que. A Your Experience	Que. B The Experience Of Your Minority Peers
1)	race and ethnicity.....................	[_____]	[_____]
2)	colorism (shades of color).............	[_____]	[_____]
3)	gender (sex)...........................	[_____]	[_____]
4)	age....................................	[_____]	[_____]
5)	political views/attitudes.............	[_____]	[_____]
6)	education:		
	a) prestige of the university attended.	[_____]	[_____]
	b) college performance.................	[_____]	[_____]
	c) perception of ability..............	[_____]	[_____]
7)	previous work experience..............	[_____]	[_____]
8)	quality of job performance............	[_____]	[_____]
9)	supervisors...........................	[_____]	[_____]
10)	lack of upward mobility opportunities..	[_____]	[_____]
11)	lack of formal corporate networks......	[_____]	[_____]
12)	political savvy/office politics........	[_____]	[_____]
13)	lack of informal social networks.......	[_____]	[_____]
14)	cronyism (not being part of the dominant group).....................	[_____]	[_____]
15)	external social networks..............	[_____]	[_____]

---

12. (Cont'd): Using the scale immediately below, answer parts 16 & 17 of
     question 10:

SCALE:	Great Extent (5)	Large Extent (4)	Some Extent (3)	Little Extent (2)	Not at all (1)

	Que. A Your Experience	Que. B The Experience Of Your Minority Peers

16) difficulty in finding the following
    people with values similar to my
    own:

    a) peers............................ [_____]   [_____]

    b) supervisors...................... [_____]   [_____]

    c) mentors.......................... [_____]   [_____]

    d) role models...................... [_____]   [_____]

17) other: specify:

    a)_____..... [_____]   [_____]

13. What key things, if any, must occur at the following strategic points
     to better facilitate the upward mobility of blacks within corporate
     environments?

     a) at entry level:

     1._____

     2._____

     3._____

     b) at mid management level:

     1._____

     2._____

     3._____

     c) at upper management level

     1._____

     2._____

     3._____

14. At your present company location, indicate approximately how many people are at, below, and above your level?
Also, for each level indicate the number of these that are black?

	TOTAL	BLACK	
a) at your level	[_____]	[_____]	[do not know____]
b) below your level	[_____]	[_____]	[do not know____]
c) above your level	[_____]	[_____]	[do not know____]
d) Company Total	[_____]	[_____]	[do not know----]

15. How important were the following in facilitating your upward mobility within your corporate environment?
(Circle the most appropriate category for each item.)

	Extremely Important	Very Important	Important	Not Important	Not Important At All
a) mentors:					
1) formal corporate..	5	4	3	2	1
2) informal social...	5	4	3	2	1
b) networks:					
1) formal corporate..	5	4	3	2	1
2) informal social...	5	4	3	2	1

5A. To what degree have your most important mentors:

	Great Degree	Large Degree	Some Degree	Little Degree	Not at All
motivated you in meeting your desired goals................	5	4	3	2	1
been instrumental in your growth and development........	5	4	3	2	1
allowed you to develop your own individual identity.......	5	4	3	2	1
maintained their objectivity towards:					
a) your own ideas...............	5	4	3	2	1
b) your career goals............	5	4	3	2	1

16B. To what extent have the following contributed to your current career
success.
(Circle the most appropriate category for each item)

	Great Extent	Large Extent	Some Extent	Little Extent	Not at All
1) family........................	5	4	3	2	1
2) yourself......................	5	4	3	2	1
3) other(s): specify:					
a) _____...	5	4	3	2	1
b) _____...	5	4	3	2	1

17. My minority status in the corporate environment has:
(Circle the most appropriate category for each item.)

	Strongly Agree	Agree	Not Sure	Disagree	Strongly Disagree
a) hindered my chances of acquiring my desired position................	5	4	3	2	1
b) produced stress on the job.....................	5	4	3	2	1
c) exposed me to productive challenges that enhanced my career growth........	5	4	3	2	1
d) inhibited me from finding mentors.................	5	4	3	2	1
e) provided opportunities for the growth and development of my administrative /supervisory skills......	5	4	3	2	1
f) other(s): specify					
1) _____...	5	4	3	2	1
2) _____...	5	4	3	2	1

QUESTIONNAIRE - SUPERVISORS OF TRAINED BLACK MANAGERS

INSTRUCTIONS: PLEASE ANSWER ALL QUESTIONS COMPLETELY.

1. a) Does your company currently sponsor   Interns?
        Yes [   ]   No [   ]   Do not know [_____]

    b) If yes, in which of the following areas is your company involved?
       (Please check all that apply.)

       1) provides financial contributions...............................[   ]

       2) provides board members...[   ]

       3) provides contributions in kind.................................[   ]

       4) provides use of its facilities.................................[   ]

       5) provides workshops facilitators................................[   ]

       6) other(s): specify

          a) _____.....[   ]

          b) _____.....[   ]

          c) _____.....[   ]

2. Approximately how long have you been the supervisor of the
    alumnus in question? ....[_____yrs. _____mos.]

3. How many   alumni are currently working for your company?
                             [_____alumni]   Do not know [_____]

4. How valuable are the following training experiences with regard to enhancing employee performance?
(Circle the most appropriate category for each item.)

TRAINING EXPERIENCES	Extremely Valuable	Very Valuable	Valuable	Not Valuable	Not Valuable At All
a) Study Skills................	5	4	3	2	1
b) Goal Setting/Life Planning..................	5	4	3	2	1
c) Corporate Etiquette.........	5	4	3	2	1
d) Money Management............	5	4	3	2	1
e) Assertiveness Training......	5	4	3	2	1
f) Career Assessment and Clarification.............	5	4	3	2	1
g) Time Management.............	5	4	3	2	1
h) Orientation to the Business World/Self Development...............	5	4	3	2	1
i) Interpersonal Relations.....	5	4	3	2	1
j) Selecting a Mentor..........	5	4	3	2	1
k) Management Skills...........	5	4	3	2	1
l) Planning/Organizing.........	5	4	3	2	1
m) Management by Objectives....	5	4	3	2	1
n) Communication Skills					
1) Oral...................	5	4	3	2	1
2) Writing...............	5	4	3	2	1
3) Listening..............	5	4	3	2	1
o) Survival of Minority Professionals in Corporate America.........	5	4	3	2	1
o) Problem Solving/Decision Making...................	5	4	3	2	1
q) Functioning in Corporate America..................	5	4	3	2	1

4. (Cont'd): Circle the most appropriate category for each item.

TRAINING EXPERIENCES	Extremely Valuable	Very Valuable	Valuable	Not Valuable	Not Valuable At All
r) Office Politics.............	5	4	3	2	1
s) Leadership Skills..........	5	4	3	2	1
t) Supervisory/Administrative Skills....................	5	4	3	2	1
u) Technical Skills...........	5	4	3	2	1
v) Business Skills............	5	4	3	2	1
w) Stress Management..........	5	4	3	2	1
x) Corporate Realities and Professionalism..........	5	4	3	2	1
y) Business Operations........	5	4	3	2	1
z) Negotiation Skills.........	5	4	3	2	1
aa) Women in Business/ Balancing Career and Family..................	5	4	3	2	1
bb) Personal Financial Planning.................	5	4	3	2	1
cc) Interviewing Skills........	5	4	3	2	1
dd) Resume Writing.............	5	4	3	2	1
ee) Values Clarification.......	5	4	3	2	1
ff) Economics..................	5	4	3	2	1
gg) Analysis of Financial Statements...............	5	4	3	2	1
hh) Evaluating the Job Offer...	5	4	3	2	1
ii) Other(s): Specify:					
1) _____	5	4	3	2	1
2) _____	5	4	3	2	1
3) _____	5	4	3	2	1

5. In your opinion, what characteristics other than those required of a typical corporate employee do minorities need?
    (Specify a maximum of four for each item.)

    a) to gain employment in your corporate business:

    1) _____

    2) _____

    3) _____

    4) _____

    b) to survive within your corporate environment:

    1) _____

    2) _____

    3) _____

    4) _____

    c) to achieve upward mobility in your corporation:

    1) _____

    2) _____

    3) _____

    4) _____

6. How important are the following in facilitating the upward mobility of minorities in your corporate environment?
    (Circle the most appropriate category for each item.)

	Extremely Important	Very Important	Important	Not Important	Not Important At All
a) mentors:					
1) formal corporate.........	5	4	3	2	1
2) informal social..........	5	4	3	2	1
b) networks:					
1) formal corporate.........	5	4	3	2	1
2) informal social..........	5	4	3	2	1

7. In general, how would you rate the level of performance of the
    alumnus in your own corporate environment?

    a) Excellent............. [   ]   d) Below average........... [   ]
    b) Above average......... [   ]   e) Poor.................... [   ]
    c) Average............... [   ]   f) No basis for
                                            evaluation......... [   ]

8. In your corporate setting, how would you compare the performance of the
        alumnus in relation to his/her minority counterparts who have not
    received this training?

    a) Much better than...... [   ]   d) Worse than.............. [   ]
    b) Better than........... [   ]   e) Much worse than......... [   ]
    c) Equal to.............. [   ]   f) No basis for
                                            evaluation......... [   ]

9. What special skills, if any, did the   alumnus bring to the job
    as compared to the following:
    (Specify a maximum of four skills for each item.)

    a) your staff in general:

        1) _____

        2) _____

        3) _____

        4) _____

    b) his/her minority counterparts:

        1) _____

        2) _____

        3) _____

        4) _____

QUESTIONNAIRE - TRAINED BLACK MANAGERS

This questionnaire should take you approximately
60 minutes to complete.

SECTION 1 -- 20 minutes

SECTION 2 -- 20 minutes

SECTION 3 -- 10 minutes

SECTION 4 -- 10 minutes

SECTION 1 - BIOGRAPHICAL DATA AND GENERAL INFORMATION

Instructions: Please fill in all of the blank spaces below.

```
.  a) I.D.:_____          e) Race: Black............[___]
   b) Date:_____/_____/_____               Hispanic.........[___]
   c) Date of Birth:____/____/____             Native
   d) Sex (circle):  M____ F____                American.......[___]
```

```
.  a) 1) Name of Current Employer_____
           or
      2) Name of Own Business_____

   b) Address of Current Employer
      or Own Business_____

   c) Name of Immediate Supervisor_____

   d) Name of Department_____

   e) Type of Industry:
      1) Banking................[___]      6) Construction..............[___]
      2) Financial Services.....[___]      7) Insurance.................[___]
      3) Manufacturing..........[___]      8) Retailing.................[___]
      4) Transportation.........[___]      9) Communications............[___]
      5) Utilities..............[___]     10) Other: (Specify):
                                                     _____ [___]
```

Indicate your Academic/Professional qualifications.
(Circle the ones that apply for each item and complete the table.)

Qualifications (circle one for each item)	G.P.A. (4 pt. scale)	Major	Month/ Year Gained	School	Public/ Private
B.A./B.S./B.Ed.	_____	_____	__/__	_____	_____
M.A./M.S./Ed.M.	_____	_____	__/__	_____	_____
M.P.A./M.B.A./ M.F.A.	_____	_____	__/__	_____	_____
Ph.D./Ed.D./ D.B.A./D.P.A.	_____	_____	__/__	_____	_____
Other: Specify					
1) _____	_____	_____	__/__	_____	_____

4A. Indicate the job title for each of your parents on the job category line
     which best describes his and her employment status while you were an
          intern. (Check the one that applies for each parent.)

Job Category	Father (Job Title)	Mother (Job Title)
1) managerial..............	_____	_____
2) administrative..........	_____	_____
3) technical...............	_____	_____
4) professional............	_____	_____
5) clerical/secretarial....	_____	_____
6) trade...................	_____	_____
7) sales...................	_____	_____
8) service.................	_____	_____
9) unemployed (usual occupation).............	_____	_____
10) retired................	_____	_____
11) not applicable (deceased)............	_____	_____
12) other(s): specify		
a)_____...	_____	_____
b)_____...	_____	_____

4B. During the time you were an   intern, what was your family's
     approximate total annual income?   [$_____]

4C. Who was the head of your household while you were an   intern?
     1) Father [____]   2) Mother [____]   3) Other (specify)
                                                 _____ [____]

4D. While you were an   intern, what was the highest year of schooling
     each of your parents had completed?

	Grade School	High School	College	Graduate School
1) Father	[____]	[____]	[____]	[____]
2) Mother	[____]	[____]	[____]	[____]
3) Other (specify)				
_____	[____]	[____]	[____]	[____]

4E. Indicate the number of siblings (brothers and sisters, excluding yourself)
     in your family, who were living with you, while you were an   intern.
          [_____]

5A. In which month/year did you: month/year

   1) complete high school.................................... [____/____]

   2) begin your   internship........................... [____/____]

   3) graduate from   .... [____/____]

   4) begin looking for a full-time professional position
      after graduating from   .... [____/____]

   5) get your first job....................................... [____/____]

5B. How many years and months of work experience relevant to your career goals
    do you actually have?..................[____ yrs. ____ mos.]

6A. Upon graduating from   was your first job with your sponsoring
    company?   Yes [____]   No [____]

6B. If not, why?
    (Check the ones that apply and rank them from the most important to the
    least important -- 1 being the most important.)

                                                        CHECK   RANK ORDER

   1) was not made an offer...................... [_____]   [_____]

   2) insufficient advancement opportunities...... [_____]   [_____]

   3) position offered not consistent with
      career interest........................... [_____]   [_____]

   4) better opportunity elsewhere............... [_____]   [_____]

   5) attended graduate school................... [_____]   [_____]

   6) inadequate salary.......................... [_____]   [_____]

   7) other (specify):

      a) _____.... [_____]   [_____]

C. Did this first job afford you the opportunity to use your acquired skills
   and expertise?   Yes [____]   No [____]

D. If not, why? (Give 3 main reasons)

   1) _____

   2) _____

   3) _____

7A. Please list below in chronological order the jobs you have held since
    graduating from

    **Note: Under Column 1 (position held) use titles such as:
           Technical, Professional, Supervisor, Manager, Senior Staff,
           Assistant Vice President, President, C.E.O., etc.

    Note: Also under Column 1 (position held), write "L" if the move from your
          previous position was a lateral one, write "V" if it was vertical.

Name of Company	1. Position ** Held	Duration (in months)	Salary	Reason for Leaving
1) _____	_____	____	____	_____
2) _____	_____	____	____	_____
3) _____	_____	____	____	_____
4) _____	_____	____	____	_____
5) _____	_____	____	____	_____

7B. When you graduated from   did you have a career objective (ultimate
    position) that you wanted to achieve?   Yes [____]   No [____]

7C. If yes, what was this career objective (ultimate position)?

    _____

7D. Is your present position the one which you ultimately wanted when you first
    completed
        Yes [____] -- go to 7I   No [____] -- go to 7E through 7I

7E. If not, approximately how many promotions within your current company would
    be needed to arrive at your ultimate position?   [____ promotions]

7F. Are you experiencing difficulty in moving up within your current company?
        Yes [____]   No [____]

7G. If yes, what is your next move?
    1) remain at present company... [____]
    2) leave present company... [____]
    3) speak to supervisor... [____]
    4) other (specify): _____ ... [____]

7H. If you have not achieved your ultimate position, how many more years do you
    think it will take you to achieve it?   [____ years]

7I. When you graduated from   what was your expectation on the number of
    years you thought it would take you to achieve your ultimate position?
        [____ years]

8. Indicate the following for your first job after graduating from   and for your current job.

	FIRST JOB	CURRENT JOB
a) Number of people you supervise(d) directly..	[_____]	[_____]

b) How often did/do you participate in the
   policy making decisions of your company?
   (Choose one only.)

   (Policy decisions are those that establish--
   rather than implement--the fundamental
   direction, major goals or orientation of
   the organization.)

	FIRST JOB	CURRENT JOB
1) frequently.................................	[_____]	[_____]
2) occasionally..............................	[_____]	[_____]
3) never.....................................	[_____]	[_____]
c) Approximate yearly salary...................	[$_____]	[$_____]
d) Staff or Line position......................	[_____]	[_____]

9. At your present company location, indicate approximately how many people are
   at, below and above your level?
   Also, for each level indicate the number of these that are black.

	TOTAL	BLACK	
a) at your level	[_____]	[_____]	[do not know____]
b) below your level	[_____]	[_____]	[do not know____]
c) above your level	[_____]	[_____]	[do not know____]
d) Company Total	[_____]	[_____]	[do not know____]

10A. Is there a particular level in your company beyond which you believe minorities have little or no chance of achieving?
         Yes [____] -- go to 10B through 10F
         No [____] -- go to 10C through 10F

     EXPLAIN:
     _____
     _____
     _____

10B. How far are you from this level (number of promotions necessary)?
                [_____ promotions]

10C. Do you <u>want</u> to reach the very pinnacle of your organization?
     (e.g., President/C.E.O.)   Yes [____]   No [____]

10D. Do you <u>believe</u> you can reach the very pinnacle of your organization?
     (e.g., President/C.E.O.)   Yes [____]   No [____]

10E. If yes, what factors and/or attributes would be necessary?

     1) _____
     2) _____
     3) _____

10F. If no, what factors and/or attributes would inhibit you?

     1) _____
     2) _____
     3) _____

11A. <u>Rank</u> the following criteria in order of importance, based on your definition of success. (1 = least important) (5 - most important)

     [_____] power
     [_____] money
     [_____] status
     [_____] other (specify) _____

11B. How successful are you in terms of your career aspirations?

     5) Extremely successful   [_____]   2) Not so successful   [_____]
     4) Very successful   [_____]   1) Not successful at all   [_____]
     3) Successful   [_____]

11C. What occurrences have happened to you in your career that have led you to this conclusion? (Specify a maximum of three occurrences.)

     1) _____
     2) _____
     3) _____

SECTION 2. ALUMNI PERCEPTION OF THE ADEQUACY OF   SERVICES.

Instructions: Below is a list of statements concerning
               Please read all statements very carefully and respond on the
               basis of your belief.

12. Circle the most appropriate category for each item.

	Strongly Agree	Agree	Not Sure	Disagree	Strongly Disagree
a) The internship experience instilled in me the pursuit of excellence.......	5	4	3	2	1
b) adequately prepared me to work effectively in the corporate environment..........	5	4	3	2	1
c) The value of the experience is over-estimated....	5	4	3	2	1
d) provided me with the following that proved to be valuable to my success in the world of work:					
1) formal mentoring service:					
i) corporate supervisor......	5	4	3	2	1
ii) corporate advisor/mentor/ business sponsor..........	5	4	3	2	1
iii) business coordinator......	5	4	3	2	1
2) informal mentoring service...	5	4	3	2	1
3) formal corporate networks..;.	5	4	3	2	1
4) informal social networks.....	5	4	3	2	1
e) The basic goals and objectives of were instrumental in fulfilling:					
1) my corporate/professional needs........................	5	4	3	2	1
2) my career goals..............	5	4	3	2	1

12. (cont'd): Circle the most appropriate category for each item.

	Strongly Agree	Agree	Not Sure	Disagree	Strongly Disagree
f) The training I received at sensitized me:					
1) to corporate culture.........	5	4	3	2	1
2) to be more effective in intercultural communication within my corporate setting..	5	4	3	2	1
3) to work more effectively with people within my professional orientation.....	5	4	3	2	1
g) _____ adequately prepared me to assume managerial/staff professional positions in:					
1) corporate America............	5	4	3	2	1
2) the community................	5	4	3	2	1
h) _____ adequately prepared me to assume leadership positions in:					
1) corporate America............	5	4	3	2	1
2) the community................	5	4	3	2	1

13A. My minority status in the corporate environment has:
(Circle the most appropriate category for each item.)

	Strongly Agree	Agree	Not Sure	Disagree	Strongly Disagree
) hindered my chances of acquiring my desired position.............	5	4	3	2	1
) produced stress on the job......	5	4	3	2	1
) exposed me to productive challenges that enhanced my career growth..................	5	4	3	2	1
) inhibited me from finding mentors........................	5	4	3	2	1
provided opportunities for the growth and development of my administrative/supervisory skills.........................	5	4	3	2	1
other(s): specify					
a)_____...	5	4	3	2	1
b)_____...	5	4	3	2	1

B. Did   prepare you to deal with the issues mentioned in the previous question (#13A)? (Check one or more that apply)

1a) If yes (which ones): (1)____ (2)____ (3)____ (4)____ (5)____ (6)____
-- (go to 13C)

1b) If no (which ones): (1)____ (2)____ (3)____ (4)____ (5)____ (6)____
-- (go to 13D)

. If yes, in what ways? (Specify a maximum of five ways)

1) _____

2) _____

3) _____

4) _____

5) _____

13D. If no, in what ways could _____ have prepared you?
(Specify a maximum of three ways)

1) _____

2) _____

3) _____

14. On a scale of 1 to 5 rate_ each of the following services provided by
_____ terms of its importance in helping you as an individual to be
successful in corporate America.
(1 = least important .... 5 = most important)

a) [   ].... summer work experiences
b) [   ].... four-year career development plan
c) [   ].... counseling
d) [   ].... training workshops
e) [   ].... regional training institute (overnighter)
f) [   ].... national training institute
g) [   ].... access to networks
h) [   ].... academic requirements to be maintained
i) [   ].... input from corporate sponsors/mentors
j) [   ].... tutors
k) [   ].... other(s): specify _____

_____

15A. Using the scale immediately below, indicate the extent to which the
      following:

      Q.1) have been obstacles to achieving your career advancement
           within your work environment?

      Q.2) have been obstacles to other non-   minorities
           within your company?

      SCALE: Great   Large   Some   Little   Not at
               Extent   Extent   Extent   Extent   All
               (5)   (4)   (3)   (2)   (1)

	Q.1 Your Experience	Q.2 The Experience of Other Non-Minorities
1) race and ethnicity...........................	[_____]	[_____]
2) colorism (shades of color)...................	[_____]	[_____]
3) gender (sex).................................	[_____]	[_____]
4) age...	[_____]	[_____]
5) political views/attitudes...................	[_____]	[_____]
6) education:		
a) prestige of the university attended......	[_____]	[_____]
b) college performance......................	[_____]	[_____]
c) perception of own ability................	[_____]	[_____]
7) previous work experience/internships........	[_____]	[_____]
8) quality of job performance..................	[_____]	[_____]
9) supervisors.................................	[_____]	[_____]
0) lack of upward mobility opportunities.......	[_____]	[_____]
1) lack of formal corporate networks...........	[_____]	[_____]
2) political savvy/office politics.............	[_____]	[_____]
3) lack of informal social networks............	[_____]	[_____]

11

15A. (Cont'd): Using the scale immediately below, indicate the extent to which
      the following:

SCALE:	Great Extent (5)	Large Extent (4)	Some Extent (3)	Little Extent (2)	Not at All (1)

	Q.1 Your Experience	Q.2 The Experience of Other Non-Minorities
14) cronyism (not being part of the dominant group).............................	[_____]	[_____]
15) external social networks....................	[_____]	[_____]
16) difficulty in finding the following people with values similar to my own:		
a) peers......................................	[_____]	[_____]
b) supervisors...............................	[_____]	[_____]
c) mentors...................................	[_____]	[_____]
d) role models...............................	[_____]	[_____]
17) other(s): specify:		
a)_____ ...	[_____]	[_____]
b)_____ ...	[_____]	[_____]

15B. With respect to your responses in the previous question (#15A), indicate
the extent to which _____ has provided <u>you</u> with the necessary skills
and expertise to adequately deal with the following.
(Circle the most appropriate category for each item)

	Great Extent	Large Extent	Some Extent	Little Extent	Not at All
1) race and ethnicity...................	5	4	3	2	1
2) colorism (shades of color)..........	5	4	3	2	1
3) gender (sex)........................	5	4	3	2	1
4) age.................................	5	4	3	2	1
5) political views/attitudes...........	5	4	3	2	1
6) education:					
a) prestige of the university attended.........................	5	4	3	2	1
b) college performance..............	5	4	3	2	1
c) perception of own ability........	5	4	3	2	1
7) corporate attitude towards previous work experience/ interships......................	5	4	3	2	1
8) job performance.....................	5	4	3	2	1
9) supervisors........................	5	4	3	2	1
10) lack of upward mobility opportunities.......................	5	4	3	2	1
11) lack of formal corporate networks...	5	4	3	2	1
12) political savvy/office politics.....	5	4	3	2	1
13) lack of informal social networks....	5	4	3	2	1
14) cronyism (not being part of the dominant group).................	5	4	3	2	1

15B. (Cont'd): Circle the most appropriate category for each item.
     the following:

	Great Extent	Large Extent	Some Extent	Little Extent	Not at All
15) external social networks............	5	4	3	2	1
16) difficulty in finding the following people with values similar to my own:					
a) peers...........................	5	4	3	2	1
b) supervisors.....................	5	4	3	2	1
c) mentors.........................	5	4	3	2	1
d) role models.....................	5	4	3	2	1
17) other(s): specify:					
a)_____...					
b)_____...	5	4	3	2	1

16. List what you consider to be the major weaknesses of   programs (e.g.,
    counseling, training workshops, summer work experience, alumni component).
    (Specify a maximum of five)

    a) _____

    _____

    b) _____

    _____

    c) _____

    _____

    d) _____

    _____

    e) _____

    _____

17A. Do you believe that the skills, expertise and experience you acquired as
      an   intern enhanced your chances:

    1) of being employed? ...... Yes [   ]   No [   ]   Do not know [   ]

    2) for upward mobility? .... Yes [   ]   No [   ]   Do not know [   ]

17B. Do you believe that just being an   alumnus in name only enhanced
      your chances:

    1) of being employed? ...... Yes [   ]   No [   ]   Do not know [   ]

    2) for upward mobility? .... Yes [   ]   No [   ]   Do not know [   ]

18A. Did your participation in   allow you to enter the corporate
      environment at a higher level than non-   minorities?
                Yes [   ]   No [   ]

18B. If yes, how?

    1) _____

    2) _____

    3) _____

8C. If yes, how long do you believe it would take a non-   minority to
      rise to your entry level? ....[____ yrs. ____ mos.]

9A. Do you believe that there are characteristics of successful people in
      your corporate environment that   services (summer work experience,
      training workshops, etc.) cannot develop?
                Yes [   ]   No [   ]

9B. If yes, state the characteristics and explain. (Specify a maximum of four)

    1) _____

    2) _____

    3) _____

    4) _____

20A. Do you think that   was the major vehicle for you into the corporate
      environment?   Yes [   ]   No [   ]

20B. If yes, in what ways? (Specify a maximum of three)

      1) _____

      2) _____

      3) _____

20C. If no, what was that major vehicle?

      _____

      _____

20D. What percentage of your minority peers at college (not   alumni)
      got onto their corporate career path through:

      1) programs such as   .... [_____%]

      2) attending Ivy League schools.............................. [_____%]

      3) attending schools where major corporations recruit........ [_____%]

      4) other(s): specify

         a) _____..... [_____%]

         b) _____..... [_____%]

S T O P

IT MIGHT BE A GOOD IDEA TO TAKE A SHORT BREAK AT THIS POINT

SECTION 3: ALUMNI EVALUATION OF THE COMPONENTS OF

21.   Listed below are various workshops conducted by   Assess the value of the
      content of each of these workshops in facilitating your upward mobility and success
      in the corporate environment. Respond only to those components that were a part of
      your training while at   If you did not experience a particular component
      circle (0).
      (Circle the most appropriate category for each item.

	Extremely Valuable	Very Valuable	Valuable	Not Valuable	Not Valuable At All	Did Not Parti- cipate
a) Study Skills Series.........	5	4	3	2	1	0
b) Goal Setting/Life Planning...................	5	4	3	2	1	0
c) Corporate Etiquette.........	5	4	3	2	1	0
d) Money Management............	5	4	3	2	1	0
e) Assertiveness Training......	5	4	3	2	1	0
f) Career Assessment and Clarification.............	5	4	3	2	1	0
g) Time Management.............	5	4	3	2	1	0
h) Orientation to the Business World/Self Development....	5	4	3	2	1	0
i) Interpersonal Relations.....	5	4	3	2	1	0
j) Selecting a Mentor..........	5	4	3	2	1	0
k) Management Skills...........	5	4	3	2	1	0
l) Planning/Organizing.........	5	4	3	2	1	0
m) Management by Objectives....	5	4	3	2	1	0
n) Communication Skills 1) Oral....................	5	4	3	2	1	0
2) Writing................	5	4	3	2	1	0
3) Listening.............	5	4	3	2	1	0
o) Survival of Minority Professionals in Corporate America.........	5	4	3	2	1	0
p) Problem Solving/Decision Making...................	5	4	3	2	1	0

21. (Cont'd): Circle the most appropriate for each item)

	Extremely Valuable	Very Valuable	Valuable	Not Valuable	Not Valuable At All	Did Not Parti- cipate
q) Functioning in Corporate America..................	5	4	3	2	1	0
r) Office Politics............	5	4	3	2	1	0
s) Leadership Skills..........	5	4	3	2	1	0
t) Supervisory/Administrative Skills...................	5	4	3	2	1	0
u) Technical Skills...........	5	4	3	2	1	0
v) Business Skills............	5	4	3	2	1	0
w) Stress Management..........	5	4	3	2	1	0
x) Corporate Realities and Professionalism..........	5	4	3	2	1	0
y) Business Operations........	5	4	3	2	1	0
z) Negotiation Skills.........	5	4	3	2	1	0
aa) Women in Business/Balancing Career and Family........	5	4	3	2	1	0
bb) Personal Financial Planning.................	5	4	3	2	1	0
cc) Interviewing Skills........	5	4	3	2	1	0
dd) Resume Writing.............	5	4	3	2	1	0
ee) Values Clarification.......	5	4	3	2	1	0
ff) Economics..................	5	4	3	2	1	0
gg) Analysis of Financial Statements...............	5	4	3	2	1	0
hh) Evaluating the Job Offer...	5	4	3	2	1	0
ii) Other(s): Specify:						
1) _____	5	4	3	2	1	0
2) _____	5	4	3	2	1	0
3) _____	5	4	3	2	1	0

22. Below is a list of statements concerning   program components.
     Read all statements very carefully and respond on the basis of your belief.
     (Circle the most appropriate category for each item)

	Strongly Agree	Agree	Not Sure	Disagree	Strongly Disagree
a) training/curriculum workshops are based on clearly defined educational and professional principles........	5	4	3	2	1
b) The summer work experience of services proved useful in my subsequent place of work.........................	5	4	3	2	1
c) My four-year career development plan allowed me:					
1) to focus on my career goals and objectives..............	5	4	3	2	1
2) to plan, more clearly, my own career development......	5	4	3	2	1
3) to choose appropriate courses at college..........	5	4	3	2	1
d) The career development and counseling services provided by					
1) assisted me in making appropriate academic course choices related to my interests and career aspirations................	5	4	3	2	1
2) provided me with appropriate information and preparation with regard to my career and my professional growth and development................	5	4	3	2	1

22. (Cont'd): Circle the most appropriate category for each item.

	Strongly Agree	Agree	Not Sure	Disagree	Strongly Disagree
e) The summer work experience allowed me to stay informed about the following within corporate environment(s):					
1) new technology..............	5	4	3	2	1
2) opportunities for minorities..................	5	4	3	2	1
3) management techniques.......	5	4	3	2	1
4) other(s): specify:					
a)_____...	5	4	3	2	1
b)_____....	5	4	3	2	1
c)_____...	5	4	3	2	1

23A. My participation in _____ enhanced my ability within my work environment:
(Circle the most appropriate category for each item)

	Strongly Agree	Agree	Not Sure	Disagree	Strongly Disagree
1) to be resistant to stress......	5	4	3	2	1
2) to be receptive to new idea....	5	4	3	2	1
3) to grasp information quickly...	5	4	3	2	1
4) to be objective................	5	4	3	2	1
5) to be persistent...............	5	4	3	2	1

23B. With respect to your responses, on which you either agreed or strongly
agreed, in the previous question (#23A-items 1, 2, 3, 4, 5), which of
the following aspects of _____ services contributed in this respect?
(Check one or more than apply for each item)

	resistance to stress	new ideas	info.	objec- tive	persis- tence
1) summer work experience.....	[(1)___	(2)___	(3)___	(4)___	(5)___]
2) counseling................	[(1)___	(2)___	(3)___	(4)___	(5)___]
3) regional training institute (overnighter)...	[(1)___	(2)___	(3)___	(4)___	(5)___]
4) national training institute................	[(1)___	(2)___	(3)___	(4)___	(5)___]
5) workshops.................	[(1)___	(2)___	(3)___	(4)___	(5)___]
6) other(s): specify:					
a) _____..	[(1)___	(2)___	(3)___	(4)___	(5)___]
b) _____..	[(1)___	(2)___	(3)___	(4)___	(5)___]

23C. With respect to question (#23A): In the areas which you disagree or
strongly disagree that _____ enhanced, what could _____ have done
to further facilitate your ability in these areas?
(Specify a maximum of four suggestions)

1)_____

2)_____

3)_____

4)_____

24A. Did you come in contact with any of the following while at
(If <u>no</u>, check Column 1; if <u>yes</u>, complete Columns 2 to 4)

	Col. 1	Col. 2	Col 3	Col 4
	NO	Was this person a <u>mentor</u>? (Yes or No)	Was this person a <u>role model</u>? (Yes or No)	Level of Importance to <u>Career Success</u> [Very(V), Little(L), None(N)]
1) Staff				
a) President............. ___				
b) Vice President......... ___				
c) Regional Director(s)... ___				
d) Director(s)............ ___				
e) Assistant Director(s).. ___				
f) Co-ordinator(s)........ ___				
g) Tutor(s).............. ___				
h) Alumni................ ___				
i) Peer(s)............... ___				
Internship experience				
a) Corporate advisor/ mentor/business sponsor............... ___				
b) Corporate supervisor... ___				
c) Business coordinator... ___				
Other(s): Specify:				
a) _____ ... ___				
b) _____ ... ___				
c) _____ ... ___				

24B. With respect to question 24A: To what degree have your most important mentors:

	Great Degree	Large Degree	Some Degree	Little Degree	Not at All
1) motivated you in meeting your desired goals......................	5	4	3	2	1
2) been instrumental in your growth and development....................	5	4	3	2	1
3) allowed you to develop your own individual identity.................	5	4	3	2	1
4) maintained their objectivity towards:					
a) your own ideas...................	5	4	3	2	1
b) your career goals...............	5	4	3	2	1
5) other(s): specify					
a)_____ ...	5	4	3	2	1
b)_____ ...	5	4	3	2	1
c)_____ ...	5	4	3	2	1

25. While you were an _____ intern, other people might have contributed to your current career success. To what extent were they important? (Circle the most appropriate category for each item)

	Great Extent	Large Extent	Some Extent	Little Extent	Not at All
a) family.............................	5	4	3	2	1
b) yourself...........................	5	4	3	2	1
c) other(s): specify:					
1)_____ ...	5	4	3	2	1
2)_____ ...	5	4	3	2	1
3)_____ ...	5	4	3	2	1

S T O P

IT MIGHT BE A GOOD IDEA TO TAKE A SHORT BREAK AT THIS POINT

SECTION 4: ALUMNI SUGGESTIONS REGARDING IMPROVEMENTS OF

Instructions: Please answer completely all of the following.

26. Based on your experiences within corporate environment(s), what new elements
     do you believe should be added to the following   components?
     (Specify a maximum of four suggestions for each item)

     a) Training workshops topics: (If you need to refresh your memory, refer
        to Question 21, pages 18 and 19.)

        1) _____

        2) _____

        3) _____

        4) _____

     b) Practical aspects of training workshops: (e.g., quality of presentations,
        facilitators, facilities, etc.)

        1) _____

        2) _____

        3) _____

        4) _____

     c) Summer work experience:

        1) _____

        2) _____

        3) _____

        4) _____

     d) Counseling:

        1) _____

        2) _____

        3) _____

        4) _____

26. (Cont'd)

   e) Alumni component: (Specify a maximum of six suggestions for this item)

   1) _____

   2) _____

   3) _____

   4) _____

   5) _____

   6) _____

27. Based on your corporate experiences, what services other than workshops, summer work experience and counseling do you think   should provide to minorities:
   (Specify a maximum of four suggestions for each item)

   a) to become employable?

   1) _____

   2) _____

   3) _____

   4) _____

   b) to survive within corporate settings?

   1) _____

   2) _____

   3) _____

   4) _____

   c) to achieve upward mobility?

   1) _____

   2) _____

   3) _____

   4) _____

28. What additional skills other than those acquired from   do you
    currently need to assist in your upward mobility within the company in
    which you are presently employed? List in order of importance.
    (Specify a maximum of five)

    a)_____

    b)_____

    c)_____

    d)_____

    e)_____

29. As an   alumnus, what future contributions are you willing to make
    to   Indicate to what extent you are willing to make these
    contributions.
    (Circle the most appropriate category for each item)

	A Great Deal	A Little	Not at All	Currently Doing
a) participation as mentor/role model in:				
1) pre-college component...............	4	3	2	1
2) college component...................	4	3	2	1
b) financial contributions................	4	3	2	1
c) becoming a business advisor............	4	3	2	1
d) recruiting corporate sponsors for at the company at which you are presently working..................	4	3	2	1
e) conducting workshops...................	4	3	2	1
f) recruiting students for	4	3	2	1
g) being an active member of the alumni association.............	4	3	2	1
h) other(s): specify:				
1) _____...	4	3	2	1
2) _____...	4	3	2	1
3) _____...	4	3	2	1

30. As an _____ alumnus, what future contributions are you willing to make
to the community? Indicate to what extent you are willing to make these
contributions.
(Circle the most appropriate category for each item)

	A Great Deal	A Little	Not at All	Currently Doing
a) assisting in minority development......	4	3	2	1
b) serving on community boards............	4	3	2	1
c) serving as a mentor/role model.........	4	3	2	1
d) financial contributions................	4	3	2	1
e) other(s): specify:				
1) _____...	4	3	2	1
2) _____...	4	3	2	1
3) _____...	4	3	2	1

(GO TO THE NEXT PAGE)

YOUR INFORMATION IS IMPORTANT.

NOW THAT YOU HAVE REACHED THE END OF
THE QUESTIONNAIRE, PLEASE COMPLETE ANY ITEMS
MARKED "OTHER" THAT YOU MIGHT HAVE NEGLECTED
TO FILL OUT.

THANK YOU FOR YOUR TIME.

Description of the Special Corporate Training Program

The training organization used in this study offers training specifically geared to meet the corporate needs of minorities and is a national career development and recruitment organization. This organization grew out of the vision of a businessman who believed that the best way to facilitate the employment of economically disadvantaged minority students in the corporate world was first to identify talented minority students and then give corporations the opportunity to further this talent within their particular company settings. Thus, in 1970 the training organization was born out of a joint mission between businesses and minorities to prepare talented minority youth from low income inner-city backgrounds for positions of corporate and community leadership.

Corporations rely on this training organization for the recruitment of the best and brightest minorities. They perceive this organization as providing participants with the skills, abilities, and experienc e corporate leaders and researchers contend that minorities need to be successful with American corporations. Thus, graduates of the program were chosen because they would have met all corporate criteria that minorities are thought/perceived to need beyond academic qualifications to be successful for employability and corporate advancement.

At the time of the study, the program had over 2,000 alumni and more than 800 corporate sponsors. Approximately 80% of its alumni became professionals and managers in more than 300 of the Fortune 500 companies. The target audience for this study were individuals from this program with four or more years of corporate experience.

The following sections will outline the training organization's goals and components.

GOALS

The major goals of the training organization included the following:

a. To expand students' knowledge of their career fields and to assist them in choosing academic courses pertaining to their interests and career goals;

b. To develop students' abilities to deal with the ambiguities and dynamics that operate within corporate settings;

c. To teach students how to balance their desires for personal achievement with the needs of their community;

d. To produce individuals who have completed four summer internships at sponsoring companies and are immediately employable upon graduation from college;

e. To ensure that corporate sponsors provide a Corporate Advisor, Business Coordinator, Supervisor, and a four-year Career Development Plan for each intern they sponsor, as well as other key elements of the program for which they have assumed responsibility; and

f. To be an efficient and effective training organization in achieving its mission.

The achievement of these ambitious goals required a definite commitment among sponsoring companies, staff, interns, program alumni, and the organization.

PRE-COLLEGE COMPONENT

The pre-college component of the training organization recruited top minority students from public and private high schools and provided them with extensive supplemental academic instruction, tutoring, skill building programs, career counseling, field trips, and other activities necessary for successful entry into the program's college internship component. These activities were also geared to enhance the students' ability to successfully enter and complete bachelor degree programs at the university level. The academic curriculum of this component consisted of mathematics, English and communications, computer science, and general economics courses and developmental activities. Curriculum activities were designed to address different aspects of personal development, career awareness, and college preparation.

The organization sees its year-round counseling of high school students as one of the program's greatest strengths. The pre-college staff members were responsible for guiding the students through a path to greater academic performance and personal development. Along with this staff, teachers and trainers continuously addressed students' needs in order to provide continuity of learning, promote students' growth and development, and challenge students at every step of the program to pursue their career aspirations.

Curricula and activities for the pre-college participants were developed by a joint committee of the training organization's staff and the local affiliate's pre-college staff. Students' training needs were based on their initial standardized test results and the staff's observation of the students' developmental needs. In most cases, the program's academic core curriculum for pre-college students paralleled their high school curriculum. The pre-college program consisted of the following features:

i   *Core Curriculum*: Pre-college students were exposed to at least 30 hours of mathematics, 30 hours of English and communications, 24 hours of computer instruction, 20 hours of science (physics and chemistry), and 12 hours of economics. During the academic year, classes were conducted on college entrance examination preparation, dressing for success, interview and resume preparation, and interpersonal skills development.

ii. *Training Workshops*: A series of workshops was given in the areas of personal development, career awareness, and preparation for college.

iii. *Counseling*: The program's staff assisted students in handling typical adolescent issues. In particular, advice was given regarding personal life concerns and academic issues such as selecting majors or careers.

iv. *Tutoring*: Students experiencing difficulty in mastering their academic courses were offered year-round tutoring. Students who wanted to complete advanced course work or increase their grade point average also received tutoring.

v.   *Other Training Activities*: Students participated in field trips to corporations during the summer months. They were also involved in annual team projects where they had the opportunity to apply mathematical and technical concepts.

COLLEGE COMPONENT

The organization's college component is a professional development program for minority youth geared toward areas of business, engineering, and the applied sciences. This component is designed to equip students with the skills and experiences necessary for continued academic achievement and to enhance their employability and upward mobility within the corporate arena. This process involved year-round recruitment, counseling, tutoring, training, academic instruction, and early intern exposure to sponsoring companies. Typically, student training occurred over a four-year period (divided into four levels: freshman, sophomore, junior, and senior). Early identification and consistent mentoring of students were key features.

In particular, the college component included the following processes: 1) recruitment, selection, and placement in a corporation and assignment to a staff person (the organization acted as the intermediary between the sponsoring company and the intern); 2) counseling at least once a month; 3) training based on a core curriculum; and 4) on-the-job mentoring. Also, a four-year career development plan for each intern was developed by the corporate sponsor, with input from the training staff and the particular intern. Every intern was evaluated each summer against the goals and objectives contained in these plans.

In order to graduate from this special corporate training program, each student must have maintained a grade point average (GPA) of at least 2.5 on a 4.0 scale. In addition, each participant must have attended at least 80% of the training and development sessions, received counseling from the program staff at least once a month, completed a four-year summer internship, and maintained a good intern evaluation from his or her corporate sponsor.

The strength of the program's college component is its systematic training and mentoring process. The strong ties between the organization and corporations allowed for corporate executive commitment to and participation in the organization's training process. This commitment further ensured that interns obtained the kinds of skills, training, and expertise needed for success in the corporate arena.

The training needs of each of the program's participants were evaluated by several different sources. A special committee from within the program determined the core training curriculum which consisted of approximately 34 different workshops taken over a four-year period. The training staff evaluated the students' training needs, based on their direct interaction with participants as well as the staff's knowledge of the developmental needs of minority students pursuing business-related careers. The students also identified their training needs through self-assessment instruments based on their internship experience. Finally, corporate sponsors ascertained their interns' training needs based on the sponsors' firsthand knowledge of what it takes to be successful in corporate environments as well as their judgments of the students' levels of performance throughout their internship.

The college component's training system includes:

i. *Core Curriculum*: The core curriculum covered a four-year period of essential workshops and other activities offered in given years throughout the student's stay in the training program. They included subject areas such as math, science, and the like.

ii. *Training Workshops*: Most of the program's workshops were in lecture format; however, facilitators also provided skill-building training that was more participatory and engaging in nature. When appropriate, as a means of generating discussion, facilitators drew from their own experiences as well as from those of interns and professionals. Much of the information shared was applied by the students during their summer work internships and/or during the academic year at college.

iii. *Counseling*: Year-round counseling sessions were held between the program's staff and interns to discuss various aspects of the training process and to monitor how the interns implemented and integrated the knowledge and skills they acquired during their summer internship and academic studies.

iv. *Tutoring*: The training organization provided tutors for any intern who needed or asked for help. Furthermore, any intern whose GPA fell below the accepted level was required to seek tutoring for subjects in which the intern was performing poorly. Tutors were selected by either the intern or the training staff. The organization financed any tutoring required irrespective of GPA level since academic excellence was an important ingredient to the intern's development.

v. *Regional Training Institute*: On an annual basis, each of the regional chapters of the training organization conducted its own special set of training and development sessions designed to further expose interns to the core curriculum, fellow alumni

from other affiliate cities, and employees of other corporate
sponsoring companies.

vi. *National Training Institute*: As an extension of the Regional
Training Institutes, special training activities took place on a
national scale once every four years. This gave students another
opportunity to enhance their personal and professional skills
while at the same time broadening their network base.

vii. *Summer Work Experience*: Interns were required to participate
in successive summer work experiences at their sponsoring
companies. These work experiences were designed to enhance
the intern's personal and professional development through
exposure to diverse corporate experiences at the same company
over a four-year period.

viii. *Community Activities*: Commitment to investing in the
community   was reinforced in the interns through their
year-round involvement   in a variety of community
activities.

ix. *Other Types of Training*: Interns participated in additional
training activities such as banquets, alumni socials, and
luncheons with corporate sponsors and community leaders in
order to familiarize themselves with the social skills needed to
assimilate into corporate and community environments.

ALUMNI COMPONENT

The purpose of the Alumni Component of the program is to provide
alumni with avenues to contribute to the organization, increase their
own personal development, and facilitate networking among themselves
and other local and national professional groups. In support of these
objectives, the program's Alumni Component had two dimensions at
the time of the study.

One dimension consisted of the program staff assisting in the
growth and development of the program's alumni associations in their
respective affiliate cities. This assistance included developing a local and
national alumni directory, providing secretarial support to the affiliate's
alumni association, and sponsoring training programs for alumni.

The second dimension consisted of the National Alumni
Association and its member alumni associations in cities affiliated with
the training organization. Each local alumni association planned and
conducted training events for fellow alumni. The local association also

organized activities in which program graduates recruited potential interns and corporate sponsors. The alumni also mentored current interns and pre-college students, organized social events, and raised funds for scholarships for interns through the Annual Alumni Personal Giving Drive. The local associations also provided management development training for their members.

The Alumni Component was established to provide participants with opportunities to reinvest in the organization. Since alumni had begun to move up to middle and upper levels of management, their continued involvement meant that they were vital links between the students, the corporate world, and the community. Alumni promoted the organization within their communities, recruited companies as corporate sponsors, or increased their companies' involvement in the training program.

The organization assessed its graduates' needs based on information provided by the alumni and the staff's knowledge of alumni's needs in general. The organization offered training and development programs to assist alumni in their personal and career development. In addition, graduates identified their needs themselves and created their own workshops. They kept the organization abreast of what they perceived to be required of employees in order for them to be effective and upwardly mobile within corporate environments.

At the time of the study, the Alumni Component consisted of:

  i. *Core Curriculum*: The core curriculum was dictated based on the immediate needs of alumni.
 ii. *Training Workshops*: The organization offered a wide array of workshops based on graduates' current and anticipated needs. Some workshops were also offered at the Regional and National Training Institutes.
iii. *Counseling*: The program's staff talked with alumni on an ongoing basis. Graduates contacted their affiliate's staff frequently, sharing areas of concern, seeking guidance in career decision making, and inquiring about employment positions available at sponsoring corporations.
 iv. *Community Activities*: Each local alumni association determined the nature and scope of its community related activities. The training organization expected that at least ten percent of its alumni would serve on Boards of Directors of community groups and at least 15 percent would contribute to the Annual Alumni Personal Giving Drive.

Determining Academic Credentials Index

A series of face-to-face telephone interviews was conducted with seven human resource managers and six senior level managers from ten Fortune 500 companies in the East and Midwest regions of the country. A resulting index of requisite academic credentials was developed based on the information gathered from these interviews. The index reflected the nature and type of academic qualifications required by these employers for various career tracks in technical and non-technical areas. The general consensus of the 13 corporate representatives was that academic requirements vary by profession. In technical areas (which require a specific degree) such as finance, engineering, and law, the recognized degrees are bachelor's, master's, and professional master's degrees. Among the certificates such as CPA, CFP, CMA, CPM, and ABI, the CPA carries the most weight and is recognized by many companies as the most prestigious. However, one of the technical areas in which CPA and professional master's degrees is not as significant is in Research and Development. Bachelor's, master's, and Ph.D. or M.D. degrees are the important accreditation required in this area. In non-technical areas such as human resources and operations, the academic qualifications most often recognized are bachelor's and master's degrees; a professional master's degree is only marginally significant in these instances.

Independent Variables Used in the Statistical Analysis

The ten independent variables used for the regression analysis, discussed in the section "Quantifiable Factors Contributing to Upward Mobility" of Chapter III, were measured as follows:

a. *Gender* (male or female), a categorical variable, was coded "1" for male and coded "0" for female.

b. *Group membership* variable was divided into three categories: trained black managers, black managers and white managers. For regression analysis purposes each category was coded "1" for membership in a particular group category and "0" for non-membership.

c. *Level of academic credentials* obtained at time of employment, an ordinal variable, was divided into four categories: undergraduate degree[1], master's degree, professional master's degree, and base degree[2] plus CPA. Although CPA is a certification[3], it is highly recognized and valued. Normally, ordinal variables can be used as interval variables in regression analysis. However, in this case it was not known if a linear relationship existed between the academic credential variables and the dependent variables. Additionally, within the corporate arena, the comparative difference in value between any two academic credential categories may vary. For example, the difference in the value of an undergraduate degree and a master's degree may be less than the difference in the value of an undergraduate degree and a professional master's degree. As a result, using the academic degree variable as an interval variable would have produced inaccuracies and biases in this measure. Thus, for the purposes of this study, this variable was used as a categorical variable. Dummy variables were created to represent academic credential categories for regression analysis purposes.

The acquisition of advanced degrees is one means of achieving greater career mobility (Salmon 1979; Forbes and Piercy 1991; Wernick 1994). While no significant differences were present between the three study groups in level of academic credentials at time of initial employment, significant differences were found to be present between study groups on this variable at the time of the study[4]. A degree change variable (dummy variable) was created and included in the regression equation to reflect changes in levels of academic credentials between the time of initial employment and the time of the study. If changes in academic credentials occurred between the time of initial employment and the time of the study, the change variable was coded as "1", and if no change in degree occurred over that time period the change variable was coded as "0". This coding approach eliminated the problem of assigning weights to academic credential variables, since it is difficult or almost impossible to assign consistent weights to measure the impact of changes from one degree to another.

d. *Academic major* at time of initial employment, a categorical variable, was divided into three categories: business[5], engineering, and other[6]. The categories were collapsed into "business" and "other" due to the focus on business related skills that was required as one moved into higher levels of management in the corporate hierarchy (see Chapter II). Dummy codings were applied to the two categories (i.e., "business" and "other").

The acquisition of advanced degrees is one means of achieving greater career mobility, especially when the degree is in an area related to one's occupation (Salmon 1979; Forbes and Piercy 1991). While no significant differences were present between the three study groups in the distribution of the academic majors at the time of initial employment, significant differences were found to be present in the distribution of major at the time of the study[7]. A change variable (dummy variable) for major was created to reflect changes in major between the time of initial employment and the time of the study. The change variable was included in the regression equation. If an individual obtained a higher degree after being employed and that degree change was in a new discipline—such as business—the change variable was coded as "1". Otherwise, the change variable was coded as "0".

e. *School prestige rating* at time of initial employment is an interval variable and was measured on a five-point scale.

f. *Initial hierarchical position* at the time of initial employment is an ordinal variable and was originally divided into five categories: top, upper-middle, upper-entry, entry and clerical levels. Since the relative importance of hierarchical position titles varies from company to company, this variable should only reflect an individual's relative position within the structure of his/her company. As a result, this variable used by itself could be somewhat misleading. Additionally, it was not known whether a linear relationship exists between initial hierarchical position and the dependent variables. Thus, determination of the relative weights between the various positional levels remains uncertain.

Because of the inaccuracies and potential biases inherent in this variable, hierarchical position at the time of initial employment was defined as a categorical variable. For regression analysis purposes, dummy variables were created to represent initial hierarchical position categories. Since there were no individuals in the upper management categories at the time of initial employment and because of the limited number of members in certain categories, hierarchical position was redefined. The hierarchical position variable was divided into two categories: middle level and lower level. For regression analysis, dummy variables were created to represent this variable—middle management level was coded as "1" and lower management levels were coded as "0". This categorization still provided an appropriate representation of corporate position ordering.

g. *Type of position* (staff or line) at time of initial employment is a categorical variable. For regression analysis purposes, staff position was coded as "0" and line positions were coded as "1".

h. *Type of industry* at the time of initial employment was divided into four categories: service[8]; financial services[9]; transportation and communications[10]; and manufacturing. Dummy variables were created to represent these categories for the regression analysis.

   i. *Change in industry* between initial job and job held at the time of the study was considered to be an important variable to be controlled for in the regression analysis. In drawing the three study samples, attempts were made to obtain and match respondents across industries. Perfect one-to-one matching did not occur because each study group had an unequal number of respondents. No significant differences were present between the three study groups with respect to industry type at the time of initial employment or at the time of the study[11]. However, any differences in salary growth could have been attributable to changes from one type of industry to another made between initial job and job held at the time of the study. As a result, a variable measuring change in industry type between initial job and job held at the time of the study was used to determine whether changes in the dependent variables (salary growth and rates of vertical promotion) were due to a change in industry type. Thus, a change variable (dummy variable) was developed and coded as "1" if an industry change occurred between the time of initial employment and the time of the study and "0" if no change took place.

   j. *Company size* at the time of the study is an interval variable and was included in the regression equation by applying transformations using natural log for the "company size" variable. This reflected the number of employees in a company on a nationwide basis. This transformation had to be conducted since this variable was not normally distributed.

NOTES

1. Since only one person from the black manager's groups had an associate degree, this degree category was included in the undergraduate degree category.

2. Base degree was either an undergraduate degree, a master's degree, or professional master's degree.

3. See discussion on academic credentials in Chapter III.

4. Preliminary analysis of study data using chi-square yielded $X^2=9.5033$; df.=6; p >.1472 at the time of their initial employment and $X^2=14.9591$; df.=6; p <.0206 at the time of the study.

5. The "Business" category contains academic majors in the fields of accounting, MIS-computers, marketing, business management, economics, finance, and corporate law.

6. The "Other" category includes academic majors in the fields of social sciences, pure sciences, and education.

7. Preliminary analysis of study data using chi-square yielded X^2=7.7953; df.=4; p > .0994 at the time of their initial employment and X^2=2.1922; df.=4; p >.7005 at the time of the study.

8. Service industry includes: consulting, medical services, education, government, MIS-computers, legal, and retailing.

9. Financial services includes banking and insurance.

10. Transportation and communication includes utilities.

11. Preliminary analysis of study data using chi-square yielded X^2=3.2526; df.=6; p > .7765 at the time of the participants' initial employment and X^2=4.9890; df.=6; p >.5452 at the time of the study.

Pretest and Data Collection Processes

This appendix discusses the procedures implemented to pilot test the questionnaires used in the study and provides a detailed account of the data collection process.

TRAINED BLACK MANAGERS

Pretest Process

The pretest process consisted of three phases. During Phase I, three upper level management personnel of the training organization were asked to evaluate each question of the questionnaire to determine whether each component of the special corporate training program was clearly represented in the questions. This group was chosen because they—as managers in charge of implementing the training process—had the best understanding of the particular training program. Following this evaluation, these managers were asked to assess each question in terms of its clarity, ambiguity, and validity in requesting the information needed for the purposes of the study.

During Phase II, six graduates of the training program were asked to evaluate each question of the revised questionnaire (from Phase I) to determine whether they felt that each aspect of the special corporate training program was clearly represented in the study questionnaire. Graduates were chosen because, as past recipients of the special corporate training, they represented the individuals best able to describe the training that participants actually received. To avoid using the already small number of graduates eligible for participation in the study, graduates who had not met the study's selection criteria of four or more years of work experience in the corporate arena were chosen to participate in the pretest process. The graduates also judged whether the language used in the questionnaire clearly stated the intent of each question.

Finally, during Phase III, two current participants of the training program were asked to evaluate the revised questionnaire (from Phase II) to further clarify any ambiguous language used and to anticipate the ways in which the actual study population would interpret the questionnaire items. Only two subjects from the study population were selected because of the small size of the actual study population (443 graduates of the training program). These two subjects were not included as part of the actual study.

Data Collection Process

The data collection process for the group of trained black managers consisted of eight phases.

Phase I

Directors of the training program in eight affiliated cities were asked to identify all of their graduates between 1974 and 1988 who had met the criteria (see Chapter III) for inclusion in this particular target group. Once these graduates were identified, the training program's managing directors made efforts to locate these individuals through their own internal records.

Phase II

The author and the training program's directors sent letters to eligible graduates whom they were able to locate. These letters invited the eligible graduates to events (e.g., luncheons, meetings, and workshops) at which questionnaires were distributed and completed. Graduates who attended these events but did not complete the questionnaire were requested to complete the questionnaire and mail it to their respective directors who, in turn, forwarded them to the author.

Phase III

The author telephoned graduates who had not turned in completed questionnaires during Phase II and encouraged them to complete and return them. Questionnaire packets also were sent to graduates who had not participated in an event during Phase II. Accompanying the mailed questionnaires was a letter from the Regional Vice President of the training organization, informing each potential respondent about the purpose of the study and the importance of their response.

Phase IV

During this phase, graduates of the program (some of whom were eligible study participants) were asked to assist in the data collection process by making calls to eligible study participants, encouraging the return of the completed questionnaires.

Phase V

The author made a series of follow-up phone calls to non-responding graduates, urging them to return their questionnaires. The author also made appointments, seeking to obtain the completed questionnaires in person.

Phase VI

To obtain completed questionnaires from the remaining eligible graduates, the author requested the assistance of the President of the training organization who then encouraged the directors to further assist in the data collection process. Some directors mailed additional questionnaire packets which included letters urging alumni participation in the study. This step was followed by telephone calls from the directors to ensure that the potential participants received the questionnaire packets. Some directors solicited support from local alumni associations. Other directors held receptions for graduates who met the study criteria but had not yet completed the questionnaire. Those who attended these receptions completed their questionnaires on site, while those who had not attended these receptions were mailed questionnaires.

Phase VII

The author again made a series of telephone calls to eligible graduates who still had not returned completed questionnaires.

Phase VIII

Upon receipt of each questionnaire, the author telephoned respondents whose questionnaire answers were incomplete or unclear.

BLACK MANAGERS

Pretest Process

The purpose of the pretest process for the black managers' group was to determine whether each question of the study questionnaire was stated in terms which clearly requested the desired information. To accomplish this task, a group of ten black managers from various companies and industries who occupied positions within the same range as those of the trained black managers were asked to evaluate the questions in the questionnaire. These managers were identified by corporate personnel (white and black) from various companies, industries, and cities. None of the managers were in the same companies as the trained black managers selected for the actual study.

Data Collection Process

The data collection process for the group of black managers consisted of six phases.

Phase I

Each trained black manager was requested to identify a black counterpart holding a position parallel to his or her own within the same company. The three entrepreneurs in the sample of trained black managers were asked to identify black entrepreneurial counterparts within the same industry and city.

Phase II

Once these black managers were identified, they each received a questionnaire, either by mail or directly from the trained black manager who identified him or her.

Phase III

Approximately one week after the black managers received their questionnaire packets, the author telephoned the trained black managers of the black counterparts who had not yet returned their packets to find out whether the black managers had received the questionnaires.

Phase IV

The author telephoned black managers who had not returned completed questionnaires to emphasize the importance of the study and to urge the return of the questionnaires.

Phase V

The author made appointments with some of the black managers who had not yet returned their questionnaires to collect the completed questionnaires in person.

Phase VI

Upon receipt of the questionnaires, the author phoned respondents whose questionnaire answers were incomplete or unclear.

WHITE MANAGERS

Pretest Process

The pretest process for the study group of white managers consisted of two phases. During Phase I, a group of ten white managers from various companies and industries who occupied positions within the same range as those of the trained black managers were asked to evaluate the questionnaire in terms of how clearly it requested the desired information. These managers were identified by corporate personnel (white and black) from various companies, industries, and cities. None of the managers were in the same companies as the trained black managers selected for the study.

This phase revealed that because of the sensitive nature of the subject of race, the response rate or the accuracy of information obtained would be undermined if questions pertaining to race were included in the questionnaire for the white managers' study group. Moreover, the personal background information was deemed more important to be obtained from this group in order to make comparisons with the other two parallel groups. In addition, pretest results indicated that the removal of race-related questions would reduce the questionnaire's length to the point where answers to study questions could be easily solicited by phone and thus would likely increase the response rate.

Based on the recommendations made during Phase I of the pretest process, Phase II was begun. The revised questionnaire was again pretested by telephone on five additional white managers to determine whether each question was stated in terms which clearly requested the information sought with no ambiguities in meaning. The same identification process used to locate the ten white managers in Phase I was used to identify the five white managers in Phase II.

Data Collection Process

The data collection process for the group of white managers consisted of five phases.

Phase I

Each trained black manager was requested to identify a white counterpart holding a position parallel to his or her own within the same company. The three entrepreneurs in the sample of trained black managers were asked to identify white entrepreneurial counterparts within the same industry and city.

Phase II

Once parallel white managers were identified and located, four- to five-minute interviews were conducted by phone to solicit answers to the questionnaire. The questionnaire was mailed to those who did not wish to give information by phone.

Phase III

After approximately one week, the author telephoned white managers who had not returned telephone messages left by her. The purpose of these calls was to emphasize the importance of the study and to solicit answers to the questionnaire by telephone. Additionally, telephone calls were made by the author to white managers who requested that the study questionnaire be sent to them but from whom questionnaires had not yet been received. This was done to emphasize the importance of the study and to urge the return of the questionnaires.

Phase IV

Another round of calls were made by the author to those who had not yet responded to telephone calls and to those who had not yet returned their questionnaires. This was done to solicit answers to study questions by telephone or to urge the return of the questionnaires.

Phase V

Upon receipt of the questionnaires, the author telephoned those respondents to clarify questionnaire answers that were incomplete or unclear.

BLACK CORPORATE EXECUTIVES

Pretest Process

The pretest process for the study questionnaire for black corporate executives consisted of one phase. This phase determined whether each question of the study questionnaire was worded in terms which clearly requested the information sought with no ambiguities in meaning. A group of six black middle and upper-middle managers from various companies, industries, and cities were asked to evaluate the questions. Additionally, a group of four black entrepreneurs from various industries were asked to evaluate the questions in the questionnaire.

Top corporate executives (black and white) were asked to name black corporate executives and entrepreneurs who were considered leaders in their respective fields. However, since it was necessary to maintain a sizeable population of black corporate executives for the study sample and since this population was relatively small, six black middle and upper-middle managers and four black entrepreneurs were chosen for the pretest evaluation. None of the ten evaluators were graduates of the special corporate training program.

A consistent concern of this pretest group was anonymity. Because of the perceived controversial nature of some of the study questions, the evaluators felt that the black corporate executives would be concerned about maintaining their anonymity. These evaluators were also concerned about the length of this questionnaire (15 pages). As a result, the pretest group recommended that the study questions should not be reduced but should be divided into two parts: part 1—a questionnaire format which should be used to seek quantitative data, and part 2—an interview format which should be used to seek qualitative data.

Interestingly, the evaluators did not recommend removing any original questions because they felt that these black corporate executives represented a chosen few blacks who had achieved upper management status within the corporate arena. They viewed these black corporate executives as a valuable resource of information in the area of corporate upward mobility for black employees. Therefore, the pretest group felt that the number and nature of questions asked were necessary to obtain a substantial amount of pertinent information from this study group.

Data Collection Process

The data collection process for the group of black corporate executives consisted of seven phases.

Phase I

The author identified potential participants through various top level corporate and entrepreneurial contacts (white and black).

Phase II

The identified black corporate executives were telephoned by the author to obtain agreement to participate and to set interview appointments.

Phase III

Prior to face-to-face interview sessions, questionnaires were forwarded by the author to black corporate executives who consented to be interviewed. However, if interviews were conducted on short notice, questionnaires were distributed on the day of the interview.

Phase IV

The author conducted interviews and collected completed questionnaires from the black corporate executives at the end of each interview session. Because a nationwide sample was sought and because the author could not physically be present at some of the interviews, some were conducted by telephone. In these cases, questionnaires were mailed to the participants prior to the interview and were returned to the author by mail.

Phase V

If questionnaires were not returned at the end of the interview or after a specified time period, the author telephoned those black corporate executives to determine the status of the questionnaires and expected date of return.

Phase VI

For those who still had not returned questionnaires, the author made appointments to collect them personally or obtained the information needed by telephone.

Phase VII

Upon receipt of the questionnaires, the author made telephone calls to respondents whose questionnaire answers were incomplete or unclear. Any additional concerns about respondents' answers to study questions were clarified over the telephone.

Gathering Insights from Corporate Personnel (Supervisors of the Trained Black Managers)

SAMPLE SELECTION

The literature reviewed in Chapter II revealed that the level and quality of an individual's on-the-job performance are important criteria for measuring career mobility. Because some researchers and corporate leaders have strongly suggested that the slow rates of upward mobility experienced by black employees are due to their inferior work performance (Chapter II), job performance was considered another important predictor of upward mobility. In order to obtain information regarding job performance levels, the supervisors of the trained black managers (Group 4) were surveyed to evaluate the competence and performance of the trained black managers (Group 1) within their respective work environments. The supervisors were in the same general departments and areas as the group of trained black managers, but they held higher level management positions than the trained black managers. The purpose for obtaining the performance ratings of the trained black managers was to establish the performance levels they achieved within their work environments. Thus, the supervisors' perspectives of the quality and nature of their performance were important.

The availability of this sample was contingent on the ability of the group of trained black managers to identify their respective immediate supervisors and on the supervisors' willingness to participate in the study. Group 4 was not limited to immediate supervisors, because at the time of the study some of the black managers indicated that they had been in their current positions for a very short period of time, and thus their immediate supervisors were not in a position to evaluate them. They indicated that their immediate supervisors expressed the same concern. These trained black managers suggested that their former supervisors would be more able to evaluate their job performance since they had supervised them over an extended period of time. In these cases the previous supervisor was at the company in which the trained black manager was employed at the time of the study.

A total of 91 out of 117 (78%) supervisors completed and returned questionnaires. Among the 26 supervisors who did not respond to the study questionnaire, the most frequently given reasons for not participating were as follows: a) they had negative feelings about being involved in a study addressing issues pertaining to race; b) the trained black managers were unwilling to call their supervisors' attention to their minority status; and c) the trained black managers were unwilling to let their supervisors know that they had attended a special training program designed to enhance the employability and upward mobility of blacks and other minorities within the corporate arena. This unwillingness reportedly was due to a desire, on the part of the trained black managers, to avoid stereotyping based on being black.

QUESTIONNAIRE DESIGN AND ADMINISTRATION

A five-page questionnaire, which was designed and administered to each member of the corporate supervisors' group, requested information about the work performance level of the trained black managers. These supervisory personnel were asked to evaluate the performance levels of the trained black managers in comparison to their corporate peers in general and in comparison to their minority peers in particular. Information was also requested about the influence of a variety of training experiences[1] which were thought to enhance employee performance. Finally, the supervisors were asked to specify the nature and type of involvement that their corporations had in the training program in which the group of trained blacks had participated. This information was sought to determine their companies' level of participation in the special corporate training program and their level of commitment to minority development[2]. No academic and professional background data were requested from the supervisors since this group was used simply as a means of validating the performance levels of the trained black managers. Additionally, since pretest results indicated that anonymity was key to obtaining study data from this group of supervisory personnel, no background data were sought.

Pretest Process

The questionnaire for this group was pretested to remove ambiguous language or questions. This process was also used to identify any concerns of the supervisory personnel regarding study questions which could slow the rate of questionnaire return. A group of ten supervisory personnel from various position levels, companies, and industries were asked to evaluate the study questions to determine whether each was phrased in terms that clearly requested the desired information, with no ambiguities in meaning. The supervisory personnel used for the pretest were chosen by top management executives (white and black) who were asked to identify corporate managers who managed diverse groups of employees. Race was not a factor in the identification or selection process used for this pretest, and none of the ten were supervisors of the trained black managers.

A recurring concern of the pretest personnel was that certain study questions might be intimidating to white supervisory personnel. For example, they believed that some of their peers might be reluctant to offer different responses for black and white employees to the question: "In your opinion, what characteristics other than those required of a typical corporate employee do minorities need to achieve upward mobility in your corporation?" These protesters contended that their white peers might hesitate to answer questions of this nature because their response could imply that they were prejudiced. For example, if a corporate supervisor answers the above question by saying that blacks need certain characteristics beyond those normally required of a typical employee, he or she may be seen as admitting that different criteria exist for black and white employees. However, the members of the pretest group believed that even though this reluctance might produce a high degree of non-response to certain questions, the questions addressed fundamental issues pertaining to race within the corporate environment. They also indicated that even if a high non-response rate to these questions occurred, these non-responses would in and of themselves be important indications of the level of sensitivity among supervisory personnel. For these reasons, the group of ten supervisory personnel suggested that these kinds of questions should be retained as long the participants' anonymity was maintained.

Data Collection Process

The trained black managers were asked to distribute a five-page study questionnaire to their respective supervisors. In order to ensure data integrity and maximum response rates for this group, a four-phase data collection process, which took approximately one year, was implemented. The same procedure, used for Groups 1, 2, 3, and 5 in addressing problems of missing data or inconsistencies found in data, was implemented for the group of supervisors. The following provides a detailed description of the actual data collection process:

Phase I

Included in each trained black manager's questionnaire packet was a separate study questionnaire to be completed by his or her supervisor. This was done to provide these trained black managers with the opportunity to become familiar with the nature of the information requested of their supervisors. Additionally, this sprocedure was used to increase the probability of delivery to their supervisors. In most cases, the trained black managers hand delivered questionnaires to their immediate supervisors. However, in cases where either the trained black manager or the immediate supervisor was new to his or her position at the time of the study, the trained black manager delivered the questionnaire to his or her former supervisor. Along with the supervisory personnel questionnaire, a letter of introduction was sent to these supervisors explaining the nature of the study and the importance of their participation. The letter also assured them that a certain level of confidentiality would be maintained through anonymity and that the completed questionnaire should be returned directly to the author.

Phase II

Approximately two weeks after the trained black managers received their questionnaire packets, telephone calls were made by the author to the trained black managers whose supervisors had not returned their questionnaires. These calls were made to determine the status of their supervisors' questionnaires and to discuss possible steps that could be implemented to increase the return rate.

Phase III

Another series of telephone calls were made by the author to the trained black managers whose supervisors had not yet returned questionnaires. Additionally, upon the request of some trained black managers, telephone calls were made directly to their supervisors. In each case, the importance of the study was reemphasized as was the need for the return of the questionnaires.

Phase IV

Upon receipt of the questionnaires, the author telephoned respondents whose questionnaire answers were incomplete or unclear. Any additional concerns about the respondents' answers to study questions were clarified over the telephone.

NOTES

1. These training experiences did not pertain specifically to the corporate training program for minorities in which these black trained managers had participated.

2. Much of the information obtained from this group was used to develop a confidential report for the training organization.

Detailed Analysis of the Two Upward Mobility Measures Using CHAID

The basis for Chi-Square Automatic Interaction Detector's (CHAID) exploration is the chi-square test. Initially, CHAID examines each independent variable to determine if any categories within the variable may be collapsed. Two categories can be collapsed by CHAID if, based on a chi-square test, no statistically significant difference exists between the dependent variable distribution of the categories. For variables with ordered categories, the user may tell CHAID only to collapse adjoining categories. Once this is done, CHAID identifies which independent variable best predicts the value of the dependent variable by selecting the independent variable whose two-way cross tabulation with the dependent variable yields the most significant chi-square. After selecting an independent variable, CHAID drops that variable and repeats the process on each of its categories. CHAID continues in this manner until no other significant predictors can be found or when a category falls below a minimum sample size. A "tree" type graph summarizes the findings of the CHAID analysis and specifies the relationships between the dependent and independent variables. For further details of the statistical aspects of CHAID see: Kass 1980, Perreault and Barksdale 1980, and Magidson 1982.

PREDICTING AVERAGE CAGR IN SALARIES

Since average growth rate in salaries is a continuous measure, it was first made categorical for use in CHAID. Although one may be tempted to make many categories with small ranges, statistical literature suggests that each cell of a chi-square must have a sample size of at least five observations to be valid. Keeping this in mind, the compound annual growth rate (CAGR) in salaries variable was categorized as follows:

1 = less than 2.0%
2 = from 2% to 5.9%
3 = 6% or more

CHAID, using average salary growth rate as the dependent variable, found the group variable (comprised of the three study groups) to be the independent variable most associated with the average CAGR in salaries. In addition, CHAID collapsed the trained black managers' group with the black managers' group because it found no significant difference in the average growth rate in salary between these groups. However, CHAID detected statistically significant differences between the white managers' group and the two black managers' groups at the .05 level of significance. An examination of the dependent variable distribution by the group variable suggested that the white managers had a higher average CAGR in salaries as compared to the two black managers' group, as illustrated in Table 4-14.

Table 4-14: Salary Growth Rates By Study Groups*

GROUP	less than 2.0%	from 2.0 to 5.9%	more than 6.0%
Trained Black Managers/Black Managers	43.5% (63)	25.5% (37)	31.0% (45)
White managers	13.7% (7)	25.5% (13)	60.8% (31)

* row percentages add up to 100

It was not surprising that position level is a predictor of CAGR in salaries for black managers, since it is generally known that promotions and large salary increases are harder to come by in middle management. However, the distribution in Table 4-14 also shows that the cell counts for the middle managers with higher CAGR in salaries are quite small—small enough that some might question the validity of the chi-square at this level[1]

PREDICTING AVERAGE RATE OF VERTICAL PROMOTION

CHAID was also used to explore the relationships between the same independent variables used in the previous analysis and the second dependent variable, average rate of vertical promotion. Since rate of vertical promotion is a continuous measure, it must first be made into a categorical measure for use in CHAID. Although one may be tempted to make many categories with small ranges, statistical literature suggested that each cell of the chi-square must have a sample size of at least five observations to be valid. Therefore, the rate of vertical promotion variable was categorized as follows:

1 = less than 3.3 years
2 = from 3.3 years to 4.5 years
3 = 4.5 years or more

CHAID found group (comprised of the three study groups) to be the independent variable most associated with the average rate of vertical promotion. Additionally, it should be noted that CHAID again collapsed the trained black managers' group with the black managers' group because it found no significant differences in the average rate of vertical promotion between these two groups. However, CHAID detected statistically significant differences between the white managers' group and the two black managers' groups at the .05 level of significance. An examination of the dependent variable distribution by group suggested that the white managers had faster average rates of vertical promotion as compared to the two black study groups, as illustrated in Table 4-15.

Table 4-15: Salary Growth Rates By Study Groups*

GROUP	less than 2.0%	from 2.0 to 5.9%	more than 6.0%
Trained Black Managers/Black Managers	19.5% (23)	39.8% (47)	40.7% (48)
White managers	34.0% (16)	53.2% (25)	12.8% (6)

* row percentages add up to 100

Among the white managers' group and the trained black and black managers' groups, CHAID found no additional significant predictors of average rate of vertical promotion.

NOTES

1. It is possible that the "position level" variable would have predicted CAGR in salaries among white managers if more of them had started their careers in middle management level positions.

Sample Questions from Which Data Were Obtained to Conduct the Qualitative Analyses

To conduct empirical analyses of qualitative data, information from questionnaires completed by the group of black senior corporate executives was used. In order to obtain information about various key categories, several study questions generated the needed information. The following reflects the key categories with their accompanying relevant questions.

ACCESSING CORPORATE NETWORK SYSTEMS

1. Indicate the extent to which lack of informal social networks and lack of formal corporate networks have been a) obstacles to achieving your career advancement within your work environments and b) also obstacles to your minority peers within your company.
2. How successful are you in terms of your career aspirations and what occurrences have happened to you in your career that have led you to this conclusion?
3. How did you succeed/why did you not succeed and what plans do you have for the future that would enhance/continue to enhance your success within the corporate environment?
4. Do you believe you can reach the very pinnacle of your organization? If no, what factors and/or attributes would inhibit you?

5. What key things, if any, must occur at the following strategic points to better facilitate the upward mobility of blacks within corporate environments: at entry level, at mid-management level, and at upper management level?
6. What are the characteristics of successful people in your corporate environment?
7. What differentiates those blacks who succeed from those who do not?
8. Based on your corporate experiences, what characteristics other than those required of a typical employee do blacks need to a) gain employment in your corporate business; b) survive within your corporate environment; and c) achieve upward mobility in your corporation?
9. Have you experienced difficulty in moving up within your current company? If yes, what type of difficulties have you experienced and what do you plan to do next?

COMMUNICATION SKILLS

1. Do you believe you can reach the very pinnacle of your organization? If no, what factors and/or attributes would inhibit you?
2. What key things, if any, must occur at the following strategic points to better facilitate the upward mobility of blacks within corporate environments: at entry level, at mid-management level, and at upper management level?
3. What are the characteristics of successful people in your corporate environment?
4. What differentiates those blacks who succeed from those who do not?
5. Based on your corporate experiences, what characteristics other than those required of a typical employee do blacks need to a) gain employment in your corporate business; b) survive within your corporate environment; and c) achieve upward mobility in your corporation?
6. How did you succeed/why did you not succeed and what plans do you have for the future that would enhance/continue to enhance your success within the corporate environment?

7. Have you experienced difficulty in moving up within your current company? If yes, what type of difficulties have you experienced and what do you plan to do next?

8. How valuable is a training experience that focuses on communication skills with regard to facilitating the upward mobility and success of blacks within the corporate environment?

ACCESS TO MENTORS

1. How successful are you in terms of your career aspirations and what occurrences have happened to you in your career that have led you to this conclusion?

2. How did you succeed/why did you not succeed and what plans do you have for the future that would enhance/continue to enhance your success within the corporate environment?

3. Do you believe you can reach the very pinnacle of your organization? If no, what factors and/or attributes would inhibit you?

4. What key things, if any, must occur at the following strategic points to better facilitate the upward mobility of blacks within corporate environments: at entry level, at mid-management level, and at upper management level?

5. What are the characteristics of successful people in your corporate environment?

6. What differentiates those blacks who succeed from those who do not?

7. Based on your corporate experiences, what characteristics other than those required of a typical employee do blacks need to a) gain employment in your corporate business; b) survive within your corporate environment; and c) achieve upward mobility in your corporation?

8. Have you experienced difficulty in moving up within your current company? If yes, what type of difficulties have you experienced and what do you plan to do next?

9. Indicate a) the extent to which difficulty finding mentors with values similar to your own has been an obstacle to achieving your career advancement within your work environment and b) the extent to which difficulty finding mentors with values

similar to your own has been an obstacle to your minority peers within your company.

ABILITY TO FIT INTO CORPORATE CULTURE

1.   Do you believe you can reach the very pinnacle of your organization? If no, what factors and/or attributes would inhibit you?

2.   Have you experienced difficulty in moving up within your current company? If yes, what type of difficulties have you experienced and what do you plan to do next?

3.   Indicate the extent to which lack of political savvy and not being part of the dominant group a) have been obstacles to achieving your career advancement within your work environments and b) have been obstacles to your minority peers within your company.

4.   How did you succeed/why did you not succeed and what plans do you have for the future that would enhance/continue to enhance your success within the corporate environment?

5.   What key things, if any, must occur at the following strategic points to better facilitate the upward mobility of blacks within corporate environments: at entry level, at mid-management level, and at upper management level?

6.   What are the characteristics of successful people in your corporate environment?

7.   What differentiates those blacks who succeed from those who do not?

8.   Based on your corporate experiences, what characteristics other than those required of a typical employee do blacks need to a) gain employment in your corporate business; b) survive within your corporate environment; and c) achieve upward mobility in your corporation?

9.   How successful are you in terms of your career aspirations and what occurrences have happened to you in your career that have led you to this conclusion?

APPRAISAL PROCESS

1.   Do you believe you can reach the very pinnacle of your organization? If no, what factors and/or attributes would inhibit you?

2.   How successful are you in terms of your career aspirations and what occurrences have happened to you in your career that have led you to this conclusion?

3. How did you succeed/why did you not succeed and what plans do you have for the future that would enhance/continue to enhance your success within the corporate environment?

4. Have you experienced difficulty in moving up within your current company? If yes, what type of difficulties have you experienced and what do you plan to do next?

STEREOTYPES

1. What factors and/or attributes would inhibit you from reaching the top of your organization?

2. How successful are you in terms of your career aspirations and what occurrences have happened to you in your career that have led you to this conclusion?

3. How did you succeed/why did you not succeed and what plans do you have for the future that would enhance/continue to enhance your success within the corporate environment?

4. Have you experienced difficulty in moving up within your current company? If yes, what type of difficulties have you experienced and what do you plan to do next?

5. Indicate the extent to which race and ethnicity have been obstacles to a) achieving your career advancement and b) the advancement of your minority peers within your work environment.

DIFFERENCES IN SOCIOECONOMIC BACKGROUNDS

1. Do you believe you can reach the very pinnacle of your organization? If no, what factors and/or attributes would inhibit you?

2. Have you experienced difficulty in moving up within your current company? If yes, what type of difficulties have you experienced and what do you plan to do next?

3. What are the characteristics of successful people in your corporate environment?

4. How did you succeed/why did you not succeed and what plans do you have for the future that would enhance/continue to enhance your success within the corporate environment?

REQUISITE SKILLS AND QUALIFICATIONS

1. What key things, if any, must occur at the following strategic points to better facilitate the upward mobility of blacks within

corporate environments: at entry level, at mid-management level, and at upper management level?

    2.   Based on your corporate experiences, what characteristics other than those required of a typical employee do blacks need to a) gain employment in your corporate business; b) survive within your corporate environment; and c) achieve upward mobility in your corporation?

Bibliography

Agresti, Alan, and Barbara Finlay. *Statistical Methods for the Social Sciences*. San Francisco: Dellen Publishing Company, 1986.

Alexander, Keith L. "Minority Women Feel Racism, Sexism Are Blocking the Path to Management." *The Wall Street Journal* (25 July 1990).

Allport, Gordon W. *The Nature of Prejudice*. Cambridge, MA: Addison-Wesley Publishing Company, Inc., 1954.

America, Richard F., and Bernard E. Anderson. "Moving Ahead: Black Managers in American Business." *MBA* (Dec. 1978/Jan. 1979): 40-49.

————. "Black Men at Work: Must Black Executives Be Superstars?" *The Wharton Magazine* (Spring 1979): 44-58.

————. *Soul in Management: How African-American Managers Thrive in the Competitive Corporate Environment*. Secaucus, NJ: Carol Publishing, Inc., 1996.

American Assembly of Collegiate Schools of Business (AACSB). *Minorities in Management*. U.S.: The Program to Increase Minorities in Business (PIMB, n.d.).

Apostle, Richard A., C. Y. Glock, R. Piazza, and M. Suelzle. *The Anatomy of Racial Attitudes*. Berkeley: University of California Press, 1983.

Argyle, Michael. *The Social Psychology of Work*. New York: Taplinger Publishing Co., 1972.

Ariss, Sonny S., and Sherman A. Timmins. "Employee Education and Job Performance: Does Education Matter?" *Public Personnel Management* 18, no. 1 (Spring 1989): 1-9.

Arthur, Michael B., Douglas T. Hall, and Barbara S. Lawrence. *Handbook of Career Theory*. New York: Cambridge University Press, 1989.

321

Baker, Octave V. "Meeting the Challenge of Managing Cultural Diversity." In *Managing in the Age of Change: Essential Skills to Manage Today's Diverse Workforce*, edited by Roger A. Ritvo, Anne H. Litwin, and Lee Butler, 169-180. New York: Irwin Professional Publishing, 1995.

Barclay, David R. "Allies or Enemies? Affirmative Action and Management Diversity." In *The Diversity Factor: Capturing the Competitive Advantage of a Changing Workforce*, edited by Elsie Y. Cross and Margaret Blackburn White, 47-55. New York: Irwin Professional Publishing, 1996.

Baron, James N., and Jeffrey Pfeffer. "The Social Psychology of Organizations and Inequality." *Social Psychology Quarterly* 57 (1994): 190-209.

Bates, Timothy. "Utilization of Minority Employees in Small Business: A Comparison of Nonminority and Black-Owned Urban Enterprises." *Review of Black Political Economy* 23 (1994): 113- 121.

Becker, Gary S. *The Economics of Discrimination*. Chicago: The University of Chicago Press, 1957.

Human Capital: A Theoretical and Empirical Analysis, with Special Reference to Education. New York: National Bureau of Economic Research, 1964.

Becker, Howard S., and A. Strauss. "Careers, Personality, and Adult Socialization." *American Journal of Sociology* 62 (November 1956): 253-263.

Bell, Chip R. *Managers As Mentors*. San Francisco: Berrett-Koehler Publishers, 1996.

Bennett, Linda. "Economic Value Added Defined." *HR Focus* (July 1995): 5.

Benton, Joe. "Progress Report on the Black Executive: The Top Spots.Are Still Elusive." *Business Week* (20 February 1984): 104-105.

Bergmann, Barbara R. *In Defense of Affirmative Action*. New York: Basic Books, 1996.

Bernstein, Aaron, Richard W. Anderson, and Wendy Zellner. "Help Wanted: America Faces An Era of Worker Scarcity That May Last to the Year 2000." *Business Week* (10 August 1987): 48-53.

Bienvenu, Bernard J. *New Priorities in Training: A Guide for Industry*. New York: American Management Association, Inc., 1969.

Blackwell, James E. *Mainstreaming Outsiders: The Production of Black Professionals*. 2nd ed. New York: General Hall, Inc., 1987.

Blau, P., and O. D. Duncan. "What Determines Occupational Success." In *Three Centuries of Social Mobility*, edited by Edward Pessan. Lexington, MA: D.C. Heath and Company, 1974.

Bowman, Garda W. "What Helps or Harms Promotability?" *Harvard Business Review,* no. 64102 (January-February 1964): 95-111.

Braham, James. "Is the Door Really Open?" *Industry Week* (16 November 1987): 64-66.

Buono, Anthony F., and Judith B. Kamm. "Marginality and the Organizational Socialization of Female Managers." *Human Relations* 12 (November 1983): 1125-1140.

Butler, Lee. "African-American Women and Men in the Workplace: Dismantling the Glass Ceiling." In *Managing in the Age of Change: Essential Skills to Manage Today's Diverse Workforce,* edited by Roger A. Ritvo, Anne H. Litwin, and Lee Butler, 241-251. New York: Irwin Professional Publishing, 1995.

Cambell, Bebe Moore. "Black Executive and Corporate Stress." *New York Times Magazine* (12 December 1982): 36.

Cameron, Randolph W. *The Minority Executives' Handbook.* New York: Warner Books, 1989.

Campbell, Donald T., and Julian T. Stanley. *Experimental and Quasi-Experimental Designs for Research.* Chicago: Rand McNally & Company, 1967.

Caplow, Theodore. *The Sociology of Work.* Minneapolis: University of Minnesota Press, 1954.

Card, David and Alan B. Krueger. *Myth and Measurement: The New Economics of the Minimum Wage.* Princeton: Princeton University Press, 1994.

Carnevale, Anthony P., and Susan P. Stone. "Diversity: Beyond the Golden Rule." *Training & Development* (October 1994): 22-39.

Chao, Georgia T. "The Socialization Process: Building Newcomer Commitment." In *Career Growth and Human Resource Strategies,* edited by Manuel London and Edward M. Mone, 49-66. New York: Quorum Books, 1988.

Chao, Georgia T., Anne M. O'Leary-Kelly, Samantha Wolf, Howard J. Klein, and Philip Gardner. "Organizational Socialization: Its Content and Consequences." *Journal of Applied Psychology* 79, no. 5 (1994): 730-743.

Charles, Reuben O., and Ken W. McCleary. "Recruitment and Retention of African-American Managers." *Cornell Hotel and Restaurant Administration Quarterly* (February 1997): 24-29.

Charme Zane, Nancie. "Theoretical Considerations in Organizational Diversity." In *The Promise of Diversity: Over 40 Voices Discuss Strategies for Eliminating Discrimination in Organizations,* edited by

Elise Y. Cross, Judith H. Katz, Frederick A. Miller, and Edith W. Seashore, 339-350. New York: Irwin Professional Publishing, 1994.

Chesler, Mark A. (Ph.D.). "Racetalk: Thinking and Talking about Racism." In *The Diversity Factor: Capturing the Competitive Advantage of a Changing Workforce*, edited by Elsie Y. Cross and Margaret Blackburn White, 47-55. New York: Irwin Professional Publishing, 1996.

Chusmir, Leonard H., and Bernadette M. Ruf. "Racial and Ethnic Differences in Importance of Success and Relationship to Job Outcomes." *Journal of Social and Behavioral Sciences* 37, no. 1 (Winter 1992) 43-60.

Clarke, Richard. *The Status of Minorities in American Corporations*. New York: Richard Clarke Associates, Inc., 1987.

[Clinton, William] *Economic Report of the President*. Washington: U.S. Government Printing Office, February 1997.

Coate, Stephen and Glen C. Loury. "Will Affirmative-Action Policies Eliminate Negative Stereotypes?" *The American Economic Review* 83, no. 5 (December 1993): 1220-1240.

Coles, Flournoy A., Jr. "The Economics of Minorities." *The Review of Black Political Economy* 4, no. 4 (1974): 47-123.

Collins, Sharon M. "Black Mobility in White Corporations: Up the Corporate Ladder But Out on a Limb." *Social Problems* 44, no. 1 (February 1997): 55-67.

———. *Black Corporate Executives: The Making and Breaking of a Black Middle Class*. Philadelphia: Temple University Press, 1997.

Cox, T. *Cultural Diversity in Organization: Theory, Research, and Practice*. San Francisco: Berrett-Koehler, 1993.

Cox, T. H., S. A. Lobel, and P. L. McLeod. "Effects of Ethnic Group Cultural Differences on Cooperative and Competitive Behavior on a Group Task." *Academy of Management Journal* 34, no. 4 (1991): 827-847.

Cox, Taylor Jr., and Carol Smolinski. *Managing Diversity and Glass Ceiling Initiative as National Economic Imperatives*. A report to the U. S. Department of Labor, Glass Ceiling Commission, January 1994.

Crosby, Faye, and Susan Clayton. "Affirmative Action and the Issue of Expectancies." *Journal of Social Issues* 46, no. 2 (1990): 61-79.

Cross, Elsie Y. "Managing Diversity: A Continuous Process of Change." In *The Diversity Factor: Capturing the Competitive Advantage of a Changing Workforce*, edited by Elsie Y. Cross and Margaret Blackburn White, 17-23. New York: Irwin Professional Publishing, 1996.

Cross, Elsie Y., Judith H. Katz, Frederick A. Miller, and Edith W. Seashore. *The Promise of Diversity: Over 40 Voices Discuss Strategies for*

Eliminating Discrimination in Organizations. New York: Irwin Professional Publishing, 1994.

Cruise, Harold. *The Crisis of the Negro Intellectual: A Historical Analysis of the Failure of Black Leadership.* New York: Quill, 1967.

Crump, Wilbert S. "Executive Accountability." In *Ensuring Minority Success in Corporate Management,* edited by Donna E. Thompson and Nancy DiTomaso, 253-258. New York: Plemum Press, 1988.

Cummings, Thomas G., and Christopher G. Worley. *Organization Development and Change.* 6th ed. Cincinnati: South-Western College Publishing, 1997.

Curry, George E., ed. *The Affirmative Action Debate.* New York: Addison-Wesley Publishing Company, Inc., 1997.

Davis, George. "The Changing Agenda: New Era, New Perspectives". In *Ensuring Minority Success in Corporate Management,* edited by Donna E. Thompson and Nancy DiTomaso, 101-113. New York: Plenum Press, 1988.

Davis, G., and G. Watson. *Black Life in Corporate America.* New York: Doubleday, 1982.

Del Grande, J. J., G. F. D. Duffe, and J. C. Egsgard. *Mathematics 12.* 2nd ed. Toronto: Gage Educational Publishing Limited, 1970.

Devries, David L., A. M. Morrison, S. L. Shullman, and M. L. Gerlach. *Performance Appraisal on the Line.* New York: John Wiley & Sons, 1981.

Dickens, Floyd, Jr., and Jacqueline B. Dickens. *The Black Manager.* New York: Amacom, 1982.

Dimpka, Prince. "Organizational Climate, Job Expectations and Their Impact on Job Satisfaction: Comparing Black and White Managers." *Journal of Social and Behavioral Sciences* 37, no. 1 (Winter 1992): 1-12.

DiTomaso, Nancy, and Donna E. Thompson. "A Summary of Small- Group Discussions on the Advancement of Minority Managers: Perspectives of Academics and Experienced Managers." In *Ensuring Minority Success in Corporate Management,* edited by Donna E. Thompson and Nancy DiTomaso, 137-148. New York: Plenum Press, 1988.

———. "Minority Success in Corporate Management." In *Ensuring Minority Success in Corporate Management,* edited by Donna E. Thompson and Nancy DiTomaso, 3-24. New York: Plenum Press, 1988.

DiTomaso, Nancy; Donna E. Thompson, and David H. Blake. "Corporate Perspectives on the Advancement of Minority Managers." In *Ensuring*

Minority Success in Corporate Management, edited by Donna E. Thompson and Nancy DiTomaso, 119-136. New York: Plenum Press, 1988.

DiTomaso, N., and S. A. Smith. "Race and Ethnic Minorities and White Women in Management: Changes and Challenges." In *Women and Minorities in American Professions*, edited by J. Tang and E. Smith, 87-109. Albany: SUNY Press, 1996.

Doeringer, Peter B., and Michael J. Piore. *Internal Labor Markets and Manpower Analysis*. Lexington, MA: Heath Books, 1971.

Doka, K. J. "Dealing with Diversity: The Coming Challenge to American Business." *Business Horizon* 39 (1996): 67-71.

Dottori, Dino; George Khill, and John Seymour. *Applied Mathematics for Today: Intermediate Book*. 2nd ed. Toronto: McGraw-HIll Ryerson Limited, 1976.

Dottori, Dino; George Knill, and James Stewart. *Foundation of Mathematics for Tomorrow: Senior Simetric*. Toronto : McGraw-Hill Ryerson Limited, 1979.

Dovidio, John, F., and Samuel L. Gaertner. "Affirmative Action, Unintentional Racial Biases, and Intergroup Relations." *Journal of Social Issues* 52, no. 4 (1996): 51-75.

Dreyfuss, Joel. "Get Ready for the New Work Force." *Fortune* (23 April 1990):165-181.

The Economist 318, no. 7700 (30 March 1991): 17-21.

Enkelis, Liane. "Blacks Who Leave Dead-End Jobs to Go It Alone." *Business Week* (20 February 1984): 106.

Farley, Reynolds. *Blacks and Whites: Narrowing the Gap?* Cambridge: Harvard Press, 1984.

Farnham, Alan. "Holding Firm on Affirmative Action." *Fortune* (13 March 1989): 87-88.

Farrell, Christopher; J. Weber, and M. Schroeder. "Why We Should Invest in Human Capital." *Business Week* (17 December 1990): 88- 90.

Farish, Phillip. "Corporate Culture." *Urban Focus* (August 1985): 6, 17.

Federal Glass Ceiling Commission. *A Solid Investment: Making Full Use of the Nation's Human Capital*. Washington: U.S. Government Printing Office, November 1995.

Ferguson, Marilyn. *The Aquarian Conspiracy: Personal and Social Transformation in the 1980's*. Los Angeles: J. P. Tarcher, Inc., 1980.

Fernandez, John P. *Black Managers in White Corporations*. New York: John Wiley & Sons, Inc., 1975.

————. *Racism and Sexism in Corporate Life: Changing Values in American Business.* Lexington, MA: Lexington Books, 1981.

————. "Racism and Sexism in Corporate America: Still Not Color- or Gender-Blind in the 1980s." In *Ensuring Minority Success in Corporate America*, edited by Donna E. Thompson and Nancy DiTomaso, 71-98. New York: Plenum Press, 1988.

————. "Human Resources and the Extraordinary Problems Minorities Face." In *Career Growth and Human Resource Strategies*, edited by Manuel London and Edward M. Mone, 227- 240. New York: Quorum Books, 1988.

Fernandez, John, and Mary Barr. *The Diversity Advantage: How American Business Can Out-perform Japanese and European Companies in the Global Marketplace.* New York: Lexington Books, 1993.

Fisher, Sethard. *From Margin to Mainstream.* New York: Praeger Publishers, 1982.

Fix, Michael and Raymond J. Struyk. *Clear and Convincing Evidence: Measurement of Discrimination in America.* Washington: Urban Institute Press, 1993.

Forbes, J. Benjamin, and James E. Piercy. *Corporate Mobility and Paths to the Top: Studies for Human Resource and Management Development Specialists.* New York: Quorum Books, 1991.

Ford, David L. "Minority and Nonminority MBA Progress in Business." In *Ensuring Minority Success in Corporate Management*, edited by Nancy DiTomaso and Donna E. Thompson, 57-70. New York: Plenum Press, 1988.

Frances Berry, Mary. "Affirmative Action: Why We Need It, Why It Is Under Attack." In *The Affirmative Action Debate*, edited by George E. Curry, 299-313. New York: Addison-Wesley Publishing Company, Inc., 1997.

Francis, Dave, and Mike Woodcock. *Unblocking Organizational Values.* Glenview, IL: Scott, Foresman and Company, 1990.

Freedman, Arthur M. "Why Managers Don't Manage." In *Managing in the Age of Change: Essential Skills to Manage Today's Diverse Workforce*, edited by Roger A. Ritvo, Anne H. Litwin, and Lee Butler, 3-13. New York: Irwin Professional Publishing, 1995.

Fullerton, Howard N., Jr. "Another Look at the Labor Force." *Monthly Labor Review*, no. 11 (November 1993).

Garcia, Frances. "What Minorities Should Know About Business." *Business Week's Guide to Careers* (1982).

Gleckman, Howard; Tim Smart, Paula Dwyer, Troy Segal, and Joseph Weber. "Race in the Workplace: Is Affirmative Action Working?" *Business Week* (8 July 1991): 50-62.

Graves, C. W. "The Future for Black Urban Administrators." *Public Management* (June 1982): 15-16.

Greenhause, Jeffrey H., Saroj Parasuraman, and Wayne M. Wormley. "Effects of Race on Organization Experiences, Job Performance Evaluations, and Career Outcomes." *Academy of Management Journal*, 33 (March 1990): 64-84.

Gross, Edward. "The Worker and Society," In *Man in A World At Work,* edited by Henry Borrow. Boston: Houghton & Mifflin, 1964.

Hacker, Andrew. *Two Nations Black and White Separate, Hostile, Unequal.* New York: Ballantine Books, 1995.

Hall, Francine S., and Maryann H. Albrecht. *The Management of Affirmative Action.* Santa Monica: Goodyear Publishing Company, Inc., 1979.

Hanner, W. C., J. S. Kim, L. Baird, and G. Bigoness. "Race and Sex Determinants of Ratings of Potential Employees in a Simulated Work Sampling Task." *Journal of Applied Psychology* 59, (1994): 705-711.

Harris, Louis. "The Future of Affirmative Action." In *The Affirmative Action Debate*, edited by George E. Curry, 326-335. New York: Addison-Wesley Publishing Company, Inc., 1997.

Hartmann, Heidi. "Who Has Benefited from Affirmative Action Employment." In *The Affirmative Action Debate*, edited by George E. Curry, 77-96. New York: Addison-Wesley Publishing Company, Inc., 1997.

Heilman, M. E. "Affirmative Action: Some Unintended Consequences for Working Women." *Research in Organizational Behavior* 16 (1994): 125-169.

Heilman, Madeline E., Jonathan A. Lucas, and Caryn J. Block. "Presumed Incompetent? Stigmatization and Affirmative Action Efforts." *Journal of Applied Psychology* 77, no. 4 (1992): 536-544.

Henderson, Richard I. *Practical Guide to Performance Appraisal.* Reston, VA: Reston Publishing Company, Inc., 1984.

Hoerr, John, Leah N. Spiro, Larry Armstrong, and James B. Treece. "Culture Shock at Home: Working for a Foreign Boss." *Business Week* (17 December 1990): 80-84.

Hofstader, Robert A. "An Affirmative Action Advisory Committee." In *Ensuring Minority Success in Corporate America*, edited by Donna E.

Thompson and Nancy DiTomaso, 249-252. New York: Plenum Press, 1988.

Holmes Norton, Eleanor. "Affirmative Action in the Workplace." In *The Affirmative Action Debate*, edited by George E. Curry, 39-48. New York: Addison-Wesley Publishing Company, Inc., 1997.

Holsendolph, Ernest. "Black Executives in a Nearly All-White World." *Fortune* (September 1972): 86-140.

Holzer, Harry J. "Employer Hiring Decisions and Antidiscrimination Policy." Discussion Paper 1085-1096. Madison: Institute for Research on Poverty, 1996.

———. "Employer Skill Needs and Labor Market Outcomes by Race and Gender." Discussion Paper 1087-1096. Madison: Institute for Research on Poverty. 1996.

Howard, Gary R. "White Americans in a Multicultural Society: Rethinking Our Role." In *The Diversity Factor: Capturing the Competitive Advantage of a Changing Workforce*, edited by Elsie Y. Cross and Margaret Blackburn White, 108-118. New York: Irwin Professional Publishing, 1996.

Hoy, Judith C. "Women in Organizations: The Struggle for Equity Continues." In *The Promise of Diversity: Over 40 Voices Discuss Strategies for Eliminating Discrimination in Organizations*, edited by Elise Y. Cross, Judith H. Katz, Frederick A. Miller, and Edith W. Seashore, 179-187. New York: Irwin Professional Publishing,1994.

Hudson Institute, Inc. *Workforce 2000: Work and Workers For The 21st Century*. Indianapolis: Herman Kahn Center, June, 1987.

Huse, Edgar F., and Thomas G. Cummings. *Organizational Development and Change*. St. Paul: West Publishing Co., 1985.

Hymowitz, Carol. "Taking a Chance: Many Blacks Jump Off the Corporate Ladder to Be Entrepreneurs." *The Wall Street Journal* (2 August 1989).

Igbaria, Magid, and Wayne M. Wormley. "Race Differences in Job Performance and Career Success." *Communications of the ACM* 38, no. 3 (March, 1995): 82-92.

Irons, Edward D., and Gilbert W. Moore. *Black Managers: The Case of the Banking Industry*. New York: Praeger Publishers, 1985.

Jackson-Leslie, Llenda. "Race, Sex, and Meritocracy." *The Black Scholar* 25, no. 3 (1995): 24-29.

James, Frank E. "More Blacks Quitting White-Run Firms." *The Wall Street Journal* (7 June 1988).

Jeffries, John M., and Richard L. Schaffer. "Changes in the Economy and Labor Market Status of Black Americans." In *Urban League State of*

Black America Report,12-77. New York: National Urban League Inc., 1996.

Jencks, Christopher. *Who Gets Ahead: The Determinants of Economic Success in America*. New York: Basic Books, Inc., 1979.

Johnson, Berman E. "Black Success: Counseling Is Crucial." *Community and Junior College Journal* (November 1982): 36, 38.

Johnson, Roy S. "The New Black Power." *Fortune* (4 August 1997): 46- 47.

Jones, Edward W., Jr. "What It's Like to Be a Black Manager." *Harvard Business Review* (July-August 1973): 108-116

————. "Black Managers: The Dream Deferred." *Harvard Business Review* 64, no. 3 (May-June 1986): 84-93.

Judge, Gail. "Shifting Markets, Shifting Structures." In *Ensuring Minority Success in Corporate Management*, edited by Donna E. Thompson and Nancy DiTomaso, 245-248. New York: Plenum Press, 1998.

Judy, Richard W., and Carol D'Amico. *Workforce 2020: Work and Workers in the 21st Century*. Indianapolis: Hudson Institute, 1997.

Kanter, Rosabeth Moss. *Men and Women of the Corporation*. New York: Basic Books, Inc., 1977.

————. "Ensuring Minority Achievement in Corporations: The Importance of Structural Theory and Structural Change." In *Ensuring Minority Success in Corporate America*, edited by Donna E. Thompson and Nancy DiTomaso, 331-345. New York: Plenum Press, 1988.

Kasey, Robert Eugene. "Human Resource Management and the African American Worker: Research in Support of Proactive Affirmative Action Initiatives" *Journal of Black Studies* 27, no. 6 (July 1997): 751-767.

Kass, G. V. "An Exploratory Technique for Investigating Large Quantities of Categorical Data." *Applications in Statistics* 29, no. 2 (1980): 119-127.

Katz, Lawrence F. "Active Labor Market Policies to Expand Employment and Opportunity." In *Reducing Unemployment: Current Issues and Policy Options*, 239-290. Symposium sponsored by the Federal Reserve Bank of Kansas City, Missouri, 1994.

Kaufman, Jonathan. "Black Executives Say Prejudice Still Impedes Their Path to the Top." *The Wall Street Journal* (3 March 1985).

Kay, Kim R., Robert E. Henne, and Richard Bohlander, eds. *Peterson's Higher Education Directory*. Princeton: Peterson's Guides, 1988.

Kennedy, Robert. "Inroads That Go Beyond Affirmative Action." *The Wall Street Journal* (10 September 1990).

Kidder, Louise H. *Research Methods in Social Relations*. New York: Holt, Rinehart, Winston, 1981.

Kiechel, Walter III. "Management Winners." *Fortune (29* November 1982): 159-160.

Kirschenman, Joleen, Philip Moss, and Chris Tilly. "Employer Screening Methods and Racial Exclusion: Evidence for New In-Depth Interviews with Employers." *Working Paper.* New York: Russell Sage Foundation (1995).

Klagge, Jay. "The Executive in the Year 2000: A Reinvented Role." *Journal of Management Inquiry* 6, no. 4 (December 1997): 298-307.

Knowles, Louis L., and Kenneth Prewitt. *Institutional Racism In America.* Upper Saddle River, NJ: Prentice-Hall, Inc., 1969.

Kochman, Thomas. "Black and White Cultural Styles in Pluralistic Perspective." In *The Promise of Diversity: Over 40 Voices Discuss Strategies for Eliminating Discrimination in Organizations,* edited by Elise Y. Cross, Judith H. Katz, Frederick A. Miller, and Edith W. Seashore, 198-204. New York: Irwin Professional Publishing, 1994.

Korn/Ferry International. *Korn/Ferry International's Executive Profile 1990: A Survey of Corporate Leaders.* 1990.

Kraiger, Kurt, and Kevin J. Ford. "A Meta-Analysis of Ratee Race Effects in Performance Ratings." *Journal of Applied Psychology* 70, no. 1 (February 1985): 56-65.

Kram, Kathy E. *Mentoring at Work.* Lanham, MD: University Press of America, 1988.

———. *Mentoring at Work: Developmental Relationships in Organizational Life.* Chicago: Scott, Foresman and Company, 1985.

Kutscher, Ronald E. *Outlook:1990-2005: New BLS Projections: Findings and Implications.* Bulletin of the U. S. Department of Labor, Bureau of Labor Statistics, 1-10. Washington: Government Printing Office, May 1992.

Landau, Jacqueline. "The Relationship of Race and Gender to Manager's Ratings of Promotion Potential." *Journal of Organizational Behavior* 16 (1995): 391-400.

Larkins, Daniel, Larry R. Moran, Ralph W. Morris, and Deborah Y. Sieff. "Survey of Current Business: Business Situation." *Report of the U. S. Department of Commerce, Economics and Statistics Administration, Bureau of Economic Analysis* 78: 1-6. Washington: Government Printing Office, May 1998.

Lee, Nancy. *Targeting the Top.* New York: Ballantine Books, 1980.

Leggon, Cheryl. "Theoretical Perspectives on Race and Ethnic Relations: A Social-Historical Approach." *Research in Race and Ethnic Relations* 1, JAI Press, (1979): 1-15.

Leibowitz, Zandy B., Caela Farren, and Beverly L. Kaye. *Designing Career Development Systems.* San Francisco: Jossey-Bass Publishers, 1986.

Leinster, Colin. "Black Executives: How They're Doing." *Fortune* (18 January 1988) 109-120.

Leonard, Jonathan. "The Impact of Affirmative Action Regulations and Equal Employment Law on Black Employment." *Journal of Economic Perspectives* 4 (1990): 47-63.

———. "Wage Disparities and Affirmative Action in 1980's." *American Economic Review Papers and Proceedings* 86 (1996): 285-289.

Lichtmen, Judy L., Jocelyn C. Frye., and Helen Norton. "Why Women Need Affirmative Action." In *The Affirmative Action Debate*, edited by George E. Curry, 175-183. New York: Addison-Wesley Publishing Company, Inc., 1997.

Lipset, S., and R. Bendix. "Intra-Generational Occupational Mobility in Oakland," In *Three Centuries of Social Mobility in America*, edited by Edward Pessen. Lexington, MA: D. C. Heath & Co., 1974.

Lipset, Seymour Martin. "Beyond Affirmative Action." *The New Democrat* (May/June 1995).

Livingston, J. Sterling. "Myth of the Well-Educated Manager." *Harvard Business Review,* no. 71108 (January-February 1971): 63-73.

Loden, Marilyn. *Implementing Diversity.* Chicago: Irwin Professional Publishing, 1996.

Magidson, Jay. "Some Common Pitfalls in Causal Analysis of Categorical Data." *Journal of Marketing Research* 19 (November 1982): 461-471.

Mandel, Michael J. "Dispelling the Myths That are Holding Us Back." *Business Week* (17 December 1990): 66-70.

Matejka, J. Kenneth, and Richard J. Dunsing. "Opening Doors: Good Relationships as Good Management." *Personnel* (September 1988): 74-78.

McBride, Nicholas. "In U.S. Corporations, Minorities Are Stuck at Mid-Level Jobs; Can't Jump Hurdles to Top Posts." *The Christian Science Monitor* (20 January 1987).

McComas, Maggie. "Atop the Fortune 500: A Survey of the C.E.O.'s." *Fortune* (28 April 1986): 26-31.

McCoy, Frank. "Shattering Glass Ceilings." *Black Enterprise* 2, no. 2 (September 1995): 22.

Mercer, Joye. "Sixth Annual Retention Conference Brings Warnings, Predictions." *Black Issues in Higher Education* 22 (November 1990): 8-9.

Mincer, Jacob. *Schooling, Experience, and Earnings.* New York: National Bureau of Economic Research, 1974.

Moss, Philip, and Chris Tilly. "Raised Hurdles for Black Men: Evidence from Interviews with Employers." *Working Paper.* New York: Russell Sage Foundation, 1995.

Muckler, Frederick A. "Evaluation Productivity." In *Human Performance and Productivity: Human Capability Assessment,* edited by Marvin D. Dunnette and Edwin A. Fleishman, 13-48. Hillsdale, NJ: Lawrence Erlbaum Associates, Inc., 1982.

Naisbitt, John. *Megatrends: Ten New Directions Transforming Our Lives.* New York: Warner Books, Inc., 1982.

Neely, George M., and Tracie Carter. "Workforce 2000 and Potential Contributions From Organizational Behavior." *Journal of Social and Behavioral Sciences,* 36, no. 4 (Fall 1990/1991): 193-209.

Newsweek (23 May 1983): 60-61.

Nixon, Regina. *Black Managers in Corporate America: Alienation or Integration.* National Urban League, 1983.

Okun, Arthur M. *Equality and Efficiency: The Big Tradeoff.* Washington: The Brookings Institution, 1975.

Patterson, Orlando. "Affirmative Action, On the Merit System" *New York Times.* (7 August 1995).

Pennar, Karen. "Yes, We're Down. No, We're Not Out." *Business Week* (17 December 1990): 62-63.

Perreault, William D., and Hiram C. Barksdale, Jr. "A Model-Free Approach for Analysis of Complex Contingency Data in Survey Research." *Journal of Marketing Research* 17 (November 1980): 503-515.

Pfleeger, Shari Lawrence, and Norma Mertz. "Executive Mentoring: What Makes It Work?" *Communications of the ACM* 38, no. 1 (January 1995): 63-73.

Podolny, Joel M. and James N. Baron. "Resources and Relationships: Social Networks and Mobility in the Workplace." *American Sociological Review* 62 (October 1997): 673-693.

Price, Hugh B. "Building A 21st Century Community: The State of Black America 1996." In *The Urban League State of Black America Report,* 7-11. New York: National Urban League, Inc., 1996.

Price, Lee. "Economic Assumptions of Outlook 1998." *U. S. Industry and Trade Outlook 1998* (1998): xiii-xviii.

Rasnic, Carol D. "The Supreme Court and Affirmative Action: An Evolving Standard or Compounded Confusion?" *Employee Relations Law Journal* (Autumn 1988): 175-190.

Reibstein, Larry. "Many Hurdles, Old and New, Keep Black Managers Out of Top Jobs." *The Wall Street Journal* (10 July 1986).

Ritvo, Roger A., Anne H. Litwin, and Lee Butler. *Managing in the Age of Change: Essential Skills to Manage Today's Diverse Workforce.* New York: Irwin Professional Publishing, 1995.

Rosenbaum, James E. *Career Mobility in a Corporate Hierarchy.* Orlando: Academic Press, Inc., 1984.

Russell Reynolds Associates, Inc. *Men, Women, and Leadership in the American Corporation.* New York: 1990.

Sackett, Paul R., Cathy L. DuBois, and Ann Wiggins Noe. "Tokenism in Performance Evaluation: The Effects of Work Group Representation on Male-Female and White-Black Differences in Performance Ratings." *Journal of Applied Psychology* 76, no. 2 (1991): 263-267.

Salmon, Jaslin U. *Black Executives in White Businesses.* Washington: University Press of America, Inc., 1979.

Schein, Edgar H. *Career Dynamics: Matching Individual and Organizational Needs.* Reading, MA.: Addison-Wesley Publishing Company, 1978.

Schuman, David, and Dick W. Olufs, III. *Public Administration in the United States.* Lexington, MA: D.C. Heath and Company, 1988.

Scullock, William E. and Glenwood C. Brooks, Jr. "Measuring Racial Attitudes in a Situational Context." *Psychological Reports* 27 (1970): 971.

Shea, Gordon F. *Mentoring.* New York: American Management Association, 1994.

Sheridan, J. E., J. W. Slocum, R. Buda, and R. Thompson. "Effects of Corporate Sponsorship and Departmental Power on Career Tournaments." *Academy of Management Journal* 33 (1990): 578- 602.

Silber, Mark B., and Clayton Sherman. *Managerial Performance and Promotability: The Making of an Executive.* New York: AMACOM, 1974.

Silverzweig, Stan, and Robert F. Allen. "Changing the Corporate Culture." *Sloan Management Review* (Spring 1979): 33-49.

Silvestri, George, and John Lukasiewicz. *Outlook:1990-2005: Occupational Employment Projections.* Bulletin of the U. S. Department of Labor, Bureau of Labor Statistics, 62-99. Washington: Government Printing Office, May 1992.

Sobel, Lester A., ed. *Quotas and Affirmative Action.* New York: Facts on File, 1980.

Somerick, Nancy M. "Strategies for Improving Employee Relations by Using Performance Appraisals More Effectively." *Public Relations Quarterly* (Fall 1993): 37-39.

South, Oron. "All Culture Change Is Not the Same." In *The Promise of Diversity: Over 40 Voices Discuss Strategies for Eliminating Discrimination in Organizations*, edited by Elise Y. Cross, Judith H. Katz, Frederick A. Miller, and Edith W. Seashore, 87-93. New York: Irwin Professional Publishing,1994.

Sowell, Thomas. *Civil Rights: Rhetoric or Reality*. New York: William Morrow and Company, Inc., 1984.

————. "Economics and Black People." *Review of Black Political Economy* 1 (Winter/Spring 1971): 3-34.

Spilerman, Seymour. "Sources of Minority Underrepresentation in Corporate Employment." In *Ensuring Minority Success in Corporate Management*, edited by Donna E. Thompson and Nancy DiTomaso, 25-36. New York: Plenum Press,1988.

Straughn, Charles T., III, and B. L. Straughn, eds. *Lovejoy's College Guide*. New York: Monarch Press, 1987.

Swanger, Clare C. "Perspectives on the History of Ameliorating Oppression and Supporting Diversity in United States Organizations." In *The Promise of Diversity: Over 40 Voices Discuss Strategies for Eliminating Discrimination in Organizations*, edited by Elise Y. Cross, Judith H. Katz, Frederick A. Miller, and Edith W. Seashore, 3-21. New York: Irwin Professional Publishing, 1994.

Tabb, William K. *The Political Economy of the Black Ghetto*. New York: W. W. Norton & Company, Inc., 1970.

Taylor, D. Garth. *Racial Disparity in the Labor Market: Second Report in a Series on the Status of African Americans in the Chicago Area Economy*. Chicago: Chicago Urban League Department of Research and Planning (August, 1990).

Thomas, David A. "An Organization Analysis of Black and White Patterns of Sponsorship and the Dynamics of Cross-Racial Mentoring." (Unpublished Dissertation). Yale University, 1986.

————. "The Impact of Race on Managers' Experiences of Developmental Relationships (Mentoring and Sponsorship): An Intra-organizational Study." *Journal of Organizational Behavior* 11 (1990): 479-492.

Thomas, David A., and Kathy E. Kram. "Promoting Career-Enhancing Relationships in Organizations: The Role of the Human Resource Professional." In *Career Growth and Human Resource Strategies,* edited by Manuel London and Edward M. Mone, 49-66. New York: Quorum Books, 1988.

Thomas, Roosevelt, Jeff Porterfield, John Hutcheson, and Carol Pierannuzi. *The Impact of Recruitment, Selection, Promotion and Compensation Policies and Practices on the Glass Ceiling.* A Report to the Department of Labor, Glass Ceiling Commission, April 1994.

Thurow, Lester C. *Generating Inequality: Mechanisms of Distribution in the U.S. Economy.* New York: Basic Books Inc., 1975.

Tomaskovic-Devey, Donald (Ph.D). *Gender & Racial Inequality at Work: The Sources & Consequences of Job Segregation.* New York: ILR Press, 1993.

———. *Race, Ethnic and Gender Earnings Inequality: The Sources and Consequences of Employment Segregation.* A report to the U.S. Department of Labor, Glass Ceiling Commission, January 1994.

Ugorji, Ugorji O. "Career-Impeding Supervisory Behaviors: Perceptions of African American and European American Professionals." *Public Administration Review* 57, no. 3 (May/June 1997): 250-255.

U. S. Bureau of Census. *Statistical Abstract of the United States.* Washington D.C.: U.S. Government Printing Office, 1990.

———. Current Population Reports. *The Black Population in the United States: March 1990 and 1989.* Washington D.C.: U.S. Government Printing Office, 1991.

U. S. Department of Commerce. Bureau of the Census. *Statistical Abstract of the United States.* Washington: U. S. Government Printing Office, 1987.

———. Bureau of the Census. *Statistical Abstract of the United States.* Washington: U. S. Government Printing Office, 1996.

———. Bureau of the Census. *Statistical Abstract of the United States.* Washington: U. S. Government Printing Office, 1997.

U.S. Department of Labor. Bureau of Labor Statistics. *Outlook 2000.* Washington D.C.: U. S. Government Printing Office, 1990.

———. *A Report on the Glass Ceiling Initiative.* Washington: U. S. Government Printing Office, 1991.

———. *Pipelines of Progress: A Status Report on the Glass Ceiling.* Washington: U. S. Government Printing Office, August 1992.

———. *Report on the American Workforce.* Washington: U. S. Government Printing Office, 1997.

———. Employment Standards Administration, Office of Federal Contract Compliance Program. *The Glass Ceiling Initiative: Are There Cracks In*

The Ceiling? Washington: U. S. Government Printing Office, June 1997.

U.S. Equal Employment Opportunity Commission. *Job Patterns for Minorities and Women in Private Industry.* Washington D.C.: U.S. Government Printing Office, 1989.

————. *Job Patterns for Minorities & Women in Private Industry.* Washington: U. S. Government Printing Office, 1994.

————. *Job Patterns for Minorities & Women in Private Industry.* Washington: U. S. Government Printing Office, 1996.

————. Office of Program Operations. *Indicators of Equal Employment Opportunity—Status and Trends.* Washington: U. S. Government Printing Office, December 1995.

Villere, Maurice and Sandra Hartman. "What's Affirmative About Affirmative Action?" *Business Horizons* (September-October 1989): 22-27.

Wernick, Ellen D. *Preparedness, Career Advancement, and the Glass Ceiling.* A report to the U. S. Department of Labor, Glass Ceiling Commission, May 1994.

Work, John H. *Race, Economics and Corporate America.* Wilmington, DE: Scholarly Resources Inc., 1984.

Yarborough, Deborah. "Reflections on the Not-So-Level Playing Field." In *The Promise of Diversity: Over 40 Voices Discuss Strategies for Eliminating Discrimination in Organizations,* edited by Elise Y. Cross, Judith H. Katz, Frederick A. Miller, and Edith W. Seashore, 123-129. New York: Irwin Professional Publishing,1994.

Zweigenhaft, Richard. *Who Gets to the Top: Executive Suite Discrimination in the Eighties.* New York: The American Jewish Committee, Institute of Human Relations, 1984.

Index

Profile

Dr. Ulwyn L. J. Pierre is the Principal and CEO of Pierre & Associates, Inc., a full-service human resource management and organizational development consulting company with clientele in the U.S. and abroad.

Dr. Pierre consults with companies on a wide range of organizational issues. In her consulting practice she also facilitates leadership development among senior management; conducts market analyses; customizes and facilitates coaching programs for key executives and managers; develops and deploys strategies; re-engineers and restructures companies; designs and implements mentoring programs; optimizes human resources; develops processes and systems that maximize productivity and profitability; and advises on employability, upward mobility and succession planning issues. She also advises business owners from diverse industries on starting, growing and maximizing their enterprises.

Her clients in the U.S. include: Baxter Healthcare Corporation, Northern Illinois Gas, The Northern Trust Company, Kraft Foods, Areoquip Corporation, The Chicago Association for Healthcare Executives, and Turner Construction Company. In Turner Construction Company's 1997 Construction Management Training Program, of the 15 offerings, her class "Managing Stress for Business Success" was voted by participants as the best and the most beneficial.

In addition to serving as "Mentor" in the Menttium 100 Program, she is a visiting professor at DePaul University teaching "Facilitating Organizational Change" and at Purdue University (Calumet) teaching "Internal and External Marketing" to entrepreneurs. She speaks at various corporate events and at national and international conferences on a wide range of topics.

Her educational background includes: a Doctorate (Human Resource Management and Organizational Development), Master's in Educational Administration/Leadership, and Master's of Business Administration (Organizational Management and Marketing), all from Columbia University, New York; Bachelor's of Education (Mathematics) from the University of Toronto, Canada; and Bachelor's of Arts (Statistics and Applied Mathematics) from the University of Guelph, Guelph, Canada.

Dr. Pierre plays an active role in client relations. She believes that to be a stellar consultant/change master one has to be an educator, leadership developer, administrator, and problem solver. Her clients affirm that her performance and results reflect her beliefs. She exercises a deep and sincere commitment to "doing it right the first time." She is listed in *International Who's Who of Entrepreneurs* (Ericson Publishing).

For Product Safety Concerns and Information please contact our EU representative GPSR@taylorandfrancis.com Taylor & Francis Verlag GmbH, Kaufingerstraße 24, 80331 München, Germany